Introduction to Teaching

Making Teacher Training Work

Barnaby Lenon and Tracey Smith

Together we unlock every learner's unique potential

At Hachette Learning (formerly Hodder Education), there's one thing we're certain about. No two students learn the same way. That's why our approach to teaching begins by recognising the needs of individuals first.

Our mission is to allow every learner to fulfil their unique potential by empowering those who teach them. From our expert teaching and learning resources to our digital educational tools that make learning easier and more accessible for all, we provide solutions designed to maximise the impact of learning for every teacher, parent and student.

Aligned to our parent company, Hachette Livre, founded in 1826, we pride ourselves on being a learning solutions provider with a global footprint.

www.hachettelearning.com

Although every effort has been made to ensure that website addresses are correct at time of going to press, Hachette Learning cannot be held responsible for the content of any website mentioned in this book. It is sometimes possible to find a relocated web page by typing in the address of the home page for a website in the URL window of your browser.

Hachette UK's policy is to use papers that are natural, renewable and recyclable products and made from wood grown in well-managed forests and other controlled sources. The logging and manufacturing processes are expected to conform to the environmental regulations of the country of origin.

To order, please visit www.HachetteLearning.com or contact Customer Service at education@hachette.co.uk / +44 (0)1235 827827.

ISBN: 9781036010393

© Barnaby Lenon and Tracey Smith 2025

First published in 2025 by
Hachette Learning (a trading division of Hodder & Stoughton Limited),
An Hachette UK Company
Carmelite House
50 Victoria Embankment
London EC4Y 0DZ
www.HachetteLearning.com

The authorised representative in the EEA is Hachette Ireland, 8 Castlecourt Centre, Dublin 15, D15 XTP3, Ireland (email: info@hbgi.ie)

Impression number   10 9 8 7 6 5 4 3 2 1
Year   2029 2028 2027 2026 2025

Illustrations by DC Graphic Design Limited, Hextable, Kent.
Typeset in the UK.
Printed in the UK.

A catalogue record for this title is available from the British Library.

MIX
Paper | Supporting
responsible forestry
FSC™ C104740

About the authors

Barnaby Lenon taught at Eton College, Holland Park School, Sherborne School, Highgate School and was the head of Trinity School, Croydon and Harrow School. He has been a governor of 23 schools, state and independent, and was the founding chairman of governors of a state free school, the London Academy of Excellence. He was on the board of Ofqual during the period of extensive reform to the curriculum and exams in the 2010s. He is currently Dean of Education at the University of Buckingham, one of the largest teacher training providers in the UK and is a trustee of the Yellow Submarine charity for young people with learning disabilities in Oxford. He was awarded a CBE for services to education.

Tracey Smith taught at Stadhampton and St Francis primary schools in Oxfordshire and then was Headteacher at Bladon, Tower Hill and New Marston primary Schools in Oxfordshire, before becoming Head of Primary Teacher Training at the University of Buckingham. Tracey returned to Headship as Executive Headteacher of two Faringdon primary Schools before continuing working with teacher training and supervision at the University of Buckingham.

Contents

Chapter 1
Good teaching

Why go into teaching?

There are numerous reasons for being a teacher:

- You may be good at teaching, and that will give you great job satisfaction.
- You want to make a difference in the lives of children, and you will certainly do that by teaching.
- You enjoy your workplace – a school full of lively children or young people and colleagues who are intelligent and like-minded.
- You engage every day with a subject you love.
- You get school holidays, which is especially important if you are a parent.
- The pay is reasonable when you start and can rise to a high level if you are promoted; the Teachers' Pension Scheme is excellent.

The truth about teaching

Teaching is often fun, but it is quite physically and emotionally draining. You have to work hard in term time. Not everyone is suited to the job.

What makes a good teacher?

Secondary

This is a tough question, because 'good' teachers can operate in quite different ways. I know good teachers who are brilliantly organised, give their pupils excellent notes and create lessons that are full of fun and variety. But I have recently come across an A-level history teacher who remains firmly stuck in an old armchair and whose only activity was talking through topics – but he does this in such an interesting way that his pupils love him and learn a great deal.

There is probably no right way to teach, and in any case, it depends on the age of the pupils and the subject you are teaching. But if we had to generalise, we would say the characteristics of good teachers tend to be:

- Good subject knowledge, because such teachers are often more enthusiastic and more interesting. They are more capable of stretching and stimulating the most able pupils and they know the syllabus, so they don't have to spend much time preparing, which enables them to devote their energy to other things, such as individual pupils. Pupils soon pick up if a teacher has great subject knowledge, and that gives them confidence in that teacher.

- A strong enough character to maintain control – if a teacher cannot control the pupils, nothing can be achieved.
- A warm person beneath the exterior – they exude energy, and their enthusiasm rubs off on pupils.
- A sense of humour, which pupils really appreciate.
- High expectations of every pupil, and ambition for all of them.
- A hard-working attitude.
- Organising skills. For example, a good teacher always has spare copies of the necessary equipment – even PE kit – for the pupil who for some reason has forgotten it.
- A clear sense of what works and doesn't work in the classroom, which comes from experience.
- Patience when dealing with pupils, especially younger children.
- Pupils look to them if they are in difficulty, and the teacher cares.

But there is no one formula for creating a good teacher. Different age groups, types of children and subjects require different methods. Experienced teachers will agree with some of the things we cover in this book, but not others.

Primary

As primary teachers usually spend all day with their pupils teaching across every subject in the primary curriculum, there are some differences between primary and secondary that need to be highlighted.

While the above list of the characteristics of a good teacher hold true in primary teaching, we should emphasise the teacher's ability to forge positive relationships with their pupils, take the time to get to know them as individuals and the ability to generate trust in such a way that pupils are happy, have a sense of belonging in the school and therefore choose to behave well.

Younger pupils need a different approach than older pupils, based on the formation of warm, caring relationships. This is easier for primary teachers to build and maintain since we spend all day with the same pupils. I recently interviewed an Early Career Teacher (ECT) in her first year, who told me:

> At the start of September, I felt at a loss as to how I was ever going to control the behaviour in my Year 1 class. The teacher I was with last year made it seem so effortless, and I wasn't really sure how she managed it.

What I started to realise was that I had to get to know my 5-year-olds really well as individuals. They all have different needs and respond differently to different things. Once I understood this and got to know them, they realised how much I cared for them and started responding to me differently. They started to trust me to be fair and consistent and to have their best interests in mind. For the last few months, behaviour has been really good in my class.

The teacher summarised her situation well, but I have observed her over the past few months and know that she could have also mentioned three pertinent points:

- She is even-tempered, calm and consistent in her manner.
- She has high expectations for behaviour and children understand what these are.
- She has built routines that her pupils are aware of and that are designed to maintain a calm and purposeful classroom environment.

Are good teachers born or made?

Like most things in life, the answer is a mixture of the two. Some of the characteristics listed above come easier to some people than to others, such as forceful class management or the ability to work hard. But other characteristics can be taught.

Having a strong voice is necessary – you are going to be talking a great deal. It helps to have a powerful voice, but that does not mean shouting. In fact, shouting is discouraged. Some clever teachers quieten their voice when there is chatter in the class, and this can have the effect of quietening the children.

How do we know what works?

Most experienced teachers know what works best in the classroom – in other words, what methods enable pupils to learn fastest. But it is useful to look at research that has been carried out on a larger scale to answer this question with confidence.

In England we use the Education Endowment Foundation (EEF), which publishes research into the effectiveness of different methods in their Teaching and Learning Toolkit. They give each teaching method three scores based on the cost of the method (for example, reducing class size, which is very expensive), the strength of the research evidence and the impact measured in terms of the number of months of learning gained in a year compared to pupils who have not had the benefit of the new method. For example, metacognition has low cost, strong evidence and huge impact, while physical activity has low cost, quite strong evidence and low impact.

The toolkit can be found here: educationendowmentfoundation.org.uk/ education-evidence/teaching-learning-toolkit.

Rob Coe et al.: What makes great teaching?

Let's have a look at a review undertaken by Rob Coe and colleagues in 2014, available at: http://bit.ly/2OvmvKO. This analysis concluded that the two main characteristics of great teachers were:

- **Subject knowledge.** As well as a strong understanding of the material being taught, teachers must be able to understand the ways in which students think about the content, evaluate the thinking behind their methods and identify common misconceptions.
- **Quality of instruction.** This includes effective questioning and use of assessment. Teachers adopt specific good practices, like reviewing previous learning, providing model answers for students, giving adequate time for practice and progressively supporting new learning through scaffolding.

Other factors that can help are:

- **Classroom climate, relationships and expectations.** The quality of interactions between teachers and students and teacher expectations is important in the classroom. There is a need to create a classroom that is constantly demanding more but still recognises students' self-worth. This also involves attributing student success to effort rather than ability and valuing resilience when experiencing failure.
- **Classroom management.** This refers to a teacher's abilities to make efficient use of lesson time, coordinate classroom resources and space and manage students' behaviour with clear rules that are consistently enforced.
- **Teacher beliefs.** Why teachers adopt particular practices, the purposes they aim to achieve, their theories about what learning is and how it happens and their conceptual models of the nature and role of teaching in the learning process all seem to be important.
- **Professional behaviours.** These behaviours include reflecting on and developing professional practice, participation in professional development, supporting colleagues and liaising with parents.

The review also lists things that do not work well:

- Using lavish praise (see pages 151–52).
- Allowing pupils to discover things for themselves.

- Grouping learners by ability, because doing this gives teachers the impression that the group is homogenous in terms of ability when it is not. Teachers sometimes go too fast for the pupils in the top sets or too slow for the weaker sets.
- Encouraging re-reading and highlighting to memorise the work, as these techniques are not effective.
- Addressing issues of confidence and low aspirations before teaching the content. Teachers need to teach the content well, show the pupils they can understand it and then confidence can rise.
- Presenting information to pupils in their preferred learning style, as the idea of learning styles is unfounded.
- Ensuring pupils are always active, rather than listening passively, if we want them to remember the work. If we want pupils to remember something they must be forced to think about it, but that can happen with a good teacher simply speaking in an interesting and engaging way.

More research evidence about good teaching

John Hattie, 2023, *Visible Learning: The Sequel*, Routledge. John Hattie's ground-breaking study was first published in 2008 and was based on a synthesis of over 800 meta-analyses relating to achievement. Over the last 15 years, the research base underlying the Visible Learning project has grown to more than 2,100 meta-analyses, drawn from more than 130,000 studies and involving more than 400 million students from all around the world. Hattie identifies behaviours by teachers that seem to work best.

PISA – the Programme for International Student Assessment. PISA reports on the knowledge and understanding of 15-year-olds across the world, focusing on reading, maths and science. Some 690,000 students completed the assessment in 2022, representing about 29 million 15-year-olds in the schools of 81 participating countries or economies. In addition to saying 'which countries do best', the analysis tries to explain why some countries do better than others.

Three myths about teaching

- **Teachers are born, not made.** Well, successful teachers come in many shapes and sizes, which is why it's odd to believe that it's the teacher's inborn personality that matters. What's more, experience shows that good training can create very effective teachers.
- **If you know a subject, you can teach it.** No, you have to know *how* to teach a subject. Subject knowledge is not enough.

- **Teaching isn't hard.** No, teaching is a hard task that can take years to master.

What is the point of this book?

The point of this book is to flesh out what we believe are the most effective practices of good teachers and the research evidence that lies behind our recommendations. The book is relevant to anyone doing teacher training, including those taking the international QTS course and those embarking on the Early Career Framework (ECF) while working in schools.

But there are several things this book can't do:

- It can't make you implement the recommendations in your school – that is up to you. But in initial teacher training and the ECF, you should try out as many of our suggestions as possible. Too many teachers develop their own style or method very early on and never try anything new. So, we hope that in your teacher training you will try out as many methods as possible and receive feedback from your mentors on how successful you are.
- It can't make you skilful any more than reading a book about 'how to drive a car' can make you a good driver. You have to learn the basics and then try them out. Gradually, you will become more and more skilful. Jonathan Smith, the former head of English at Tonbridge School, once said that the characteristics of good teaching are pretty obvious, but it is 'obviousness of a tricky kind'. Yes, good teaching methods are easily stated, but they are harder to implement.
- It can't be a good substitute for effective training in the particular subject you are teaching. Every subject is different and requires different teaching methods, both in primary and secondary schools.

Avoiding over-generalisations about good teaching: The three-legged stool

There are three distinct legs to teacher training:

1. The general statements we can make about how best to teach children. For teachers in England, these are summarised in the Teachers' Standards.
2. The subject or subjects you are teaching, all of which require specific subject knowledge and slightly different approaches to teaching.
3. The age group of the children, which also determines how you are going to teach them. Can things apply equally to primary and secondary schools? Not often, which is why many chapters in this book include specific points applying to different age ranges.

It is perfectly possible to be an excellent secondary art teacher but a lousy maths teacher, or to be a good A-level teacher but a hopeless primary school teacher. Therefore, these three legs to the stool are separate but equally important to the structure.

How could a book about teaching apply equally to, say, an academically selective independent girls' school and a state comprehensive school? The answer is, it can in some ways and but not in others, so the reader must interpret things accordingly.

Chapter 2
The basics of teacher training in England

How do you become a teacher?

There are several ways to become a teacher in England. The most obvious is to gain a degree and then do teaching training – there are a variety of routes, which you can learn about on the DfE's 'Get Into Teaching' website, available at: getintoteaching.education.gov.uk.

All teacher training providers use three basic methods for developing teachers:

- Talks are given by experienced teachers, based in large part on the Teachers' Standards and ITTECF syllabus and reading useful books and articles, especially about the research evidence for teaching methods.
- Trainee teachers get **placements** or jobs in schools where they watch more experienced teachers at work and teach classes themselves. For the Qualified Teacher Status (QTS) qualification, the teachers are expected to know about the differences and similarities between four consecutive school year groups. The QTS also requires teachers to have taught in two schools so they can gain experience of different approaches to teaching, school organisation and management.
- More experienced teachers (**mentors**) observe the trainee teaching and give feedback. A mentor is appointed by the school and normally teaches the same subject as the trainee.

Teacher trainers have to show evidence that their trainees are doing well enough to pass the course. This evidence comes in two main forms:

- From the assessments made by the school mentor and any staff who visit from the training provider (such as a university). They will judge the trainee against the Teachers' Standards.
- From the reflections and essays written by the trainee over the course of a year.

The three main questions that will be asked by the training provider are:

1. Can the trainee teach well?
2. Does the trainee have a grasp of good practice and the research evidence that lies behind it?
3. Does the trainee know their subject?

What are 'key stages'?

Key stages are the blocks of years that make up the national curriculum in English schools. For teacher training, you will often need to specialise in two consecutive key stages, so you need to know the key stages and the year groups each applies to.

- **Early Years Foundation Stage (EYFS)** – for children aged 3–5, this stage includes nursery and reception years.
- **Key stage 1** – for children aged 5–7, years 1 and 2.
- **Key stage 2** – for children aged 7–11, years 3–6. The KS2 programmes of study for English, mathematics and science are presented in the national curriculum as 'lower' (years 3 and 4) and 'upper' (years 5 and 6).
- **Key stage 3** – for children aged 11–14, years 7–9.
- **Key stage 4** – for children aged 14–16, years 10–11.
- **Key stage 5** – for young people aged 16–18, this stage is commonly known as 'sixth form'.

Two important documents

The Teachers' Standards

Teachers' Standards are not a new thing – the first serious government attempt to regulate Initial Teacher Training was in 1984. Immediately before 2011, there were five booklets of Teachers' Standards each with dozens of standards that were tied to the pay and conditions of teachers, for:

- Core (41 standards)
- Qualified Teacher Status
- 'Post-threshold' teachers
- 'Excellent' teachers
- 'Advanced skills' teachers

It is not a surprise that the 2010 coalition government wanted to simplify them, and in 2011 they did just that.

What are the 2011 Teachers' Standards?

The great thing about the Teachers' Standards is that there are only nine of them:

Part one: Teaching

1. Set high expectations which inspire, motivate and challenge pupils
   - Establish a safe and stimulating environment for pupils, rooted in mutual respect.
   - Set goals that stretch and challenge pupils of all backgrounds, abilities and dispositions.
   - Demonstrate consistently the positive attitudes, values and behaviour which are expected of pupils.

2. Promote good progress and outcomes by pupils
   - Be accountable for pupils' attainment, progress and outcomes.
   - Be aware of pupils' capabilities and their prior knowledge, and plan teaching to build on these.
   - Guide pupils to reflect on the progress they have made and their emerging needs.
   - Demonstrate knowledge and understanding of how pupils learn and how this impacts on teaching.
   - Encourage pupils to take a responsible and conscientious attitude to their own work and study.

3. Demonstrate good subject and curriculum knowledge
   - Have a secure knowledge of the relevant subject(s) and curriculum areas, foster and maintain pupils' interest in the subject, and address misunderstandings.
   - Demonstrate a critical understanding of developments in the subject and curriculum areas and promote the value of scholarship.
   - Demonstrate an understanding of and take responsibility for promoting high standards of literacy, articulacy and the correct use of standard English, whatever the teacher's specialist subject.
   - If teaching early reading, demonstrate a clear understanding of systematic synthetic phonics.
   - If teaching early mathematics, demonstrate a clear understanding of appropriate teaching strategies.

4. Plan and teach well-structured lessons
   - Impart knowledge and develop understanding through effective use of lesson time.
   - Promote a love of learning and children's intellectual curiosity.

- Set homework and plan other out-of-class activities to consolidate and extend the knowledge and understanding pupils have acquired.
- Reflect systematically on the effectiveness of lessons and approaches to teaching.
- Contribute to the design and provision of an engaging curriculum within the relevant subject area(s).

5. Adapt teaching to respond to the strengths and needs of all pupils

- Know when and how to differentiate appropriately, using approaches which enable pupils to be taught effectively.
- Have a secure understanding of how a range of factors can inhibit pupils' ability to learn, and how best to overcome these.
- Demonstrate an awareness of the physical, social and intellectual development of children, and know how to adapt teaching to support pupils' education at different stages of development.
- Have a clear understanding of the needs of all pupils, including those with special educational needs; those of high ability; those with English as an additional language; those with disabilities; and be able to use and evaluate distinctive teaching approaches to engage and support them.

6. Make accurate and productive use of assessment

- Know and understand how to assess the relevant subject and curriculum areas, including statutory assessment requirements.
- Make use of formative and summative assessment to secure pupils' progress.
- Use relevant data to monitor progress, set targets, and plan subsequent lessons.
- Give pupils regular feedback, both orally and through accurate marking, and encourage pupils to respond to the feedback.

7. Manage behaviour effectively to ensure a good and safe learning environment

- Have clear rules and routines for behaviour in classrooms and take responsibility for promoting good and courteous behaviour both in classrooms and around the school, in accordance with the school's behaviour policy.
- Have high expectations of behaviour and establish a framework for discipline with a range of strategies, using praise, sanctions and rewards consistently and fairly.
- Manage classes effectively, using approaches which are appropriate to pupils' needs in order to involve and motivate them.
- Maintain good relationships with pupils, exercise appropriate authority, and act decisively when necessary.

8. Fulfil wider professional responsibilities

- Make a positive contribution to the wider life and ethos of the school.
- Develop effective professional relationships with colleagues, knowing how and when to draw on advice and specialist support.
- Deploy support staff effectively.
- Take responsibility for improving teaching through appropriate professional development, responding to advice and feedback from colleagues.
- Communicate effectively with parents with regard to pupils' achievements and wellbeing.

Part two: Personal and professional conduct

A teacher is expected to demonstrate consistently high standards of personal and professional conduct. The following statements define the behaviour and attitudes which set the required standard for conduct throughout a teacher's career.

- Teachers uphold public trust in the profession and maintain high standards of ethics and behaviour, within and outside school, by:
  - treating pupils with dignity, building relationships rooted in mutual respect, and at all times observing proper boundaries appropriate to a teacher's professional position
  - having regard for the need to safeguard pupils' well-being, in accordance with statutory provisions
  - showing tolerance of and respect for the rights of others
  - not undermining fundamental British values, including democracy, the rule of law, individual liberty and mutual respect, and tolerance of those with different faiths and beliefs
  - ensuring that personal beliefs are not expressed in ways which exploit pupils' vulnerability or might lead them to break the law.
- Teachers must have proper and professional regard for the ethos, policies and practices of the school in which they teach and maintain high standards in their own attendance and punctuality.
- Teachers must have an understanding of, and always act within, the statutory frameworks which set out their professional duties and responsibilities.

This is a sensible list of some of the qualities of good teachers. They were written by a committee convened by the schools' minister at the time, Nick Gibb. Sally Coates, an experienced teacher, was the chair, but delegated the actual writing to a much smaller sub-committee chaired by Roy Blatchford. Two of the key people on this sub-committee were Professor Anthony O'Hear, who set up the

School of Education at the University of Buckingham, and John McIntosh, the distinguished former head of the London Oratory School.

The QTS qualification, which is the main qualification for teachers in England, requires all teachers to be judged against the Teachers' Standards at the end of their course.

The Core Content Framework (CCF)

In 2019 the CCF – sometimes called the Initial Teacher Training and Early Career Framework (ITTECF) – was published. Professor Sam Twiselton of Sheffield Hallam University was the chair of the group who wrote it for the DfE. Other members included John Blake (who is now at the Office for Students), Emma Hollis of the National Association of School-Based Teacher Trainers (NASBTT) and James Noble Rogers of the Universities' Council for the Education of Teachers (UCET).

What is the CCF for?

The CCF is defined as a 'minimum entitlement for trainee teachers and places a duty on providers of initial teacher training – and their partner schools – to meet this entitlement'. In other words, the CCF is the core syllabus for teacher training. It's an attempt to elaborate on the Teachers' Standards and include some more recent research, in particular the findings of neuroscience.

The CCF is very clear that all the statements they make have research evidence behind them and have been approved by the Education Endowment Foundation (EEF). The EEF (see page 3) is a government-sponsored organisation that conducts research into 'what works' in schools and publishes a useful teacher toolkit.

The CCF was updated in 2024 and is now called the ITTECF, which is available at: gov.uk/government/publications/initial-teacher-training-and-early-career-framework. This long name shows us that there are two stages to teacher training, both following the same syllabus:

1. Initial Teacher Training, a one-year course leading to QTS qualification. The ITTECF is the syllabus.
2. The Early Career Framework, a two-year course that takes place in the school in which you are working after you have done the one-year QTS qualification. The ITTECF is once again a part of the syllabus.

It's important to appreciate that these teacher training syllabi were produced by a small group of people favoured by the government minister in charge at the time. The ITTECF was written by Ian Bauckham of Ofqual, Richard Gill of the Teaching School Hubs Council, Marie Hamer of the Ambition Institute,

Matt Hood of Oak National Academy, Reuben Moore of the National Institute of Teaching, Chris Paterson of the EEF and Professor Sam Twiselton of Sheffield Hallam University. Some of them are experienced schoolteachers, while others not.

Problems with the Teachers' Standards and ITTECF

The preamble to the CCF states:

> The ITT Core Content Framework does not set out the full ITT curriculum for trainee teachers. The complexity of the process for becoming a teacher cannot be overestimated and it remains for individual providers to design curricula appropriate for the subject, phase and age range that the trainees will be teaching.

That is an important caveat, but once a teaching training syllabus is defined in a DfE document and you learn that you will be inspected against it, that document *becomes* a large part of the syllabus. Other very important factors, such as subjects and pupil age phase, take second place, whatever the intentions of the authors of the CCF.

Both the Teachers' Standards and the CCF fail to distinguish properly between primary and secondary, even though the methods used for teaching younger children are very different to the methods used with teenagers. Of course, certain things can be equally true of young and older children, such as the need to maintain good behaviour, but the methods employed differ greatly. The Teachers' Standards and ITTECF are largely orientated to secondary schools.

Primary teachers are trained to teach 13 subjects, while secondary teachers are often trained to teach one; they are fundamentally different roles. Furthermore, the Teachers' Standards and ITTECF do not adequately acknowledge that different subjects require different teaching methods. Much of what is true of secondary maths teaching is not true of secondary art teaching.

It's perfectly possible for someone to tick all the boxes of the Teachers' Standards and achieve the QTS qualification without being a very good teacher. This is because they only have to reach a minimum standard, and the Teachers' Standards are just a basic shopping list. You can go to Tesco and buy the ingredients, but it requires a decent recipe and some acquired skills to make a good meal. The essential characteristics of a good teacher – subject knowledge and an energetic, persuasive personality, for example – are not really measured by the QTS qualification. The Teachers' Standards and the ITTECF are good lists, but they are not adequate on their own.

The gap between the written syllabus and reality in your classroom

Reading and learning the ITTECF can't make you a good teacher any more than reading a car's manual and the Highway Code can make you a good driver. The only way to understand the ITTECF is to watch other teachers try it out in a classroom before teaching classes yourself with feedback from your mentor – your driving instructor.

The Early Career Framework

The two-year Early Career Framework is called 'statutory induction' and is the bridge between initial teacher training and a career in teaching. It's carried out in the school in which you work, normally immediately after you have completed your initial teacher training. It combines a structured programme of development, support and professional dialogue with good teachers in your school (mentors) and an assessment of your performance against the Teachers' Standards.

The ECF is a programme based on the Teachers' Standards and ITTECF for teachers who have completed the Initial Teacher Training QTS course. These teachers are called ECTs – Early Career Teachers. Early Career Teachers get a 10% and 5% timetable reduction in years 1 and 2 of the programme respectively. There are two formal assessment points, one midway through induction and one at the end of the induction period, and if you do well enough you are classified as having completed your statutory induction.

Many teachers are more than satisfactory before they even begin the two-year ECF course. But the timetable reduction is helpful for all new teachers because of the amount of time they spend preparing topics they have not taught before.

Your school is responsible for managing the Early Career Framework, and they are checked by an 'appropriate body' to check they have done the job well. Your school will appoint a mentor to support you and provide coaching, and an induction tutor to carry out progress reviews.

You may wonder what the point of the ECF is. It has two purposes:

1. It is very difficult to cover all aspects of the ITTECF in only one school or university year. For example, primary teachers are expected to know about thirteen different subjects and knowing them well is impossible in a year. Secondary teachers may be expected to know about key stages 3, 4 and 5 (children aged 11–18), and again, this is too much to learn in only one year.

2. The UK government has been keen to reduce the number of teachers leaving the profession after only 1–5 years. It was felt that providing additional training on a reduced teaching timetable would help.

The two-year ECF is not compulsory; it's up to you and your school. At the time of writing, there is no legal requirement to satisfactorily complete an induction period if an ECT intends to work solely in the independent sector. Nor does the ECF have to follow the ITT year immediately – it can be done at any time.

The ECF can be done in most schools, including overseas independent schools that have been inspected by a DfE-accredited inspectorate within the last six years against the standards for inspection of British schools overseas.

The golden thread

The DfE established the term 'golden thread' to describe the thread of teacher training that runs from initial teacher training through the ECF and then on to National Professional Qualifications (NPQs), which are further courses for middle and senior management.

Qualifications for teachers

There are two main qualifications for beginner teachers in England: the QTS (Qualified Teacher Status) and the PGCE (Postgraduate Certificate in Education). They mostly last one year.

QTS

The QTS course is managed by the DfE, and the syllabus is the Teachers' Standards and the ITTECF. It is a pass/fail course. Providers of this course must have approval from the DfE to offer it, and they must teach the course and collect evidence (mainly from lesson observations) that the trainees have made good progress with the elements described in the Teachers' Standards. The providers have to employ an independent person (called an external moderator) to confirm that their processes and standards are fair and comparable with other teacher training providers. They also inspected by Ofsted, and the Ofsted reports are published.

The requirements of every QTS course are spelled out in 'Initial teacher training (ITT): criteria and supporting advice', which is an essential DFE document. It tells you exactly what you need in order to start a QTS course and what has to happen before the end. The document is available at: gov.uk/government/publications/initial-teacher-training-criteria.

One requirement of the QTS course is that you do teaching practice in at least two schools. This is called the 'second school placement', which involves three weeks in a school that contrasts with the main placement school. For example, if your main school is a special needs school, your second school placement should be in a mainstream school and may last half a term.

Another requirement is that you pass an English and maths test. This will be organised by your teacher training provider. The required syllabus is:

- Teachers should use standard English grammar, clear pronunciation and vocabulary relevant to the situation to convey instructions, questions, information, concepts and ideas with clarity. Teachers should read fluently and with good understanding.
- Writing by teachers will be seen by colleagues, pupils and parents, and as such it's important that a teacher's writing reflects the high standards of accuracy their professional role demands. They should write clearly, accurately, legibly and coherently using correct spelling and punctuation.
- Teachers should use data and graphs to interpret information, identify patterns and trends and draw appropriate conclusions. They need to interpret pupil data and understand statistics and graphs in the news, academic reports and relevant papers. Teachers should be able to complete mathematical calculations fluently with whole numbers, fractions, decimals and percentages. They should be able to solve mathematical problems using a variety of methods and approaches, including estimating and rounding, sense-checking answers, breaking down problems into simpler steps and explaining and justifying answers using appropriate language.

Apprenticeships

The Teacher Apprenticeship is a cheap way of funding a QTS course. To take the apprenticeship route, you have to be employed by a school in England even though you are not qualified as a teacher. Your school has to access the apprenticeship levy fund, but this is not difficult. You have to find a QTS provider who is on the Register of Apprenticeship Providers.

Such courses are effectively free of charge, but they have to follow apprenticeship rules, the main ones being:

- The course must last a school year and there has to be evidence that the trainee has engaged with the course every month.
- For the same reason, there must be regular calls between the trainee and the course teacher. These are known as progress reviews.
- The standards are checked by an independent expert.

Teachers overseas can gain the QTS qualification by taking the international QTS course, which is very similar to the QTS course itself.

To take a QTS course, you need to have passed GCSE English and maths or an equivalent, and a science if you want to become a primary teacher. You also need a degree taken in the UK, or one taken abroad that is an equivalent standard, and you will need to be physically fit enough to teach. The rules relating to these requirements can be found in the criteria and supporting advice document.

Another course you may come across is the Assessment Only route to QTS qualification. This course is for teachers with two or more years of experience who have to produce a portfolio of evidence and whose lessons are inspected by trained assessors. This process can be relatively quick.

PGCE

The PGCE course, which is sometimes combined with the QTS course, is run by universities and can be anything those universities want it to be. It often involves writing academic essays that are judged against 'levels' (usually level 6 or 7) that are defined by the Quality Assurance Agency (QAA) in the UK Quality Code for Higher Education.

Level 7 is defined by the QAA as students having:

- A systematic understanding of knowledge and a critical awareness of current problems and/or new insights, much of which is at, or informed by, the forefront of their academic discipline, field of study or area of professional practice.
- A comprehensive understanding of techniques applicable to their own research or advanced scholarship.
- Originality in the application of knowledge, together with a practical understanding of how established techniques of research and enquiry are used to create and interpret knowledge in the discipline.
- Conceptual understanding that enables the student:
  - To evaluate critically current research and advanced scholarship in the discipline.
  - To evaluate methodologies and develop critiques of them and, where appropriate, to propose new hypotheses.

Typically, students will be able to:

- Deal with complex issues (both systematically and creatively), make sound judgements in the absence of complete data and communicate their conclusions clearly to specialist and non-specialist audiences.

- Demonstrate self-direction and originality in tackling and solving problems and act autonomously in planning and implementing tasks at a professional or equivalent level.
- Continue to advance their knowledge and understanding and to develop new skills to a high level.

(QAA, 2024 2nd edition, *The Frameworks for Higher Education Qualifications of UK Degree-Awarding Bodies*).

Getting a level 6 or 7 qualification gives you 'credits'. The number of credits reflects the amount of work; one credit represents 10 hours of work. All UK university qualifications carry credits. These credits can be used to access other university qualifications and can reduce the length of time spent on such higher qualifications – this is called 'credit transfer'. The ways in which credit can be transferred are determined by each individual university. Credit transfer is dependent on whether the accumulated credit is relevant to the programme to which you want to transfer.

Getting a degree

Finally, you can go to a university and take a degree course such as a Bachelor of Education (BEd), which includes teacher training. The University of Buckingham, for example, offers a three-year degree in education for teaching assistants in primary schools, followed by a one-year QTS course.

Do you need these qualifications to teach in England?

You need a QTS qualification to teach in a state school. You don't need any teaching qualification to teach in an independent school, but some will expect it. Some schools will be happy to take you if you just have a good degree, as long as you do teacher training with a provider of an employment-based course within your first two years.

Intensive training and practice (ITAP): Part of the QTS course

ITAP is a form of teacher training employed for the QTS course since September 2024 and is based on the system used in the Core Practice Consortium in the USA by Dr Pam Grossman, Professor of Education at the University of Pennsylvania. The basic idea is that you need to think through a skill and practice it with an expert teacher before you use that skill in a classroom. QTS rules require ITAP training in England to cover 100 hours (or 20 days) in the training year. (See Grossman, P., 2018, *Teaching Core Practices in Teacher Education*.)

The training provider will choose 3–5 core competencies, which are skills they regard as especially important. Some of these may be particular to specific subjects and specific phases (age groups). An example of such competencies would be 'how to use formative feedback' or 'how to teach pupils with dyslexia'.

The training will then involve the following steps:

1. The training provider will use experts to explain the core competency to the trainees, linking to both theory and evidence from research findings.
2. The training provider will show them what good and bad practice for each competency looks like using films, pupil work, lesson plans, marking, classroom transcripts and classroom observations of experts. Dr Grossman calls this 'representation'. There should be in-depth critical analysis and discussion of all these (Dr Grossman calls this 'decomposition' – breaking down a complex practice into its constituent parts). The mentor or trainer shows how different strategies are available and which may be best.
3. Then trainees try out the skill, though maybe not in a full classroom at first because we want a non-stressed environment and to isolate one skill. Dr Grossman calls this 'approximations of practice' – just like a trainee pilot using a flight simulator or a surgeon practising on a dummy. This could take the form of role-play – although we may not like role-play because we are British. Instead, we can use co-teaching, where the trainee teaches a part of a lesson focusing on the core competency. Then there will be a debrief on the trainee's efforts by the mentor or other expert.
4. The trainee can then teach a whole lesson, followed by feedback and opportunities to practise further and improve.

Teacher training delivered by multi-academy trusts and some schools

At some stage, most young teachers will receive training provided by their multi-academy trust (MAT) or school. This training could be very different to the training described in this chapter, because the school where you choose to work might have particular requirements.

Some MATs and schools require teachers to teach in a very specific way and follow a script. This has two advantages and one big disadvantage. The advantages are that making teachers follow a script helps to minimise the impact of bad teachers – they are, at least, delivering an approved curriculum. And if a teacher is ever away, the cover teacher can pick up the script and carry on where the absent teacher left off.

The disadvantage is that there is little job satisfaction in delivering someone else's script, as one of the principal elements of job satisfaction is autonomy (see Daniel Pink, 2011, *Drive: The Surprising Truth About What Motivates Us*). That is why the prescriptive training offered by some MATs and schools can be dispiriting.

Another factor is that a school may have a particular ethos, and every teacher is expected to work with that ethos. Steiner schools and Montessori schools (page 292), for example, believe young children learn in a particular way, and so their teachers have to be trained accordingly.

Applying for teacher training

You can apply for teacher training at any time, but the earlier you do so in the school year the greater your chance of success. You can use the DfE 'Get Into Teaching' website (see page 9), or you can apply directly to a university or training provider.

For a QTS course, you need a UK university degree and GCSE passes in maths and English, plus a GCSE science for those training to become primary teachers. If you don't have a UK university degree or the required GCSEs, the alternatives you could use are described in the DfE's criteria and supporting advice (see page 17).

You need to decide:

- Where you want to be. Close to home or not?
- Whether you want to work and earn money while you train, such as on an employment-based course like those provided by the University of Buckingham or Teach First.
- If you are doing an employment-based course, do you want to follow the apprenticeship route?

Chapter 3
Getting ready for teacher training

The best use of your time before you start training is to discover what you will be teaching in your placement school and start building your subject knowledge. You should then find out about the resources the pupils will have, such as textbooks, and become familiar with them. If possible, discuss these things with the mentor who will be looking after you.

It's ideal to do lesson preparation before you begin training because it's difficult to prepare lessons as well as marking work after the end of every school day. Your mentor should tell you what they want you to cover in the time you are with them. They may give you a week-by-week breakdown of what you will be expected to teach with a list of resources, or schemes of work, that you can use.

Speak to your training provider or your main placement school as early as possible about the second school placement.

Things you need to do before you start teaching practice

- Make your own teaching notes, using AI if that is helpful.
- Create a summary syllabus for the pupils in each class so they and their parents can see what you're covering.
- Create a knowledge organiser for the content, concepts and key vocabulary you will be teaching.
- Know whether you are following a course bought by the school, such as White Rose maths.
- Establish whether the pupils will have textbooks.
- Create your own printed workbooks.
- Think about the organisation of your classroom (if you have one).
- Be clear about the rules and routines of your school and classroom.
- Ensure resources are ready, such as a visualiser, clock, whiteboards, whiteboard pens and rubber, textbooks, exercise books, paper, spare writing pens for pupils, files, hole punchers, computers and projectors.
- Plan any practical work in subjects like science and design and technology.
- Plan the term as a whole, and some of the first lessons.
- Plan tests and homework.
- Obtain a mark book (either digital or paper).

- Make sure you know who your pupils are in each class, something about their prior attainment and which have special needs. Prior attainment could be their primary school SATs results or, for sixth formers, their GCSE results.
- Make sure you know the teaching assistants, technicians and SENCOs.

Before you start training, you must have had training in child protection and have read the DfE's 'Keeping Children Safe in Education' and the school's safeguarding policy. You also must know that if you are worried about a child's safety or welfare, it's not your job to sort it out – your job is to report the issue to the school's designated safeguarding lead immediately.

How beginner teachers progress over time

You may go through the following stages at the beginning of your career:

- When teachers begin teaching, they focus on control of the class and having an orderly classroom. This is understandable.
- When they are more confident, they focus more on 'delivering the syllabus'.
- When they are confident about the syllabus, they start to think about individual children and building their skills and conceptual understanding.

Managing your life when doing teacher training

Teacher training is quite demanding. You may have to get up early in the morning to be in school by 8am, and you will be teaching for much of the time, especially in an employment-based course. You have not taught before, so you have to prepare lessons and build your subject knowledge. You have to prepare resources for every lesson, liaising with technicians in some subjects. You will want to do marking, yet you need to leave time for the teacher training course, which involves lectures and seminars, essays, meeting your mentor, observing other teachers and getting feedback on your own teaching.

You need to avoid getting stressed and burned out, so make sure you:

- Try to do as much of the lesson preparation, including photocopying, before the term begins, and use AI where it helps.
- Manage your marking – you do not have to write huge amounts, and you can easily set tests in a lesson that are marked by the pupils themselves.
- Devote time every weekend to preparing the week ahead but leave time for yourself.

Teaching when you have a cold and are losing your voice is hard – invest in throat lozenges.

Safeguarding is everyone's responsibility...

Before you start working in any school, you will receive safeguarding training and you will need to obtain a certificate. Any trainer will mention the phrase 'safeguarding is everyone's responsibility'. It's important that you read the latest version of 'Keeping Children Safe in Education' (sometimes referred to as KCSiE), which is published by the DfE with updates every September. Read about the changes each year to keep yourself up to date.

All teachers should have regular training that covers the essential elements of child protection and safeguarding. You may have training provided by your local authority or trust, or you may follow external courses. Many schools now provide a 'safeguarding snippet' in weekly staff newsletters or ask questions in staff meetings, and it's expected that you will always know the answers to these questions.

When starting in teaching, it's important to understand the role of safeguarding and how to keep children safe:

- **Training.** Teachers often need level 1 or 2 safeguarding training, but the levels vary between training providers. Training can be basic or advanced and can be delivered through eLearning, virtual events or face-to-face sessions.
- **Responsibilities.** Teachers should be aware of signs of abuse or neglect and be prepared to report them. They should also create a safe environment for children and teach them about safety.
- **Reporting.** Teachers should know how to report concerns and who to report them to. They should also record their concerns in accordance with good recording principles.
- **Online abuse.** If a child is being cyberbullied, teachers should report this immediately to the school safeguarding lead.
- **When you are interviewed.** When asked about safeguarding, teachers should demonstrate knowledge of proper procedures, sensitivity and the importance of confidentiality.

...however, you are not alone

An oft-quoted case in safeguarding training, the death of a child called Victoria Climbié, changed safeguarding policy in the UK. Following a public enquiry, all of the parties involved in her case were widely criticised. It was found that there were numerous instances where Victoria could have been saved, that many of the organisations involved in her care were badly run and more importantly, information was not being shared across the various agencies involved. If the information had been shared, it was likely that she would have been saved.

Every school has at least one (and usually many more) designated safeguarding lead (DSL). These members of staff can be consulted about any concerns you may have about a child or member of their family. You will be trained in the use of the school's online safeguarding system to log any small concerns you may have, but any more urgent concerns must be reported by you to the DSL immediately. An issue like unexplained bruising, for example, will need to be called in by a DSL to the local multi-agency safeguarding hub (MASH) immediately, and the MASH team may even decide that a child can't be allowed to go home at the end of the school day.

What are the key principles of safeguarding?

Several key principles underpin strong safeguarding to ensure the welfare, safety and happiness of children. These mainly include:

- A child's needs should always come first.
- It's important to help and support children as early as possible before an issue escalates.
- Safeguarding is everybody's responsibility, and everyone at a setting should act in a timely and coordinated manner to respond to any concerns about the welfare of a child. Your job is to report any concern to the DSL.
- You cannot promise a child confidentiality if they speak to you.

Common mistakes in safeguarding

Launching an investigation yourself.

- If you become aware of a potential problem, do not start investigating. Report it to a more experienced teacher.

Not reporting safeguarding concerns.

- In some instances, people are so concerned about making data breaches that they don't report legitimate safeguarding concerns to the necessary authorities. This is often due to a lack of internal training or processes covering how to handle these situations.

Making assumptions.

- There are occasions when a teacher (or teachers) may be tempted to think, 'surely that couldn't happen in that family'. This is a dangerous assumption to make. Remember, it could happen in *any* family.

Openly discussing an issue.

● You have to treat safeguarding issues as confidential. You should report your concerns, but do not engage in chat with colleagues or other people. (A friend once had to give up his safeguarding role because he was overheard discussing issues on a train.)

Thinking there are only four main categories of abuse.

● The four main categories of abuse – physical, sexual, emotional and neglect – help us understand how different types of abuse can harm children and how they can be identified. But the DfE is very clear that there are other types of abuse or welfare concerns that may not be mentioned in your school safeguarding and child protection policies, so do make sure you know what these are:

- Bullying
- Child sexual exploitation
- Children appearing in court
- Children with family in prison
- Criminal exploitation/county lines
- Cyberbullying
- Drugs
- Fabricated and induced illness syndrome
- Faith abuse
- Female genital mutilation (FGM)
- Gangs and gang culture
- Generational abuse
- Gender-based violence/violence against women and girls (VAWG)
- Grooming
- Harassment
- Hidden harm
- Homelessness
- Honour-based violence
- Invisible children
- Mental health
- Missing education
- Other forms of domestic violence and abuse
- Peer abuse
- Private fostering
- Radicalisation
- Sexting
- Teenage relationship abuse
- Trafficking

Chapter 4
High expectations

ITTECF syllabus

High expectations (Standard 1 – Set high expectations)

Learn that...	Learn how to...
1. Teachers have the ability to affect and improve the wellbeing, motivation and behaviour of their pupils. 2. Teachers are key role models, who can influence the attitudes, values and behaviours of their pupils. 3. Teacher expectations can affect pupil outcomes; setting goals that challenge and stretch pupils from their starting points is essential. 4. Setting clear expectations can help communicate shared values that improve classroom and school culture. 5. A culture of mutual trust and respect supports effective relationships. 6. High quality teaching has a long-term positive effect on pupils' life chances, particularly for pupils from disadvantaged backgrounds. 7. High quality teaching is underpinned by positive interactions between pupils, their teachers and their peers. 8. Pupils' experiences of school and their readiness to learn can be impacted by their home life and circumstances, particularly for EAL pupils, young carers and those living in poverty.	**Communicate a belief in the academic potential of all pupils, by:** a) Using intentional and consistent language that promotes challenge and aspiration. b) Setting tasks that stretch pupils, but which are achievable, within a challenging curriculum. c) Creating a positive environment where making mistakes and learning from them and the need for effort and perseverance are part of the daily routine. d) Seeking opportunities to engage parents and carers in the education of their children (e.g. proactively highlighting successes) and consider how this engagement changes depending on the age and development stage of the pupil. **Demonstrate consistently high behavioural expectations, by:** e) Creating a culture of inclusion, respect and trust in the classroom that supports all pupils to succeed (e.g. by modelling the types of courteous behaviour expected of pupils). f) Teaching and rigorously maintaining clear behavioural expectations (e.g. for contributions, volume level and concentration).

Learn that...	Learn how to...
	g) Applying rules, sanctions and rewards consistently in line with school policy, including where individual pupils have an agreed tailored approach, escalating behaviour incidents as appropriate. h) Acknowledging and praising pupil effort and emphasising progress being made.

High expectations in secondary schools

This standard deals with two separate types of high expectation: pupil behaviour and pupil academic work. The four comments on behaviour ('Learn how to...' points e) to h)) are very important, so we will come back to them in Chapter 10.

High expectations of pupil work

A higher than usual level of syllabus content and demand

The highest-achieving secondary schools often teach work during Year 7 that other schools leave to years 8 or 9. Such schools often talk about a 'knowledge-rich curriculum' and produce their own textbooks and knowledge organisers to raise the level of demand. On the whole, the lessons you teach and the work you set should be stretching but achievable.

In 2024, Sir Jonathan Bate, the Professor of English at Oxford University, suggested that some students struggle to read long novels at university because a focus on 'crowd control' in schools meant these pupils were never stretched in terms of reading. He found that some literature students struggle to finish one book in three weeks when they had previously been able to read three in just one week.

Expecting all pupils to reach a good level

Many pupils are capable of reaching a much higher level than they are actually performing at. The evidence for this comes from those schools that achieve high levels of value added with pupils from disadvantaged backgrounds (see Lenon, B., *Much Promise*, 2017, which explains exactly what these schools do). The evidence also comes from countries like Japan, which do not have the long tail of underachievement we find in England. For example, the weakest third of pupils in England do quite badly at GCSE compared to East Asian countries.

We all know what high expectations means: setting the bar fairly high for all pupils. You set the expectation that pupils work hard and do well in tests. But the key point about high expectations is what you actually do about a pupil who gets 9 out of 20 in a test, or even 14 out of 20. If you have high expectations, the next step is to ask the pupil to resit the test and carry on resitting until they reach your bar. That will require time set aside to do the retest, and possibly time to reteach some of the trickier work.

This is the crucial step that distinguishes the most dedicated teachers from the rest; it's the step that will make the difference between success and failure for weaker pupils. Simply saying, 'teachers should have high expectations' is not wrong in itself, but what really matters – and is unspecified in the ITTECF – is how that aspiration works in practice. This is an example of 'obviousness of a tricky kind'.

Two common obstacles to achievement

One obstacle is the pupil having a special need, such as dyslexia, which holds them back. In this case the school should provide SEND support, but unless the pupil's special need is quite severe you should not allow your knowledge of their needs to lead to too many allowances.

Another obstacle is that the pupil comes from a family that has not promoted the value of school or exam passes and perhaps has not taught the child to read. As a result, they have been behind all their lives. Some argue that children from low-income homes who are on free school meals struggle at school. On average this is a true statement, but there are many children on free school meals who do very well at school. So on the one hand, you may need to provide additional support to some children from low-income homes, but on the other hand you must not fall into the trap of creating self-fulfilling prophecies.

The same is true of other sub-groups, such as boys or children from a minority ethnic group (Afro-Caribbean, for example). The same principle applies: knowing the average data for a group (such as 'boys do worse than girls at GCSE') doesn't tell you much about the individual children in your class.

If a pupil has poor English, they need extra help

When a pupil struggles with English, the school should drop them from one subject and replace that time with literacy lessons if possible. As the teacher, you need to correct bad spelling and get the pupil to write out the correct spelling 3–5 times. Teach them vocabulary, including subject-specific terminology.

All pupils need help with oracy (speaking well), which includes the use of complete sentences, using academic speech and speaking with good audibility.

Try to teach children effort and perseverance. You may need to have a chat with them individually, giving encouragement – as the ITTECF suggests, good relationships make this easier.

Doug Lemov and high expectations

In Doug Lemov's books and website, *Teach Like a Champion*, he identifies a number of good techniques that work in schools in the US:

- No pupil may opt out of a question; all need to rehearse success.
- Set and defend a high standard of correctness, meaning you need to have worked out the correct answer first. What are you expecting the pupils to say or write?
- Use follow-up questions that extend knowledge; for example, ask for a better word or say, 'tell me more'.
- When pupils are speaking in class, get them to use complete sentence answers.
- Insist on audibility, correct grammar and vocabulary.
- Never apologise for things being rigorous, academic or requiring hard work.

Hard work

Most pupils (and some teachers) have no idea what hard work actually means. It's virtually impossible for a secondary age pupil to do well if they are not able to work reasonably hard.

How do you get pupils to work hard?

You have to explain why hard work is going to be worthwhile, because if pupils work hard they will achieve good results, which may well lead to a good job and a better life. You have to explain that most successful people, including footballers and musicians, have only become successful through dedicated hard work. At GCSE, the correlation between results and ability is weaker than the correlation between results and effort.

You also have to explain what hard work means. In terms of homework, if you have given pupils 30 verbs to memorise, you need to explain how they go about doing that and that the final step in the revision process is to write out the verbs from memory.

In terms of Easter holiday revision before GCSE exams begin (in May), hard work means revising every GCSE subject once. That means making notes from your notes or text and then seeing if you can write them out a third time from memory. That will take five hours a day at least, right through the Easter holidays – that is what hard work means.

Finally, you have to give pupils the experience, every day and every week, of the ways in which a bit of effort yields good results. They can do it... if they try.

Target grades

Many secondary schools give pupils target GCSE grades based on their prior attainment (such as the SATs tests they took at age 11) and what the data suggests pupils with that level of prior attainment tend to achieve. Target grades can be good, but:

- You should be aiming to get every pupil the highest grades irrespective of their targets.
- Some pupils improve greatly over time. Pupils who do not speak English much at home tend to struggle at the start of primary school but overtake those who speak English at home by the end of Year 6. Some boys take a long time to mature, but they can make great progress at ages 15 and 16.
- Some pupils are very good at some subjects and bad at others. Target grades do not always reflect this, especially if they are based on SATs scores in reading, writing and maths. What about a pupil whose main strengths are music or art?

Target *effort* grades are a good thing – all pupils should be showing a good level of effort.

The balance of sticks and carrots

This is where the skill of a teacher is important. You can see that the ITTECF places the emphasis on gentle encouragement and praise – this is correct, as often an encouraging word is needed if a pupil is going to try harder rather than give up. A skilful teacher gives a pupil work they are fairly sure they can do and then praises them for doing it.

If a pupil doesn't seem to understand how to answer a question, you should model using a worked example so they can see what is required. In maths, this may be the steps you take to solve an equation. In history, this may mean showing how to structure an answer, the correct length of the answer and level of detail expected.

Never say, 'just do your best'. After the age of 10, all pupils *want challenge* – watch them playing sport or a video game. Most work we set is too easy – 'doing work' is not enough if it lacks challenge.

What about sticks? If a pupil is intelligent but lazy – something that is true of many teenage boys – it's appropriate to give them a detention under school supervision to complete the work they have failed to do. If a pupil has simply not completed homework for no good reason, they must be required to complete it quickly.

How can high expectations apply to lower attaining pupils?

Some pupils are lazy while others seem to find learning difficult, but it's amazing what good teachers can do to get good GCSE grades with such unpromising teenagers.

Take our former colleague Eugene Higgins. Eugene is always given the bottom set for GCSE maths because he gets them good grades. How does he do this? He has a no-nonsense but perfectly warm relationship with his pupils. He knows that they all believe they are bad at maths, but they know he can drive them to glorious results.

This is what Eugene recommends:

- Build confidence – little steps can make pupils believe they are able mathematicians. They need to know that everybody can do maths.
- Give them easy assessments and tests initially. Use mini whiteboards.
- Every lesson must be fun. Whether you use a quiz or a worksheet, variation is important.
- Use past-paper questions every week, focusing on the first 12–14 easier questions – the bottom set can become good at these. Often those in the bottom set lack the ability to retain information, so repetition is essential for them.
- Get the pupils to put solutions on the whiteboard and explain these to the rest of the class. It's helpful to have the pupils talk about maths.
- Place an emphasis on memorisation, as lots of things in maths are simply rules that simply need to be learned.
- Always set high expectations.

You can see how these recommendations reflect the ITTECF:

- Teacher expectations can affect pupil outcomes; setting goals that challenge and stretch pupils from their starting points is essential.
- Use intentional and consistent language that promotes challenge and aspiration.
- Set tasks that stretch pupils, but which are achievable, within a challenging curriculum.

- Create a positive environment where making mistakes and learning from them and the need for effort and perseverance are part of the daily routine.
- A culture of mutual trust and respect supports effective relationships. Effective relationships between the teacher and pupils make it more likely the pupils will work well.

Some children may have very little idea about the purpose of school and the multitude of career opportunities out there. When I worked with bright Bangladeshi girls in East London, many had no idea what a university was, why they should think about university, how they would get there and who would pay. Most rarely left their homes, and they spoke about central London as if it was another country. For these young people, just one teacher can make all the difference if they explain the options that could be open to them. Schools can also help hugely by educating the parents.

But for many, university is not the destination. In their case, the destination may be jobs in the local economy. Careers advice from teachers or local authority careers staff are one thing, but much better are talks given by former pupils or parents who can open their eyes to a variety of options. My hairdresser runs a chain, and he only employs young school leavers with a pass in English and maths GCSEs; this example can raise the motivation and determination of some pupils.

What about the 'child genius'?

Any teacher may come across a child who is exceptional. This often manifests itself in maths, music and chess, where a child can be many years ahead of the norm. What should you do with such children?

First, there is no need for them to sit public exams much earlier than other children; they will do well whenever they sit the exam. Collecting exam grades at a young age is not necessary, or especially desirable.

Second, if the pupil is very able, there is little point in them sitting through lessons covering topics they may have mastered years ago. These pupils need a teacher who can teach or set them more difficult work that they find interesting. A top sixth form mathematician may embark on Open University modules, for example, or another subject with a mathematical element such as astronomy.

Third, very able pupils should be given a high degree of autonomy and allowed to explore knowledge for themselves. Research in China (Qin et al., 2021) looked at the likelihood of very able adolescent students suffering from depression. It found that those with high academic achievement *and* parents who gave them supportive autonomy (i.e. parents who were not controlling) were at lower risk of developing depression. Other studies have also found that a combination of care and autonomy yields the best results, while excessive parental expectations correlate with higher levels of anxiety. What damages such children is not high standards, but parents and teachers being too controlling. There can be clear expectations about what the pupil ought to achieve, but there should be plenty of freedom about how they go about achieving it.

Finally, don't overwhelm these children with excessive praise. Point them in the right direction and let them get on with it.

Dumbing-down

The results of international PISA tests confirm that children in the UK know less at age 15 than in some other countries such as Singapore and South Korea. In part this is because of 'dumbing-down' – syllabuses and exams have got easier. It's good for teachers to know how hard O-level papers were before they were replaced by GCSEs in 1986, as these old papers show what standard can be reached by children in the upper part of the ability range.

Compare the following two questions from exam papers that are 46 years apart.

O-level French paper (1974)

Translate the following passage into French:

I like reading. My father's favourite pastime is watching the television. My brother is never happier than when he is playing football. Mother is interested in the theatre.

Last Sunday, when we had finished lunch, we began to make plans for the summer holidays. Everybody wanted something different. My brother, as usual, was particularly difficult.

'I want to go to Spain,' he declared. 'The Duponts went to Alicante last year and are going back there in August. I should be able to bathe and go out in their boat with them.'

I replied, very reasonably, that it is too hot at the seaside. I would prefer to be in the country where one can sit in the shade of a tree or beside a stream or go for walks in the woods.

In the end, no doubt, we shall spend a month, as always, at my uncle's. Mother will go to the theatre with my aunt. Dad and my uncle will sleep in front of the television. Paul will be at the stadium. And I, I will be bored.

AQA GCSE French paper (2020), higher tier

Translate the following passage into French:

I get on very well with my sister, so we often go to the shopping centre together. Yesterday I gave some clothes to the homeless. I think that one must help others. After my studies at university, I hope to live abroad, where I will do voluntary work for a year.

Evidence base: John Hattie's research

John Hattie was born in New Zealand and was a professor of education and director of the Melbourne Education Research Institute at the University of Melbourne, Australia. Hattie undertook the largest ever synthesis of meta-analyses of quantitative measures of the effect of different factors on educational outcomes, leading to his 2008 book, *Visible Learning: A Synthesis of Over 800 Meta-Analyses Relating to Achievement.*

Hattie found that teachers with high expectations achieved better results with pupils. The effect size in his research was 0.5 to 1.44. An effect size of 1.0 indicates an increase of one standard deviation on the outcome – in this case, the outcome is improving school achievement. A one standard deviation increase is typically associated with advancing children's achievement by 2–3 years.

What did Hattie find the teachers with high expectations looked like? They:

- Expect their pupils to do better, so they will push them to improve.
- See themselves as agents of change.
- Don't dwell on differences between students in a class – they expect them all to improve.
- Don't use differentiated activities for different children.
- Focus on motivation, persistence and hard work.

Getting the top grades

The London Schools' Excellence Fund (LSEF) paid for a research collaboration (Sing, 2015) between state and independent schools to identify which strategies and approaches make the difference for achieving top grades in key subjects at GCSE and A-level.

The rationale for this work was based on research published by the Sutton Trust, which reported that just five schools in England sent more pupils to Oxford and Cambridge over three years than nearly 2,000 others combined. The study highlighted that many state schools struggle to get their students the top grades required to enter top universities and, as a result, state school students were under-represented in these institutions. In contrast, independent schools tend to dominate the highest A-level grade score tables. The LSEF project wanted to learn from independent schools about the KS4 and KS5 strategies and approaches used to achieve such large numbers of A/A* grades in English, maths and the sciences.

The LSEF project found that in many ways teaching in state and independent schools was similar. However, successful independent schools were more likely to have teachers with very strong subject knowledge, faster-paced lessons, high-order questioning to stretch pupils and higher levels of expectation by staff.

The project found that teachers must resist the temptation to make class conditions as easy as possible for children to 'succeed'. Instead, teachers must keep raising the bar and keeping students engaged with threshold (difficult) ideas in subjects, creating genuine struggle in lessons and exposing them to serious academic material. Teachers have to ensure pupils are regularly given the opportunity to defend their viewpoints against interrogation and criticism, and create deliberate difficulties in lessons rather than simply teaching familiar material well (Stephen and Warwick, 2015).

The only teachers who can achieve these things are those who are immersed in their subject and have a specialised way of thinking. These teachers keep students engaged with difficult and frustrating concepts that require the pupils to struggle somewhat; in this way, pupils develop deeper knowledge and cognitive skill. Successful teachers do not remove the struggle with too much scaffolding.

High expectations in primary schools

Having high expectations of pupils is probably the most important factor determining successful teaching and learning in primary schools. Communicating these expectations in a way that your pupils fully understand is an essential factor. You may recall that some of your favourite primary school teachers were the ones who expected the most from you in terms of behaviour and standards of work. You may even have referred to them as 'strict', but in all likelihood they would have been the teachers who you felt yourself succeeding with as a pupil. This is because you felt safe in their class, you would have been challenged and known how to achieve and you would have appreciated the boundaries they set so that everyone 'knew where they were' with them.

When I walk into a classroom, I immediately know if the teachers have high expectations. The pupils will also share these expectations within themselves;

they will look happy, motivated and well-behaved. There will be a sense of order and purpose. Pupils are likely to acknowledge you and explain their work to you. They know what they are doing and what success looks like.

It's sometimes challenging as a trainee or ECT to really capture how another teacher has set and communicated their high expectations with their class, and for this reason observations of others at the start of the school year are highly recommended. If possible, ask to observe with your mentor so they can point out the subtle indicators that the teacher is using with their class. It may be the tiniest look, change in body language or lowering of the voice that is making all the difference. The spoken language will be intentional and consistent. Expectations are often repeated.

Having an impact on pupils

Wellbeing

Anyone's wellbeing is negatively impacted by stress, negativity, worry, lack of appreciation and problematic relationships. We therefore need to create a classroom climate of success and positivity where everyone feels welcomed and valued. Some refer to this as the creation of a sense of belonging.

Imagine Ben's classroom. Ben welcomes his pupils at the door, positioning himself so he can see them lined in the corridor and then when they move into the classroom. Each one is greeted with a smile, a handshake and a 'good morning' or an 'alright mate', depending on his mood. Each pupil is expected to respond in the same manner so that immediate contact has been made and each pupil feels valued.

As the day progresses, Ben expects his pupils to behave well and work hard. The pupils know what this means because Ben has communicated his expectations with them repeatedly, and he is consistent. He will drop personal details into conversations when he needs to, particularly if someone is going through a difficult time. He compliments them when they work hard, showing his appreciation.

Motivation

The pupils work hard in Ben's classroom because they like him. Rather than being motivated by rewards (extrinsic motivation), they are internally (intrinsically) motivated because they like him and they want to please him. They love it when he praises them, clicks his fingers, smiles at them or says 'yes mate' because he is pleased with their effort. They know he will help them when they are stuck or unsure what to do. This happens rarely, as he always checks they understand the task in hand at the outset.

Behaviour

Rarely does Ben need to deal with challenging behaviour, because pupils are happy in his class. The work is not too hard for them (which would make it stressful), nor is it too easy (which would make it boring). They feel successful and enjoy being praised for it. Ben will compliment them on their behaviour as well as their work ethic, and he tells them he is proud of them. He does have a few pupils who struggle with communication and interaction needs, but he takes time with them to find out how to make life easier for them, whether they prefer to use ear defenders or sit in particular places, for example. Most of the time, they behave well on the playground or for supply teachers, as they know that breaches will be reported to Ben, and he won't be happy to hear about this. It matters to them what he thinks and how he thinks of them.

Teachers are key role models

You will have realised that Ben is a very positive role model for his pupils. They know he works hard and is kind to people, and they want to be like him because they admire him so much. Their attitude towards learning is positive, as is their attitude towards each other. As some people wear their hearts on their sleeve, Ben wears his values. The pupils know what is important to him and that his values are aligned with the school values. They know he values kindness, respect, aspiration and determination, and he demonstrates to them what these values look like and how we can live them. The pupils start to live these values themselves, and so their behaviours have also become influenced by Ben's role modelling.

Creating a culture of trust and respect

It could be argued that trust and respect are mutually inclusive. If I want my pupils to feel that making mistakes publicly is a good way for them – and others – to learn from their mistakes, then I need to cultivate and maintain a class environment where trust and respect are able to flourish.

Pupils need to know that making mistakes is an important aspect of learning new knowledge or skills. In a classroom where pupils are afraid to voice an opinion or attempt to answer a question, they need to be assured that they will not be laughed at or ridiculed for getting something wrong. I once worked with a Year 6 teacher, Nicky, who had a large banner at the front of her classroom which read:

> *Making mistakes is not just expected in this classroom; it is encouraged and welcomed.*

I have recently interviewed teachers, and I asked them the following questions:

- How important is it to establish trust and respect?
- How do you go about doing this?

The answers to the first question were a resounding 'very important'. One teacher, Joe, spoke of knowing that in his absence his class would behave just as well for a supply teacher or a teaching assistant. He said that putting in the extra work to build this culture of trust and expectation paid dividends tenfold, as he didn't need to waste time after the event sorting out what had gone wrong. Neither does he issue sanctions on the odd occasion that something may go awry – he holds discussions with his class about the importance of good behaviour and showing respect to every member of the school community. This ensures the pupils understand the need for respect, kindness and good behaviour, rather than being forced to 'behave well'.

How does Joe go about establishing this culture of mutual trust and respect? The answer to this question is double-sided; the word mutual is important, Joe explained. He nurtures the pupils' trust in him by always being calm, fair and consistent. He applies rules and expectations fairly across the class and expects the same standards of behaviour from all the pupils.

While Joe acknowledges the existence of neurodiversity within his classroom and sometimes puts in extra effort with certain pupils, no-one is exempt from the expectation that they will behave with respect and courtesy at all times. Likewise, he shows the pupils that he trusts them to make the right decisions and work hard. The more he shows them he expects the best from them, the more they rise to the challenge. With these methods and expectations, this demonstrates how he meets the criteria in e), f) and g) of the 'Learn how to...' statements.

High quality teaching

Numbers 6 and 7 of the 'Learn that...' statements refer to high quality teaching. So, we look back to Joe. As Joe has established his culture of high expectations for work and behaviour (which is underpinned by a culture of mutual trust and respect), it follows that he can teach high-quality lessons. Lesson time is not punctuated with behavioural issues but instead is marked by positive interactions between himself and his pupils and between the pupils themselves. The pupils understand that making mistakes is acceptable (indeed welcomed, as it is part of the learning process), and rather than ridiculing a peer who makes a mistake, pupils encourage each other.

During a maths lesson, for example, the following remarks are made by pupils:

I can understand how Jack got that answer; however, I think he forgot to add the two totals together.

I agree with what Ella said, but I would like to add some more things that I noticed about the patterns.

I think if Yasmeena had remembered to check that her numbers were in the correct columns, she would have got the correct answer.

These remarks demonstrate a culture of respect and inclusiveness. Everyone feels supported, not just by the adults in the room but also by other pupils. Sometimes the pupils work in pairs for the maths lesson, and it may be the case that pairs are mixed ability, sometimes with a pupil who is more confident in their maths ability working with another pupil who finds maths challenging. We know from EEF research that this approach benefits both pupils in such a partnership, as peer teaching helps to consolidate learning (EEF, 2021a).

Role modelling

We need to ensure that our teachers are calm, consistent and fair. We expect them to demonstrate the behaviours expected in their pupils; if a pupil holds a door open for a teacher, a simple 'thank you, that is kind of you' suffices for the pupil to understand how desirable this behaviour is and how desirable it is to repeat the behaviour. Similarly, the use of 'please' and 'thank you' from the teacher serves to model the importance of good manners to the pupil.

Use of 'thank you' can also be a pre-emptive expectation for desired behaviour. Asking a pupil to tuck their shirt in *please* is not nearly as impactful as asking the pupil to tuck their shirt in *thank you*, as the latter implies an assumption that the pupil will readily comply. Try it sometime – you will be amazed with the results.

Interventions

In any school, you will be faced with a situation where some children are way ahead while others are way behind. A good example is years 1 and 2 maths and reading, where some pupils will have been taught by their parents or in a good reception class while others were not.

In a class of 30, it's difficult dealing with this range of ability. It's hard enough hearing every pupil read every week, let alone providing extra help to the weaker pupils. Some form of intervention is needed, either by working with a small group within the context of a normal lesson while the rest do something else or by taking sub-groups out of normal lessons where they are taught additional maths or reading separately. Many schools will want to prioritise maths and reading, so these extra lessons can be taught during times when other subjects are being taught.

Increasingly in schools, pupils are not being removed from their lesson to be taught by a teaching assistant, as it is now widely acknowledged that pupils most in need of support should be spending their learning time with the most effective adult – the teacher. Where this is the case, the pupils may instead be involved in 'pre-teaching' sessions, where they are taught the concepts or vocabulary that will be necessary for them to fully engage with the main lesson.

This is what high expectations means – giving significant extra help so children who are behind can catch up. Nothing is more important, because children who are less able at maths, reading and writing when they leave primary school rarely catch up.

One major problem is funding. The extra help for small groups of children who need it is expensive, and not all schools can fund it. EEF research (2021b) in the UK highlights a number of factors with regard to this:

- One-to-one tuition and small-group tuition in sets of 2–5 do work. One-to-one tuition results in an extra five months of progress, but of course this is more expensive than small-group tuition, which results in four months of progress.
- For disadvantaged pupils, pupil premium money can be used to pay for small-group tuition.
- Group sizes larger than six reduce the effectiveness of small-group tuition.
- The quality of the teacher matters more than the size of the group.
- The staff who run this tuition require good training.

Evidence base: Some things to read

Education Endowment Foundation, 2021a, *Education Endowment Foundation Teaching and Learning Toolkit, Behaviour Interventions*. Online.

Education Endowment Foundation, 2021b, *Education Endowment Foundation Teaching and Learning Toolkit, Small Group Tuition*. Online.

Institute of Education Sciences, 2008, *Reducing Behavior Problems in the Elementary School Classroom*. Available at https://ies.ed.gov/ncee/wwc/PracticeGuide/4. A practical guide to improving behaviour in primary schools based on research in schools.

PISA, 2015, *PISA in Focus: Do teacher-student relations affect students' well-being at school?* This shows the importance of student wellbeing and the impact of better teacher-student relations on academic achievement.

Other references

Hattie, J., 2008, *Visible Learning: A Synthesis of Over 800 Meta-Analyses Relating to Achievement*, Routledge.

Hattie, J., 2023, *Visible Learning: The Sequel: A Synthesis of Over 2,100 Meta-Analyses Relating to Achievement*, Routledge.

Lemov, D., 2021, *Teach Like a Champion 3.0*, Jossey-Bass.

Lenon, B., 2017 *Much Promise: Successful Schools in England*, John Catt.

Qin, X., Kaufman, T., Laninga-Wijnen, L., Ren, P., Zhang, Y., and Veenstra, R., 2021, The impact of academic achievement and parental practices on depressive symptom trajectories among Chinese adolescents, Research on Child and Adolescent Psychopathology, 49(10), 1359–1371.

Sing, S., 2015, Pedagogical approaches to delivery of a knowledge-led, content-rich GCSE and A level curriculum: Learning with independent schools - RESEARCH REPORT, London Schools Excellence Fund.

Stephen, M. and Warwick, I., 2015, *Educating the More Able Student*, Sage.

Warwick, I. and Crossman, A., 2024, *Greater Expectations: Enabling Achievement for Disadvantaged Students*, Corwin.

Chapter 5
Promoting good progress and outcomes by pupils

ITTECF syllabus

How pupils learn (Standard 2 – Promote good progress)

Learn that...	Learn how to...
1. Learning involves a lasting change in pupils' capabilities or understanding.	**Avoid overloading working memory, by:**
	a) Taking into account pupils' prior knowledge when planning how much new information to introduce.
2. Prior knowledge plays an important role in how pupils learn; committing some key facts to their long-term memory is likely to help pupils learn more complex ideas.	b) Breaking complex material into smaller steps (e.g. using partially completed examples to focus pupils on the specific steps).
3. An important factor in learning is memory, which can be thought of as comprising two elements: working memory and long-term memory.	c) Reducing distractions that take attention away from what is being taught (e.g. keeping the complexity of a task to a minimum, so that attention is focused on the content).
4. Working memory is where information that is being actively processed is held, but its capacity is limited and can be overloaded.	**Build on pupils' prior knowledge, by:**
	d) Identifying possible misconceptions and planning how to prevent these forming.
5. Long-term memory can be considered as a store of knowledge that changes as pupils learn by integrating new ideas with existing knowledge.	e) Linking what pupils already know to what is being taught (e.g. explaining how new content builds on what is already known).
6. Pupils have different working memory capacities; some pupils with SEND may have more limited working memory capacity than their peers without SEND.	f) Sequencing lessons so that pupils secure foundational knowledge before encountering more complex content.
7. Where prior knowledge is weak, pupils are more likely to develop misconceptions, particularly if new ideas are introduced too quickly.	g) Encouraging pupils to share emerging understanding and points of confusion so that misconceptions can be addressed.
8. Regular purposeful practice of what has previously been taught can help consolidate material and help pupils remember what they have learned.	

Learn that...	Learn how to...
9. Requiring pupils to retrieve information from memory, and spacing practice so that pupils revisit ideas after a gap are also likely to strengthen recall. 10. Worked examples that take pupils through each step of a new process are also likely to support pupils to learn.	**Increase likelihood of material being retained, by:** h) Balancing exposition, repetition, practice and retrieval of critical knowledge and skills. i) Planning regular review and practice of key ideas and concepts over time (e.g. through carefully planned use of structured talk activities). j) Designing practice, generation and retrieval tasks that provide just enough support so that pupils experience a high success rate when attempting challenging work. k) Increasing challenge with practice and retrieval as knowledge becomes more secure (e.g. by removing scaffolding, lengthening spacing or introducing interacting elements).

One of the main purposes of school is for pupils to learn things that adults believe are important. Too often we teach, but the pupils do not learn. There is no point in delivering a whizzy lesson if the pupils have not learned something.

Methods that help pupils learn

Most good teachers use some of the teaching strategies described in this section – and many use them without even knowing it's a strategy. You should try them out and decide for yourself.

Strategy 1. Drive motivation

Pupils need to believe that learning the work is important and worthwhile. It's a good thing to explain why the topic you are studying is important, not least in subjects like chemistry and maths.

Older pupils need to understand the significance of good exam results and be given encouragement by the teacher. Many pupils respond to a teacher who says something positive, such as 'I believe you can do well'. The pupils will also be motivated if the teaching is good – that is, it has the right pace, it's interesting and they are all involved.

Popularity is also important. More pupils will be motivated to please the teacher if they like them and trust their judgement (consider pupils saying, 'We've got a great maths teacher this year').

In your teaching, you will need appropriate sticks and carrots to drive motivation. For example:

- **Sticks:**
  - 'You will have a retest if you do not get a high enough score.'
  - 'We will publish pupil rank orders based on the marks.'

- **Carrots:**
  - 'You will be formally recognised by me and the school for good effort or progress as opposed to just good marks.' (Some pupils are not academic enough to gain good marks, but their confidence can be maintained with good effort or progress scores.)

One of the best ways to drive motivation is to set pupils' specific goals, such as achievement goals (write five good reasons that explain why this war began) or effort goals (complete the homework set this week and hand it in on time). Another good way of motivating a pupil is to ensure they are successful, even if it's at one thing. It is often success that generates motivation, rather than the other way round.

Research evidence

Bandura, A. (1977) Self-efficacy: toward a unifying theory of behavioural change, Psychological Review, 84

Some pupils fail to perform at the level they are capable of in exams because they are fearful, much like a penalty-taker who is great in training but can't score in a real match. Bandura calls the ability to cope 'self-efficacy'.

To overcome psychological barriers, it is recommended that teachers should:

- Give pupils tasks they *can* manage to build confidence. The perceived cause of academic underperformance matters – the emotional response can profoundly affect future performance.
- Use modelling to increase the chance of pupils succeeding.
- Give pupils 'mini exams' in class to get them used to full exams.
- Discourage competition and emphasise personal progress. Focus on progress, not mistakes.
- Understand that general exhortations don't work – it must be subject-specific. For example, if the issue is algebra, teach them algebra well.

Dweck, C. and Leggett, E. (1988) A social-cognitive approach to motivation and personality, Psychological Review, 95

If a pupil believes they lack the ability to do a subject, they will not try ('fixed mindset'). If they believe they can improve, they may try ('growth mindset'). This is why too much focus on a test result is a mistake; if you give pupils a tough test and they do badly, that lowers their motivation – if they have a fixed mindset.

Of course, some children are more intelligent than others, so it's a lie to pretend that innate ability does not matter, and effort is all that counts. But what you can say is that those who struggle but keep trying do improve.

Zimmerman, B. (1989) A social cognitive view of self-regulated academic learning, Journal of Educational Psychology, 81

Independent learning is not a good way to become an independent learner. What works is clear instruction and explicit modelling of solutions and strategies – then pupils can work independently.

Students need to be motivated, and that requires:

- good teaching first, so they know what to do
- small steps so they make progress
- modelling
- verbal encouragement.

Lemov, D. (2021) *Teach Like a Champion 3.0*, Jossey-Bass

One of Doug Lemov's very simple tools ('call and response') is described in his book, *Teach Like a Champion*. Students chant key information they have been taught back to the teacher in unison, such a phrase in French or a piece of terminology. This gives even the weaker pupils a chance to pronounce key words, even if they are not quite remembering them. It generates energy and enthusiasm because everyone is involved.

Use of praise

Praise for students may be seen as affirming and positive, but a number of studies suggest that the wrong kind of praise can be harmful to learning. Stipek (2010) argues that praise that is meant to be encouraging and protective of low attaining students actually conveys a message of the teacher's low expectations. Praise for success with an easy task can therefore be interpreted by the pupil as the teacher having a low expectation of their ability, thereby diminishing confidence.

Effective use of praise in the primary classroom

1. **Praise is best when it is targeted at desired behaviours.**
   'I think it's brilliant that you persevered to the very end on that maths problem.'
   'Well done for remembering not to call out.'
2. **Make praise specific.**
   'I love the way you corrected your punctuation there.'
   'Well done, you really thought hard about the ending of your writing.'
3. **Monitor yourself and reflect on your use of praise.**
   When you are using praise, make sure it is meaningful, and drop the empty 'well done'. Children don't know what it is that they have done well unless you specifically tell them.
4. **Remember that praise, when given well, is good for self-confidence and fostering positive relationships.**

Strategy 2. Worked examples and modelling

Use worked examples to demonstrate how to do something before the pupils try it out for themselves. This is a fundamental method of teaching maths but should be used in all subjects, for example, how to write an introductory paragraph in a history essay. This is similar to modelling, where the teacher models how to do something. Examples of modelling include a design tech teacher showing how to make a dovetail joint before the pupils try for themselves or a maths teacher thinking aloud as he works out a solution on the board.

Keep the instructions as clear and simple as possible, and proceed in small steps. Then the pupils try it out; for example, they write the introduction to an essay with a different title but with the worked example in front of them. Then you put up a good answer – maybe one just written by a pupil – using a visualiser. Talk through the elements that make this a strong example.

Worked examples in primary schools

Worked examples are essential in the primary school. A common way of utilising them would be to gradually reduce scaffolding. In the context of primary mathematics, for example, worked examples can model step-by-step demonstrations of problem-solving procedures so pupils can gain an understanding of the underlying concepts and strategies. Here, worked examples become cognitive scaffolds, guiding pupils through the thought processes required to tackle a task.

Have a look at the EEF's blog on Worked Examples (2022). This is what they suggest:

> *Understanding what your pupils already know is key. Using worked examples when pupils are already proficient can potentially hinder learning. As teachers, our role is to be aware of which concepts our pupils find challenging, what prior knowledge and experience they bring with them, and adapt our teaching accordingly.*

The EEF uses the acronym 'FAME' to demonstrate strategies when using worked examples:

- **Fading** – once pupils have experienced complete worked examples, scaffolding can be reduced as they move towards independence.
- **Alternating** – alternate worked examples with opportunities for pupils to complete a similar problem.
- **Mistakes** – including mistakes in worked examples can provide further challenge. Supporting learners to explain why incorrect solutions are wrong can help pupils to develop deeper understanding than if they solely consider correct solutions.
- **Explanation** – to help pupils understand how and why the worked example has been used, teachers should model their thinking aloud. Explain what you are doing and why – out loud.

An example of this may be:

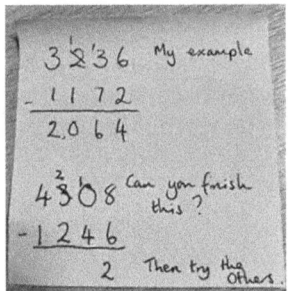

Strategy 3. Good questioning in class

Ask pupils questions, calling on them by name, not using 'hands up'. This is called 'cold calling'. If a pupil gives a wrong answer, ask another pupil. When the correct answer is found, go back to the pupils who gave the wrong answer and get them to give the correct version.

This sort of questioning is a type of formative feedback. It's not designed to formally mark and grade the pupil, rather it's designed to help them learn. It also lets the teacher know how well they are doing; for example, if you know there is a common error occurring in pupils' work, you can address this later through teaching about the problem directly. If pupils need to write in more detail, you can model what this looks like and then give them a specific, scaffolded task to help them achieve this for themselves.

Questioning will happen in most lessons. It will involve asking and answering questions orally or writing short answers on paper or a mini whiteboard. It will not involve giving marks.

Good questioning in primary

'Hands-down' questioning is just as effective in the primary classroom, as it does not simply rely on asking the pupils with their hands up, therefore ensuring full attention of the class. It's also a fantastic way to assess understanding of particular pupils. It's best if you ask the question first before saying the pupil's name, as this ensures everyone will have formulated an answer in their heads before knowing who will be asked to answer. This is often referred to as 'pose, pause, pounce, bounce'. ('Bounce' refers to bouncing the question around the class, as others may have thought of a good answer, particularly if it is an open-ended question.)

Strategy 4. Regular testing

Regular testing, or retrieval practice, is essential in order to discover what pupils have learned (and not learned) and because trying to recall things drives knowledge into the long-term memory.

Testing can be formal and higher stakes (marks are collected), or informal and low stakes. Starter quizzes and informal tests with answers written on mini whiteboards are great ways to test students' knowledge without the pressure of marks.

Research evidence

Craik, F. and Lockhart, R. (1972) Levels of processing: A framework for memory research, Journal of Verbal Learning and Verbal Behaviour, 11

How should we help pupils learn? By deep processing – in other words, really thinking about the topic. For example, copying notes off the board does not require thought, whereas making notes from a talk or book does require thought because pupils are required to paraphrase, abbreviate and focus on the most important points.

Other ways to help pupils learn include asking them to:

● Link what they are learning to their prior learning.
● Apply new knowledge to different situations.
● Explain new knowledge in their own words.
● Relate new knowledge to their personal experience.

Strategy 5. Spaced learning and interleaving

If you want to learn a poem, it's better to spend 20 minutes per day for three days than one hour in one day. In fact, revisiting a topic every 2–3 weeks can be very effective (Kim and Webb, 2022, showed this in relation to learning a second language). This is called 'spaced learning'.

Another useful method is **interleaving**, where you revisit topics while teaching different parts of the curriculum. Interleaving helps pupils identify links between different topics, which improves their understanding and makes them revisit topics they have covered through spaced learning.

Research evidence

Dunlosky, J., Rawson, K., March, E., Nathan, M., and Willingham, D. (2013) Improving students' learning with effective learning techniques: promising directions from cognitive and educational psychology, Psychological Science in the Public Interest, 14

Things that work:

● Spaced learning – 30 mins per day for four days is better than two hours in one day.
● Practice tests help pupils remember better.

Things that don't work so well:

● Rereading notes or text.
● Highlighting notes.
● Writing summaries of text that you need to learn.

Strategy 6. Desirable difficulty

One of the greatest insights in the last few years has been Robert Bjork's concept of desirable difficulties (1994), which suggests that introducing certain difficulties into the learning process can greatly improve long-term retention of the learned material. Some examples are:

- Spacing learning – include questions on past topics throughout different homework assignments or tests.
- Interleaving.
- Having pupils learn through a puzzle or other kind of active process, rather than simply reading passively.
- Varying the settings in which learning takes place.

What all of these difficulties have in common is that they seem to encourage a deeper processing of material.

It's understandable that pupils want learning to be easier and teachers want to make it easier. If a teacher tries a few different approaches to teaching some concept or material, they may conclude that the approach that leads to the most immediate and observable signs of improvement is the best one. However, when teachers try to facilitate learning by making it as easy as possible, while this may increase the immediately observable short-term performance it decreases the more important long-term retention.

Strategy 7. Scaffolding

A scaffold is a temporary support that is used to assist a pupil. These scaffolds are gradually withdrawn as pupils become more competent and include the teacher 'thinking out loud' as they solve the problem.

Scaffolding in primary

It's important that scaffolding is not simply sitting the children who have not grasped a concept at a table with the learning support assistant. Carefully considered flexible grouping often involves, for example, the teacher continuing to work to support a group of pupils with further explanation, modelling and practice before they are ready to work independently on a task. The eventual removal of scaffolding such as writing templates, word mats or times table grids is crucial and a skill of great teaching. Scaffolding provides needed support before encouraging independence.

Strategy 8. Mastery approach

When the coalition government was formed in the UK in 2010, it highlighted the fact that children in much of East Asia were ahead of children in the UK in terms of maths and science knowledge. A party was sent to Singapore to find out why, and their conclusion was important: in the UK we tried to teach too much, too fast, and our pupils were left with insecure knowledge. In countries like Singapore, the curriculum is based on the principle that the teacher does not leave a topic until it has been mastered by every pupil. *Do less but do it better.*

The mastery approach was examined by the EEF (2021), who concluded that the approach was inexpensive to introduce and on average very effective. However, there is a wide variation in the impact, the greatest being in primary schools, specifically in maths and science. Results in secondary schools were less impressive.

Mastery is not about offering new learning or pushing pupils to work at a higher level; it's about ensuring a deep mastery of each small step so new learning can be built upon strong prior knowledge. In the case of maths, primary-age children may be able to demonstrate mastery when they can represent concepts or skills in multiple ways, or when they are able to independently apply the concept to new problems in unfamiliar situations.

Strategy 9. Chunking

Otherwise known as 'small steps, chunking simply means teaching material in manageable steps – not too much at once. Pupils need to grasp each step before moving on.

Strategy 10. Link to existing knowledge (prior learning)

Linking to existing knowledge involves building new learning onto old learning by connecting to something pupils already know. This makes it much more likely the pupils will understand and remember.

It obviously helps to know what is already in your pupils' brains, because if you don't know you will either bore them to death with repetition or you run ahead too fast when they don't know the basics. This latter problem is especially serious in linear subjects such as maths and modern languages, where each lesson builds on the knowledge of a previous lesson.

In order to find out what is in the pupils' heads, you have to test them. If you discover that some pupils know more than others (which is what you might expect), then you have to take steps to bring them all up to a similar level. To look at one obvious example, there is little point in pupils taking maths to GCSE if they have not yet mastered their times tables. Pupils need to have their times tables in their long-term memories, because otherwise their working memory becomes rapidly overloaded as they try to work out simple multiplications.

It's a challenge in non-linear subjects if you discover that pupils have already been taught a topic, such as glaciation or the Romans. If this is the case, you have to work hard to build on the pupils' prior knowledge and make things interesting. Just because they studied it before, that doesn't mean their knowledge or understanding is secure.

David Ausubel was a psychologist who contributed to educational psychology and cognitive science and is best known for his work on the importance of prior knowledge. Ausubel (1968) argues that:

> *If I had to reduce all of educational psychology to just one principle, I would say this: the most important single factor influencing learning is what the learner already knows. Ascertain this and teach [them] accordingly.*

It is essential, therefore, that learning follows a logical sequence of progression.

Research evidence

Ausubel, D. (1960) The use of advance organizers in the learning and retention of meaningful verbal material, Journal of Educational Psychology, 51

Pupils learn better by relating new knowledge to their existing knowledge, so make sure the expected prior knowledge is secure before you begin. Test pupils on their prior knowledge so they bring it to mind, or you can see what they need to relearn.

Strategy 11. Avoiding cognitive overload

Thanks to neuroscience, we know that the brain has both working (short-term) memory and long-term memory. Working memory is the bit you are using most of the time in daily life. It has limited capacity, and much of what it contains, such as the things you have seen, read or done in the past day, is soon forgotten. Our working memory can handle something like 3–7 bits of information, after which it can't hold more.

The long-term memory has an unlimited capacity and, as the name suggests, it contains information that remains for months or years. The information in the long-term memory is grouped into topics and linking new knowledge to these topics helps to keep it in the long-term memory. These topics are called 'schemas' – we can visualise this concept in the diagram on page 56.

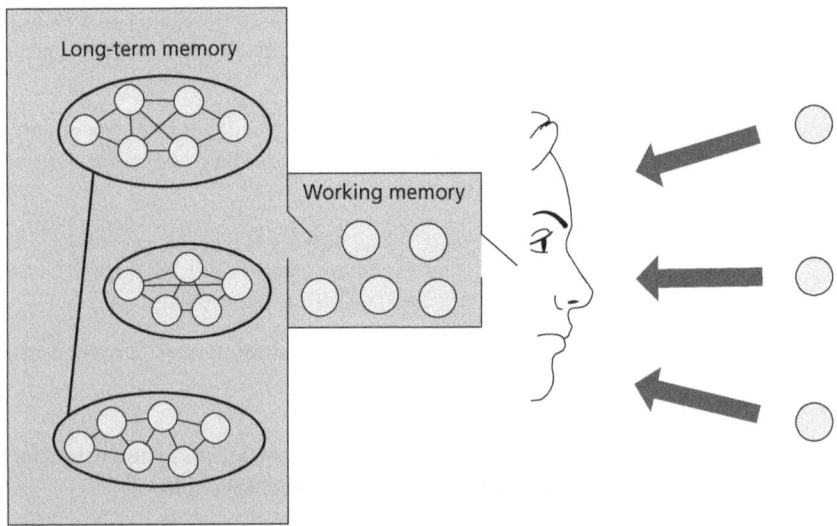

Because the working memory has limited capacity (or 'cognitive load'), if you try to do too much in one lesson it will soon become full. Once it is full, the pupils will learn little. In order to avoid wasting too much space in the working memory, we should keep things as simple as possible. For example, if pupils are working on a problem, try to keep quiet. Model problem solving through worked examples before allowing pupils to attempt the same task.

Other approaches include:

- Presenting new material in short, simple steps with plenty of opportunity to practice after each step until the pupils develop a greater understanding.
- Simplifying complex information by presenting it with both diagrams and words.
- Using explicit instruction rather than discovery-by-the-pupil methods.

Of course, this is what good teachers have always done – small steps, being very clear and using worked examples. The main point to bear in mind is that teaching is of little value if what you are teaching doesn't get into the long-term memory. Too many pupils are taught a great deal but learn nothing.

Cognitive overload in primary

Overloading working memory is also a problem in primary school. When pupils know declarative facts with quick recall, the working memory is free to concentrate on procedural knowledge. This is why there is a focus on learning number facts and phonics, so that automaticity can avoid filling space in the working memory, thereby reducing cognitive load.

Some primary teachers like to use 'brain breaks' or 'active breaks', which can help pupils literally take a break for their working memory as fatigue and sustained mental effort can increase cognitive overload. Incorporating regular breaks into learning time allows the brain an opportunity to rest and recharge, and short breaks – even just a few minutes – can improve focus, concentration and overall mental performance.

Avoiding distractions in the primary classroom

External distractions, such as noise or visual clutter, can lead to significant cognitive overload. Create a quiet and organised workspace, turn off notifications on electronic devices and eliminate other unnecessary distractions to focus your attention on the task at hand. Some gentle background music may aid concentration, particularly if there are noises coming from outside or another classroom.

It's important to avoid sensory overload for pupils – not only those with sensory processing needs, but the whole class. A common mistake in the primary classroom is to think that the overhead electric light always needs to be on, but this is not the case; sometimes muted lighting is best for everyone. If you are using slideshows, try to avoid clutter on the slides – keep it simple.

Cognitive load and working memory in the primary classroom

Here's a great example I observed in a trainee teacher's classroom. The teacher was teaching the pupils expanded noun phrases, and he took some time to talk through what these are and why it's good to use them in our writing. He then modelled them with the class before the pupils had a go in pairs at creating their own based on stimuli he had selected.

Next, he read a passage from that lesson's text. This took 15 minutes, after which I was certain his Year 3 pupils would have forgotten his input and modelling of expanded noun phrases. He wanted them to create their own expanded noun phrases from nouns in the text.

The brilliant part of this lesson was that he had planned for cognitive overload and working memory and knew that the pupils were likely to have forgotten the first part of his lesson – the modelling of expanded noun phrases. So, he repeated it, with nouns from the text. In this way, not only were the pupils able to learn twice from his examples, but they were also using retrieval of their previous learning. So in effect, he had taught them how to do this twice within 20 minutes. Consequently, when the pupils began their independent work, they could do so without help as the information had had the opportunity to 'sink in' – in other words, to move from their working memory into something longer term.

Research evidence

Sweller, J. (1988) Cognitive load during problem solving: Effects on learning, Cognitive Science, 12

The working memory has limited ability to code information. So, novice students will struggle with hard problems because they don't have the necessary background information in their long-term memory. The working memory quickly becomes overwhelmed.

One of the aims of education is to place useful knowledge in the long-term memory; doing problem solving doesn't necessarily achieve this. Pupils need knowledge before they can problem-solve, therefore attempts to get pupils to solve problems without the necessary knowledge is a waste of time.

Strategy 12. Dual coding

Dual coding involves explaining something using a diagram or picture and then using words. In other words, using two ways to understand the same thing.

Working memory has two channels: sight and sound. These are separate, and each has their own capacity. We should therefore present ideas that make the most of both channels – the visual and the auditory. Below is an example – the formation of a coastal stack.

© *Philip Bird LRPS CPAGB/Shutterstock.com*

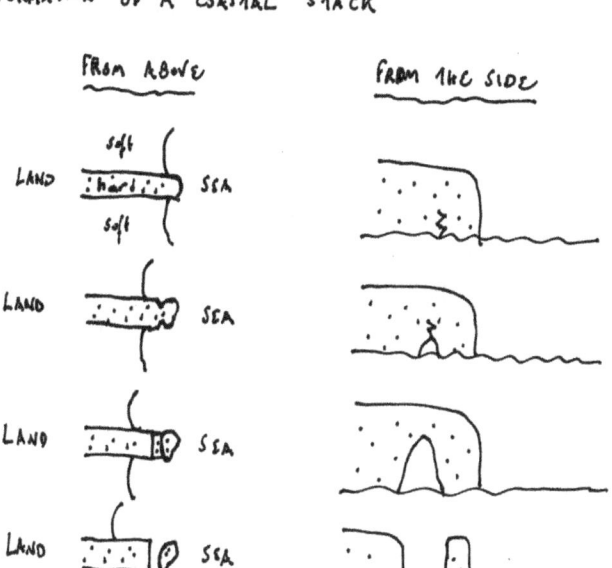

Stage 1

Show the photograph and then the diagram, which is very simple and doesn't have too much annotation. Explain that the images on the left of the diagram are taken from a helicopter looking down, and the images on the right are taken from a boat looking sideways on. Avoid too much text on the diagram to reduce cognitive load.

Stage 2

Once the pupils have understood this, ask them to annotate the diagrams with all the key terminology, which you explain:

- Formation of a headland because the rocks lie in bands at right-angles to the coast and some are harder than others. The softer rocks are eroded away.
- The headland has areas of weakness that are exposed by wave erosion. This creates a cave. If the cave cuts right through the headland, you get an arch. If the arch gets bigger and the top collapses, you are left with a stack.

By doing this annotation, the pupils are focusing partly on the visual (the diagram) and partly on the auditory (your description of the processes and terminology). But you have kept it simple.

Stage 3

Once they have understood all that, you can go into greater depth.

- Why might rocks form bands at right-angles to a coast?
- Why are some rocks more resistant to erosion than others? Why chalk?
- What might cause the weakness in a rock that allows a cave to form?
- What are the means by which the sea erodes rock?

The diagrams help a great deal. Starting with the diagrams (and a photograph of a real headland, arch and stack) makes this far easier for pupils to understand and remember. The diagrams had few notes to start with, and gradually these were added. Finally, we moved to more advanced concepts that could not easily be added to the diagrams but that the diagrams supported cognitively.

Primary

Used widely in the primary classroom, dual coding may consist of:

- Diagrams
- Icons and symbols
- Graphic organisers
- Sketch noting
- Posters
- Timelines
- Cartoon strips
- Infographics

Some examples commonly used in the primary classroom can be found across a variety of different subjects, and the principles are the same as those described above in secondary. Here are three to give you an idea:

© Peyker/Shutterstock.com   *© MarcoSa/Shutterstock.com*

Research evidence

Clark, J. and Paivio, A. (1991) Dual coding theory and education, Psychology Review, 3

You remember information if you process it both verbally and non-verbally. Words and diagrams are better than just text or diagrams alone. Do not put up a power point slide of words and them read it – this actually impedes learning. When explaining a diagram, do it verbally not through text in or around the diagram.

Kalyuga, S. and Sweller, J. (2014) The redundancy principle in multi-media learning, in Mayer, R. E. (Ed.), *The Cambridge Handbook of Multimedia Learning* **(2nd ed.), Cambridge University Press.**

If pupils have to deal with the same written and spoken words at once, they spend working-memory resources coordinating these written and spoken words, meaning less working memory is available for learning.

Strategy 13. Making good use of practical work

Science experiments and field trips help bring a subject alive, as they are memorable and an important part of the skill of the subject. They help pupils remember a topic much better than sitting listening to a talk. Unfortunately, pupils are more likely to remember the fun of the science equipment or the excitement of the trip than the purpose of either – the thing you really want them to know. So, the teacher has to train pupils to make the link in their brains between their mental image of the experiment or trip and what they were designed to demonstrate.

Strategy 14. Records of work

A set of notes or knowledge organiser for various topics make good records of the work that pupils need to learn. These should preferably be created on paper, as it's easier to learn compared to working on screen.

Good notes use colour and numbered points to organise key knowledge that has been learned. A knowledge organiser, such as the example on page 62, will probably not include all the information you want your students to know, but it's a great start and useful for a homework task (for example, 'learn this for a test').

MINI-BEASTS KNOWLEDGE ORGANISER

ESSENTIAL VOCABULARY

abdomen	The bottom part of an arthropod's body.
annelid	An animal with a long, segmented body.
antennae	The 'feelers' that arthropods use for sensing.
arachnid	An arthropod with 8 segmented legs and no wings or antennae.
arthropod	An animal with an exoskeleton, segmented body and jointed legs.
colony	A group of birds, insects or animals that live in a group together.
crustacean	An arthropod that is mainly found in water, often with a body covered in a hard shell.
exoskeleton	A hard shell covering the outside of the body.
mollusc	An animal with a soft body, no spine and often covered with a shell.
thorax	The middle part of an arthropod's body which the legs and wings are attached to.
larva	The young form of an insect.
decomposer	An organism that decomposes organic material.
metamorphosis	The process of transformation from young to an adult form.
hibernate	When some animals have long periods of deep sleep in very cold weather.
insect	A small animal that has 6 legs and generally one or two pairs of wings

Main Types of Mini-beasts

There are four main types of mini-beasts.
- Insects
- Arachnids
- Molluscs
- Crustaceans

Insects

Insects have three segments to their bodies: the head, the thorax and the abdomen. They have 6 legs and usually one or two pair of wings. Examples of insects are ants and flies.

Head
Thorax
Abdomen

Crustaceans

Crustaceans are arthropods that have two pairs of antennae and are covered in a shell.

Most crustaceans live in the sea. Examples of crustaceans are crabs and lobsters.

Molluscs

Molluscs are animals that have a soft body, no spine and are often covered in a shell. They often live in water. Examples of molluscs are snails and oysters.

Shell

Soft, spineless body

Arthropods

Arthropods all have an exoskeleton (skeleton outside their body), a segmented body and six jointed legs. Arthropods are the largest group of mini-beasts.

Arachnids

Arachnids are arthropods that have eight segmented wings and no antennae. Their bodies are divided into two parts: the head and thorax in one part and the abdomen in the other. Examples of arachnids are spiders and scorpions.

Head and thorax
Abdomen

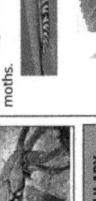

Life Cycle of Insects- metamorphosis

Remember the Very Hungry Caterpillar? The female lays eggs on a leaf, which a larva grows inside. The larva then eats a lot in preparation for the chrysalis stage. When it is ready, the insect seals itself in a protective case (a chrysalis). This is called the pupa stage. After a while, it emerges as a fully grown adult, often with wings. Insects that go through complete metamorphosis include ladybirds, butterflies and moths.

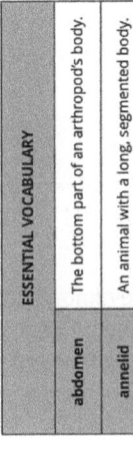

LINKS TO PREVIOUS LEARNING AND VOCABULARY

Food chain	Decomposers form part of the food chain.
Life Cycles	Insects go through metamorphosis as part of their life cycles.
Evolution	Some animals have evolved to hibernate to survive harsh winters.
Habitats	Insects are found in a variety of habitats.

Tips on testing your pupils

Okay, so you have taught well, but your pupils have learned little. Professor Rob Coe (2013) noted this when he was at Durham University and visited schools: 'there are plenty of things that make a lesson look good, but the pupils may not have learned much.' Coe listed the following as poor proxies for learning:

- The students are busy – lots of work is being done (especially written work).
- The students are engaged, interested and motivated.
- The students are getting attention through feedback and explanations.
- The classroom is ordered, calm and under control.
- The curriculum has been 'covered' (i.e. presented to students in some form).
- (At least some) students have supplied correct answers, even if they:
  - have not really understood them
  - could not reproduce them independently
  - will have forgotten them by next week
  - already know them anyway.

Teaching the curriculum well is not enough; you have to ensure it's remembered by pupils, that it's held in their long-term memory. This means you have to quiz or test the pupils regularly. The point is that in order for us to remember something we have to first make some effort to learn it, and we have to recall (or retrieve) it from the long-term memory on a fairly regular basis. If we don't, the memory fades.

There are three things to bear in mind when testing your pupils. First, you must test regularly, which you can do informally by asking questions in class or having quizzes. This should happen in most lessons. Then, for older pupils, you should give formal tests, probably every two weeks. The pupils should be given time to revise, told what the pass mark is and they should have to repeat the test if they fail. Failure to learn the work should not be the final step in the process of teaching a topic; this is what we mean by high expectations.

'How do I find the time to reteach and retest a topic to pupils who are falling behind?' This is an important question for a teacher, because pulling the weakest pupils up to the level of the rest is the most challenging job of a teacher. Your school needs a system that creates the time to do this. Some schools have times in the week set aside for extra tuition; if your school doesn't, you may need to arrange a time after school. Parents need to be informed so they know their child will be late home on that day.

Primary pupils should be asked to do 'think, pair, share', where they turn to their partner, for example, and say what they can remember from the last lesson or the last 15 minutes of this lesson. Allowing thinking time first (or writing time for older pupils) gives pupils the time needed to recall prior learning and form a decent oral or written response.

The second thing to bear in mind is that pupils should be required to recall work done in the last lesson, week or term. Therefore, every test, formal or informal, should facilitate recall. For example, a teacher could say the following:

> *On Friday we will have a 20-question test. 15 of the questions will be on the topic we have just studied, and five will be on other work we have done this year.*

This is also an example of spaced practice – you don't learn something once, but should instead keep coming back to it.

In their 2008 study, Verkoeijen et al. split pupils into three groups: group 1 was asked to reread a text they were studying immediately after a first read; group 2 waited for four days; and group 3 waited three and a half weeks. In a retest, group 2 performed best, so spaced rereading works – as long as the space is not too great.

It's common practice in some primary schools to carry out a low-stakes test in order to recall prior learning. Sometimes this may take the form of a 'flashback 4' exercise; below is an example of a flashback 4 exercise used at the beginning of a primary maths lesson.

1. How many mm in 20cm?	Recalling prior learning from **yesterday**
2. Subtract 2,375 from 8,193	Recalling learning from **last week**
3. How much change would Ellie have from £10 if she buys a toy that costs £2.83 and another that costs £5.46?	Recalling learning from **last term**
4. Subtract 49 from 73 on your number line	Recalling learning from **last year**

A third point to consider is that pupils should be discouraged from merely reading their notes or highlighting them in order to drive information into the long-term memory, they need to do more than that. A more effective method is to write out notes and then write them out again from memory, going back to anything they had forgotten.

Revision tips for secondary pupils

Between the ages of 11 and 15, I was quite bad at school. I passed the 11+ exam, got into a good school and found myself in the top set, and for this reason my teachers assumed I knew how to learn and took little trouble with me. But I didn't know how to learn, so my performance in linear subjects (subjects where every lesson builds on the last lesson, such as French and maths) deteriorated. When I was 16, my parents moved from the local area and I was fortunate to become a boarder. Here, I was able to watch the behaviour of my new friends in the boarding house; I learned to make notes from a textbook, and I learned the techniques of memorisation (see page 196).

When I was 18, I was offered a scholarship to Oxford conditional on passing the French O-level (which I had failed at the first attempt). The next sitting of the exam was five weeks after I received the letter from Oxford, so using my newly acquired skills I set out to learn 2,000 words in French and a bit of grammar. I had 'learned' French at school for six years and knew almost nothing, but I taught myself for five weeks and passed well enough. This is a reminder that pupils can improve, but also that they need to be explicitly shown the meaning of hard work and techniques of memorisation.

Now I'm a teacher and I've observed thousands of secondary pupils, I'm sure I know what works. This is what I tell them:

- Try out different revision methods and work out which are the most effective. Metacognition means awareness and understanding of your thought processes; for pupils, this includes understanding how they learn most effectively.
- Create a revision plan for the holidays before the exams.
- Work for about two hours at a time then take a 30-minute break before resuming.
- Write out the notes and make notes from the notes, and all the time, try to actively recall what you are writing. Some pupils find it very helpful to make small cards (index cards); it's the process of making the cards that matters more than the cards themselves. Driving knowledge into the long-term memory requires you to do something active – reading is not enough.
- Test yourself by writing out the notes from memory. It's the process of trying to recall information that drives it into the memory.
- Where possible, use diagrams to summarise your notes as these can be easier to learn.

Hermann Ebbinghaus and the forgetting curve

We forget things as time passes. The forgetting curve was defined by German psychologist Hermann Ebbinghaus in his book, *Memory* (1885). You need to revise at least three times as an exam approaches because your memory decays with time, but the more often you revise the slower the rate of decay. In the example on page 66, the student revised five times:

Rate of forgetting with study/repetition

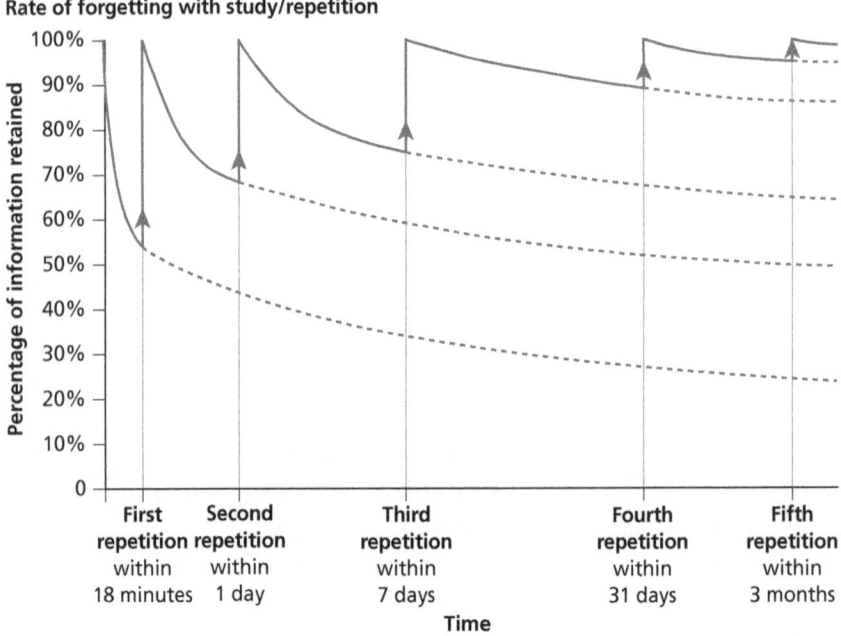

With modern languages, you will need to build up your vocabulary. So, start with a list of words you want to learn; aim for 30 words a day. Test yourself until you can do all 30, and write out the ones you forgot. Each day, go back to the words you learned on previous days.

With maths and A-level physics, you need to do practice questions. All good textbooks will have worked examples and questions for you to try.

How to make good notes

Some pupils are good at revising from handouts, a screen or even a book, but the easiest way to learn is from notes. The advantage of notes is that you can use shorthand, make shapes on the page that make it easier to memorise, add to the notes if you wish to and add colour, which also helps memorisation. Research shows that it is more effective to make notes with a pen than on a computer, as the physical process of writing increases your engagement and learning.

Read about this

Mueller, P. and Oppenheimer, D., 2014, *The pen is mightier than the keyboard: The advantages of longhand over laptop note taking*, Psychological Science, 25(6), 1159–1168.

Mangan, A. and Balsvik, L., 2016, *Pen or keyboard in beginning writing instruction? Some perspectives from embodied cognition*, Trends in Neuroscience and Education.

Lenon, B., 2017, *Much Promise* pp. 82–84.

Here is an article about Covid-19 that I have made notes on: livescience.com/why-covid-19-coronavirus-deadly-for-some-people.html. Don't trouble to read the whole article if you don't have time. Below are my handwritten notes.

<u>Why Covid-19 kills some but spares others</u>

Live Science, 2020

1. Age
   - 8/10 deaths in US aged 65+
     - .. older people have heart disease and diabetes
     - .. " " " a weaker immune system

2. Diabetes (types 1 + 2)
   - .. unclear if diabetes is directly increasing severity or it is OTHER health conditions which can go with diabetes such as cardiovascular and health problems.
   - .. may be – chronic inflammation ~ molecules called CYTOKINES
     - – increased coagulation
     - – weaker immune response
     - – direct pancreatic damage.

3. Heart disease
   - .. Covid attacks lungs & less oxygen : heart has to work harder
   - .. Covid attacks heart directly
   - .. Covid kicks-off an overblown immune response : CYTOKINE STORM & heart damage

4. Smoking
   - .. damages immune system
   - .. " respiratory tract.
   - .. increases number of ACE2 receptors in lungs and Covid plugs into them to infect cells (possibly).

These hurried notes show several things:

- A hierarchy of points – the four main headings, sub-points with dots and sub-sub-points with a dash.
- Numbered points (four) – it will help me remember these notes if I can remember that there are four main headings.
- Plenty of white space on the page, which means the notes make a pattern; this helps recall, as it's better than a whole page of text from one margin to the other. I can also add to them.
- Key terminology in capital letters; for example, 'CYTOKINE STORM'.

Highlighting the headings in colour would help too.

Making these notes forced me to identify the key points and made me think deeply about them. That is why, having made the notes, I remembered them.

Collect your pupils' files every term and check their notes – you will be in for some unpleasant surprises. Remember that notes are a simplified form of the main text, but they should not exclude facts that the pupils may need to know for the exam. Sometimes a page of brilliant and dense text turns into two pages of brilliant notes.

If pupils are revising for an exam, they need to be confident that their notes are complete. There's no point in revising incomplete notes, so check the syllabus. If anything is missing, you could use the exam board textbook to help the pupils fill in the gaps (many pupils like revision guides such as the CGP series).

How pupils should structure a good essay

Historians will know how to write a good essay – there are a few key points:

- Answer the question directly. The greatest mistake a pupil can make in an exam is simply to write out their notes.
- Before you start writing, scribble down your main points. Each point should answer the question directly and will become one paragraph.
- Write an introductory paragraph that answers the question directly – a summary of your main points. Now the reader knows you know the answer.
- Each subsequent paragraph should start with a sentence that answers the question directly – one of your points.
- In a question that asks you to evaluate something (pros and cons), you need to give both sides of the argument.
- Write a concluding paragraph that gives your own, final opinion on the question.

- If you run out of time, write out all your main points, even if this comes at the expense of some detail. But the best writers don't run out of time – they keep a close eye on the clock.

Why should we be bothered to learn anything when we can look it up?

It's still important for children and young people to commit knowledge to the long-term memory even though everything can be looked up on the internet. Daisy Christodoulou looked at this issue in her 2014 book, *Seven Myths About Education*.

Christodoulou argues that there are many reasons why we need knowledge in our long-term memory:

- Looking something up on Google uses up space in the working memory, which has limited space. So whenever we search on Google, we don't then have the capacity to process new information or combine it with other information.
- It's better to know your times tables even though you can look up the answer, or know how to spell even though you could use a dictionary, as knowing your times tables and how to spell enables you to solve more complex problems without overloading the working memory.
- Background knowledge is often needed in order to look something up successfully in the first place.
- Research in schools shows that asking children to 'research a topic on the internet' is ineffective. They don't have enough background knowledge to know what is relevant and correct.

Incidentally, teaching 'research skills' in a general way is nonsense, as good research depends on having a large body of knowledge and is subject-specific.

So, what does a good lesson look like?

A good lesson has the following characteristics:

- It's teacher led.
- The teacher has a voice that can be heard.
- The teacher asks lots of questions.
- The teacher injects pace and enthusiasm.
- New material is presented in small steps.
- Clear and detailed instructions and expectations are communicated.

- There is deliberate practice of specific sub-skills.
- Worked examples and model answers are provided.
- It uses scaffolding of knowledge.
- It includes quiet working time.
- There's a high level of pupil practice.
- The teacher gives feedback, including corrections.
- The teacher injects fun.
- The pupils are able to write good notes.

Recap

Explain the following concepts and how they could influence your teaching:

- Worked examples
- Modelling
- Formative feedback
- Retrieval practice
- Spaced learning
- Cognitive overload
- Dual coding
- Chunking
- The forgetting curve
- Scaffolding

References and more useful reading

Ausubel, D. P., 1968, *Educational Psychology: A Cognitive View.* New York: Holt, Rinehart & Winston.

Bandura, A., 1977, Self-efficacy: Toward a unifying theory of behavioural change, Psychological Review, 84(2), 191–215.

Bjork, R. A., 1994, Memory and meta-memory considerations in the training of human beings. In J. Metcalfe and A. Shimamura (Eds.), *Metacognition: Knowing About Knowing* (pp. 185–207), Cambridge MA.

Christodoulou, D., 2014, *Seven Myths about Education*, Routledge.

Coe, R., 2013, *Improving Education: Triumph of Hope Over Experience*, Centre for Evaluation and Monitoring.

Craik, F. and Lockhart, R., 1972, Levels of processing: A framework for memory research, Journal of Verbal Learning and Verbal Behaviour, 11(6), 671–684.

Deans for Impact, 2015, The Science of Learning. Online at: https://deansforimpact.org/resources/the-science-of-learning/. A summary of the research from cognitive science related to how students learn which connects this research to its practical implications for teaching and learning.

Dix, P., 2017, *When the Adults Change, Everything Changes: Seismic shifts in school behaviour*, Independent Thinking Press.

Dunlosky, J., Rawson, K., March, E., Nathan, M., and Willingham, D., 2013, Improving students' learning with effective learning techniques: Promising directions from cognitive and educational psychology, Psychological Science in the Public Interest, 14(1), 4–58.

Dweck, C. S. and Leggett, E. I., 1988, A social-cognitive approach to motivation and personality, Psychological Review, 95(2), 256–273.

Ebbinghaus, H., 1885, *Memory: A contribution to experimental psychology*. Reprinted in Annals of Neurosciences, 20(4), 155–156.

Education Endowment Foundation, 2018, Improving Secondary Science Guidance Report. Online at: EEF_ImprovingSecondaryScienceGuidanceReport. pdf. Seven great research-based recommendations about how to improve student learning.

Education Endowment Foundation, 2021. Online at: teacher-learning-toolkit/ mastery learning.

Education Endowment Foundation, 2021, Cognitive science approaches in the classroom: A review of the evidence. A great summary of the research evidence into the efficacy of spaced learning, interleaving, retrieval practice, managing cognitive load, dual coding.

Education Endowment Foundation, 2022, Working with worked examples – simple techniques to enhance their effectiveness.

Kalyuga, S. and Sweller, J., 2014, *The redundancy principle in multi media learning*. In R. E. Mayer (Ed.), *The Cambridge handbook of multimedia learning* (2nd ed). Cambridge University Press.

Kim, S. and Webb, S., 2022, The effects of spaced practice on second language learning: A meta-analysis. Language Learning: A Journal of Research in Language Studies, 72(1), 269–319.

Kirschner, P., and Hendrick, C., 2020, *How Learning Happens: Seminal Works in Educational Psychology and What They Mean in Practice*, Routledge.

Mangan, A. and Balsvik, L., 2016, *Pen or keyboard in beginning writing instruction? Some perspectives from embodied cognition*, Trends in Neuroscience and Education.

McGill, R., 2022, *The Teacher Toolkit Guide to Memory*, Bloomsbury.

Ofsted Research review series: geography (2021). Online at: Research review series: geography – GOV.UK (www.gov.uk)

Pritchard, B., 2022, EEF Blog: Working with worked examples – Simple techniques to enhance their effectiveness. Online at: educationendowmentfoundation.org.uk

Rosenshine, B., 2012, Principles of instruction: Research-based strategies that all teachers should know. American Educator, 12–20. Research-based teaching strategies that work in the classroom – a definitive work.

Stipek, D., 2010, *How do Teachers' Expectations Affect Student Learning?* Prentice Hall.

Sweller, J., 1988, *Cognitive load during problem solving: Effects on learning*, Cognitive Science, 12(2), 257–285.

Verkoeijen, P., and Delaney, P., 2008, Rote rehearsal and spacing effects in the free recall of pure and mixed lists, Journal of Memory and Language, 58(1), 35–47.

Willingham, D. T., 2009, *Why Don't Students Like School?* San Francisco, CA: Jossey-Bass. A cognitive scientist talks about how the mind works and what this means for teachers.

Zimmerman, B., 1989, A social cognitive view of self-regulated academic learning, Journal of Educational Psychology, 81(3), 329–339.

Chapter 6
Demonstrate good subject knowledge

ITTECF syllabus

Subject and curriculum (Standard 3 – Demonstrate good subject and curriculum knowledge)

Learn that...	Learn how to...
1. A school's curriculum enables it to set out its vision for the knowledge, skills and values that its pupils will learn, encompassing the national curriculum within a coherent wider vision for successful learning. 2. Secure subject knowledge helps teachers to motivate pupils and teach effectively. 3. Ensuring pupils master foundational concepts and knowledge before moving on is likely to build pupils' confidence and help them succeed. 4. Anticipating common misconceptions within particular subjects is also an important aspect of curricular knowledge; working closely with colleagues to develop an understanding of likely misconceptions is valuable. 5. Explicitly teaching pupils the knowledge and skills they need to succeed within particular subject areas is beneficial. 6. In order for pupils to think critically, they must have a secure understanding of knowledge within the subject area they are being asked to think critically about.	**Deliver a carefully sequenced and coherent curriculum, by:** a) Identifying essential concepts, knowledge, skills and principles of the subject and providing opportunity for all pupils to learn and master these critical components. b) Ensuring pupils' thinking is focused on key ideas within the subject. c) Working with experienced colleagues to accumulate and refine a collection of powerful analogies, illustrations, examples, explanations and demonstrations. d) Using resources and materials aligned with the school curriculum. (e.g. textbooks or shared resources designed by experienced colleagues that carefully sequence content). e) Being aware of common misconceptions and discussing with experienced colleagues how to help pupils, master important concepts. **Support pupils to build increasingly complex mental models, by:** f) Discussing and analysing with expert colleagues the rationale for curriculum choices, the process for arriving at current curriculum choices and how the school's curriculum materials inform lesson preparation.

Learn that...	Learn how to...
7. In all subject areas, pupils learn new ideas by linking those ideas to existing knowledge, organising this knowledge into increasingly complex mental models (or "schemata"); carefully sequencing teaching to facilitate this process is important.	g) Balancing exposition, repetition, practice of critical skills and knowledge.
	h) Revisiting the big ideas of the subject over time and teaching key concepts through a range of examples.
	i) Drawing explicit links between new content and the core concepts and principles in the subject.
8. Pupils are likely to struggle to transfer what has been learnt in one discipline to a new or unfamiliar context.	**Develop fluency, by:**
9. To access the curriculum, early literacy provides fundamental knowledge; reading comprises two elements: word reading and language comprehension; systematic synthetic phonics is the most effective approach for teaching pupils to decode.	j) Providing tasks that support pupils to learn key ideas securely (e.g. quizzing pupils so they develop fluency with times tables).
	k) Using retrieval and spaced practice to build automatic recall and application of key knowledge.
10. Every teacher can improve pupils' communication and literacy, including by explicitly teaching reading, writing and oral language skills specific to individual disciplines.	**Help pupils apply knowledge and skills to other contexts, by:**
	l) Ensuring pupils have relevant domain-specific knowledge, especially when being asked to think critically within a subject.
11. Pupils' positive dispositions and attitudes towards mathematics are associated with positive outcomes on learning.	m) Interleaving concrete and abstract examples, slowly withdrawing concrete examples and drawing attention to the underlying structure of problems.
12. Pupils' oral language skills can be supported by teaching new words and how to use and understand words within sentences or longer texts. This can help to address speech and language difficulties, especially for children in their early school years.	**Develop pupils' literacy, by:**
	n) Demonstrating a clear understanding of systematic synthetic phonics, and the necessary prerequisite knowledge, particularly if teaching early reading and spelling.
	o) Supporting younger pupils, especially those with reading difficulties, to become fluent readers by building automatic and accurate decoding with various texts and repeated reading of texts with modelling and feedback.

Learn that...	Learn how to...
	p) Teaching unfamiliar vocabulary explicitly and planning for pupils to be repeatedly exposed to high-utility and high-frequency vocabulary in what is taught.
	q) Modelling strategies that encourage active comprehension by asking questions, making predictions, and summarising when reading.
	r) Promoting reading for pleasure (e.g. by using a range of whole class reading approaches and regularly reading high quality texts to pupils).
	s) Teaching, modelling, and requiring high quality oral language, sometimes known as oracy, recognising that spoken language underpins the development of reading and writing (e.g. where appropriate, develop pupils' responses to questions into full sentences).
	t) Teaching different forms of writing by modelling planning, drafting and editing.
	u) Supporting younger pupils to become fluent writers through explicit teaching and practice of spelling and handwriting, with modelling and feedback, such as addressing both the process and product of letter formation when developing pupils' handwriting.

For many teachers, building their own subject knowledge will be the most exciting part of their training. The best teachers have good subject knowledge, meaning they are more confident and can use their superior knowledge to make lessons interesting. It's worth remembering that having a university degree does not necessarily mean your subject knowledge is good enough.

Coe et al. (2014) concluded, after gathering evidence from a wide range of sources, that strong subject knowledge is one of the most effective aspects of great teaching. Coe suggests:

The evidence to support the inclusion of content knowledge in a model of teaching effectiveness is strong, at least in curriculum areas such as maths, literacy and science. Different forms of content knowledge are required. As well as a strong, connected understanding of the material being taught, teachers must also understand the ways students think about the content, be able to evaluate the thinking behind non-standard methods and identify typical misconceptions students have.

Over the past few years, Ofsted have published subject reports and research reviews, which examine the best ways of teaching subjects. We would recommend you take a look at all the research reviews if you teach at primary and the reports of the subject you teach if you are a secondary or subject specialist teacher.

How do I know what I need to know?

Good mentors will give you the details of the courses you are supposed to be teaching, and in most cases teaching materials as well.

Primary

For KS1 and KS2 you will be given a curriculum by your school, and you also have the national curriculum to guide you. Primary teachers are likely to teach all of core and foundation subjects, although some primary and prep schools will have specialist teachers for subjects like music or PE.

You need to look at the national curriculum for the phase you are teaching in. When I first started teaching, I needed to do a good deal of preparation in the form of reading around subjects I was less familiar with. For example, I had stopped formal learning of history in Year 9, so the first time I taught the Egyptians to KS2 I had to read around the subject to ensure I knew enough about that period of history before teaching it. You will also need to understand progression in each subject, how the prior knowledge of your pupils is built upon, what has come before in their learning and where it will go next.

To build your subject knowledge, you could use textbook or look at online sources. BBC Teach and BBC Bitesize have some useful resources; similarly, you could look on the TES website or search what you are looking for within the appropriate age phase. Each of the subject sections towards the end of this chapter will give you some more subject-specific ideas.

Prep schools

Not all prep schools follow the Common Entrance syllabus, but for the many that do you need the Independent Schools Examinations Board (ISEB) current syllabuses and past papers and the accompanying textbooks from Galore Park, Hachette Learning or CGP.

Secondary

At KS3, it's recommended that you print off the national curriculum in the subjects you are teaching. For KS4 and KS5, you should also print off the exam board syllabi taught by your school as well as recent past papers in GCSE and A-level.

Textbooks are available for most subjects; at GCSE and A-level, they are often specific to a particular exam board. Having said that, all exam syllabi are quite similar because they are based on the subject specifications published by the DfE, so you can learn a lot from textbooks that are designed for a syllabus you are not teaching.

Here are the main recommendations when it comes to building subject knowledge at secondary:

- Start with standard textbooks, and make notes.
- Ask all your colleagues who have taught the relevant syllabus for help – they may have masses of teaching materials available.
- Use the exam board materials from their websites.
- Watch and read all available online resources, including media you are going to use in your lessons.
- Watch the relevant Oak Academy and BBC Bitesize lessons.
- Look at the website and publications of the relevant subject associations, such as the Geographical Association.
- Read the Ofsted research reviews and subject reports.

Avoid making a huge mistake

Somewhere, every summer, a class of A-level English pupils goes into an exam and discovers they have been taught the wrong novel or play. Of course, the head of English is fired. It's a disaster.

The reason this happens is that teachers fail to grasp the fact that most exam board syllabi change a little every year, including the list of set texts. That's why you need to check the online exam board syllabi *every year* for the exam two years ahead.

The school curriculum list

State schools follow the national curriculum, which is set out below. (Please note that at KS2, the subject title for languages is 'foreign language', whereas at KS3 it's 'modern foreign language'.)

	Key stage 1	Key stage 2	Key stage 3	Key stage 4
Age	5–7	7–11	11–14	14–16
Year groups	1–2	3–6	7–9	10–11
Core subjects				
English	✓	✓	✓	✓
Mathematics	✓	✓	✓	✓
Science	✓	✓	✓	✓
Foundation subjects				
Art and design	✓	✓	✓	
Citizenship			✓	✓
Computing	✓	✓	✓	✓
Design and technology	✓	✓	✓	
Languages		✓	✓	
Geography	✓	✓	✓	
History	✓	✓	✓	
Music	✓	✓	✓	
Physical education	✓	✓	✓	✓

The arts (comprising art and design, music, dance, drama and media arts), design and technology, the humanities (geography and history) and modern foreign languages are not compulsory national curriculum subjects after the age of 14, but all pupils in maintained schools have a statutory entitlement to be able to study a subject in each of those four areas.

	Key stage 1	Key stage 2	Key stage 3	Key stage 4
Age	5–7	7–11	11–14	14–16
Year groups	1–2	3–6	7–9	10–11
Religious education	✓	✓	✓	✓
Sex and relationship education			✓	✓

All state schools are required to make provision for a daily act of collective worship and must teach religious education to pupils at every key stage. They must also provide relationships education to pupils in primary education, relationships and sex education (RSE) to pupils in secondary education and health education to all pupils. Many schools will teach age-appropriate relationships and sex education.

Every primary school will have its own RSE policy, which is likely to guide you as to what your school has decided each year group will be learning. Do not deviate from this policy, as it's a guide for parents too. As for teaching religious education (RE), there is likely to be an 'agreed syllabus' for your county, which you can search for online, but again, schools make their own choices within these guidelines, so make sure to check the school's plan.

RE and RSE syllabuses often change over time and particularly with new governments, so keep up to date with these updates. We already know, for example, that revised RSE guidance will come into effect from the 1st September 2026. This guidance will include primary schools being 'strongly encouraged' to teach about healthy, loving relationships and 'include same-sex parents along with other family arrangements when discussing families' and lifts the previous government's ban on teaching about gender identity. You can read more about these guidelines on the GOV.UK website.

Parents have a right to request to withdraw their child from sex education delivered in secondary schools, which, unless there are exceptional circumstances, should be granted up to three terms before their child turns 16 – the legal age of sexual consent. At this point, if the child themselves wishes to receive sex education rather than be withdrawn, the school should make arrangements for this to happen in one of the three terms before the child turns 16. There is no right to withdraw from relationships education at primary or secondary.

All secondary schools are expected to teach maths, English and science to GCSE. Schools have been strongly encouraged by Ofsted not to start teaching GCSE syllabi until Year 10 and to maintain a wide range of subjects throughout KS3.

Creative subjects

Some creative subjects, most notably design and technology, drama and music, have declined in our schools since 2010; only art seems to have maintained a strong position. But the creative subjects have many advantages:

- For some pupils, creative subjects are the ones they enjoy most and are best at. I remember a sixth former who was a disaster in my geography lessons but who went on to perform as Hamlet in the school play, proving that I was totally wrong to believe that he could not commit teaching to memory. If only I had motivated him.

- For some pupils, the creative subjects at school lead to good jobs. Design and technology is surely the most important school subject for engineers.
- Eric Jensen's research (2009) shows that studying the arts may help build attention skills, memory, emotional intelligence and respect for diversity and difference (Jensen, 2009).

Beyond the curriculum list

Assigning time to each subject

Most schools will assign more time to English and maths at GCSE, for example, because these subjects are so important in terms of performance tables and the opportunities open to students in the sixth form.

At KS3, schools like to put on as many subjects as possible – tasters for the GCSE choices that follow. But this can have the negative effect that a subject like art or drama is confined to one lesson per week or two lessons per week but only for half a term. In general, a subject lacks momentum if it's not offered for two periods spaced across a week and taught every week.

In primary schools, we need to ensure that our pupils reach a good level of English and maths by Year 6 in order to prepare them adequately for secondary school. This is why KS2 SATs remain in place, as a target for expected levels of ability in Year 6. Reading is therefore the most important subject for pupils to do well, so they can access the secondary curriculum.

Many schools now teach reading as a discrete subject, but it's also expected that reading runs through everything, so it's important that we consider the reading levels of texts that we use in all subjects. The texts should not be too difficult for your pupils to access, but they should not be too easy either, as all opportunities should be taken to advance reading skills. Sometimes we need to pre-teach vocabulary before giving pupils access to a text.

Primary teachers are also told how much time we should spend teaching PE or giving pupils the opportunity to engage in physical activity, as this is important for physical health.

Options choices at secondary

Options choices are all about possible subject combinations. Can I do maths, physics and art A-levels together? Small schools can't offer as much choice as larger schools mainly because they may only be able to offer art in one of the three or four A-level option columns (all of which correspond to timetable slots). A small school can't afford to run more than one A-level art set; a larger school can have art in two columns, and that makes the possibility of combinations like maths, physics and art more likely.

So-called 'twenty-first century skills'

Some people argue that we should not be teaching traditional subjects but should instead focus on 'twenty-first century skills'. These are often presented as generic skills, such as communication and problem solving. The problem with this argument is that:

- Research shows these general skills tend to be subject-specific. For example, you have to learn critical thinking when studying history, but this is not the same thing as critical thinking in maths.
- Most skills require knowledge. In order to be a critical thinker in history you have to know a lot of history.
- Many of the so-called twenty-first century skills are actually character traits, not skills, such as teamwork, leadership or perseverance.
- Most of these twenty-first century skills have actually been important for 3,000 years.

Of course, there are some skills that truly are twenty-first century skills, such as navigating the internet intelligently and knowing about the merits and pitfalls of artificial intelligence (AI). All good schools teach these things, and you should teach them through your subject.

The alternative approach – teaching knowledge

Most of the best schools in England now say that they teach a 'knowledge-rich curriculum'. That means, teaching a lot of 'knowledge'. Why do they do this?

E. D. Hirsch was born 1928 and is now retired; he was previously the Professor of Education and Humanities at the University of Virginia. During the late 1970s, while giving tests to measure how quickly students grasped ideas from written texts, he discovered that while the readability of a text was an important factor in determining speed of comprehension, an even more important consideration was the reader's possession – or lack – of relevant background knowledge.

He found that students at the University of Virginia were able to understand a passage about Ulysses S. Grant and Robert E. Lee, while students at a Richmond community college struggled with the same passage, because they lacked a basic understanding of the American Civil War.

This led Hirsch to formulate the concept of cultural literacy – the idea that reading comprehension requires not just the skill of decoding letters and words but also wide-ranging background knowledge. He concluded that schools should not be neutral about what is taught but should teach a highly specific curriculum that would allow children to know things that writers tend to take for granted. His book on the subject, *Cultural Literacy: What Every American Needs To Know*, was published in 1987. Beginning in the 1990s Hirsch began publishing the Core Knowledge Series where each book focuses on the precise knowledge that should be taught to children at each age.

Good schools now believe that you cannot teach useful skills such as critical thinking without good background knowledge.

Reforms in 2025

The 2014 National Curriculum had been in place for a decade, when Sir Keir Starmer's Labour Government commissioned a review, headed by Professor Becky Francis. Her Interim Report, published in March 2025, called for an overhaul of the curriculum in order to respond to technological and social changes. The review made the following observations:

- Mastery teaching and learning with a subject is vital, yet not possible in some subjects due to the weight of content to be covered.
- The socio-economic gap for educational attainment remains 'stubbornly large'.
- Young people with SEND make less progress than their peers.

Ambitions for a refreshed national curriculum included:

- Support schools to provide a rigorous and knowledge-rich education, aiming for breadth across subjects and depth within subjects.
- Remain relevant and up to date while embedding and recognising the importance of cultural knowledge stemming from the past.
- Empower teachers to foster a love of learning by enabling learning to be situated in a range of local, national and global contexts, to widen horizons, and to ensure that young people see meaningful representations of themselves in what they learn, as well as encountering and recognising the perspectives of others.
- Allow schools to support the full development of their students and prepare them for their future life and work.
- Be coherently and logically sequenced and allow space for schools to support mastery of core concepts, effective transitions, and progression through each key stage of education.

- Enable students to master high-quality and aspirational learning, no matter what their individual needs or backgrounds. It should also support teachers to use their professional expertise in designing or selecting an engaging and stretching programme of learning that best suits their students' needs.

Other aims for a revised curriculum include:

- Reflect the issues and diversities of our society, ensuring all children and young people are represented in the curriculum and exposed to a wide range of perspectives that serve to broaden their horizons.
- Ensure that the system of 16–19 pathways supports all learners to hone the knowledge and skills they need to step confidently into adulthood. This includes both qualifications as well as skills (such as finance and budgeting, employment and interview skills), to support learners to develop into well-rounded individuals and to be ready for higher learning or work.
- For post-16 pupils, provide more pathways and providers to make T-levels more accessible. (The purpose of T-levels is to prepare learners for skilled employment across a range of industries.)
- Introduce Technical Occupational Entry Qualifications (TOQs) for 16- to 19-year-olds. These are smaller technical qualifications developed against specific occupational standards that are not covered by T-levels.
- Reconsider the available pathways, so that all learners have the best opportunity to reach level 2 in maths and English by the end of their 16–19 study. We also need to find ways to support and value the progress of all learners, including those who may not go on to achieve level 2.
- Examine how the assessment of writing at key stage 2 can be improved to support high and rising standards.

Oracy

No teenager should be allowed to leave school without some lessons in speaking well. Oracy means being able to speak effectively either in conversation with someone or to a group of people. Too many intelligent young people get good exam results but fail to get the best jobs because they cannot present themselves well.

There are many ways to promote oracy:

- Insist that your pupils speak up clearly in class. If a pupil gives a mumbled answer, they should be asked to say it again clearly.
- Require all pupils in a particular year group to have a short test in speaking aloud and then train up those who are weaker.

- Some pupils will learn how to speak in public by having a speaking part in a play or taking part in debating competitions.
- Many schools have reading and speech competitions where pupils have to read a passage with only a few minutes preparation and recite a passage from memory.

Oracy is vital in the primary classroom too. What we should be ensuring pupils can do is spelled out in the national curriculum. It's important that you know what is involved in each subject of the national curriculum as levels of oracy have declined in recent years. Opportunities for speaking should be built into lessons; sometimes you will need to teach the pupils how to speak properly, how to form sentences accurately and so on.

Here are some ideas for improving oracy:

- Classroom discussions.
- Show and tell.
- Role-playing and drama (great in English and history lessons).
- Vocabulary teaching and deepening.
- Creating a rich language environment (display key vocabulary, use word banks and sentence stems, make dictionaries and thesauruses easily accessible).
- Using technology.
- Personalised support.

In KS1, pupils should be taught the following skills with regard to speaking, listening and oracy:

- Listen and respond appropriately to others.
- Ask relevant questions to extend their understanding and knowledge.
- Articulate and justify answers, arguments and opinions.
- Give well-structured descriptions and explanations.

In KS2, pupils should be taught the following skills with regard to speaking, listening and oracy:

- Listen and respond appropriately to others.
- Ask relevant questions to extend their understanding and knowledge.
- Articulate and justify answers, arguments and opinions.
- Give well-structured descriptions and explanations.
- Participate in discussions, presentations, performances and debates.
- Adapt their language to suit different purposes and audiences.
- Speak fluently and confidently in a range of contexts.

What if I don't like the traditional school curriculum?

The national curriculum is the government's view about what should be taught in schools across the country. Having a national curriculum brings certain advantages:

- All pupils are studying roughly the same things at the same age, which makes it easier if a pupil (or teacher) moves school.
- It's far easier to set national tests or exams that compare all pupils fairly.
- It's likely that educational publishers will generate high-quality resources if they know what they need to cover.

The standard school subjects represent the way that adults have chosen to classify knowledge over the past century. But if a school dislikes the traditional curriculum, there are a number of things they can do:

- Teach the International Baccalaureate (IB) at sixth form. Pupils must study six subjects, one from each of six subject groups: language and literature; language acquisition; individuals and societies; sciences; mathematics; and the arts. Students take 3–4 subjects at higher level (HL) and 2–3 at standard level (SL). They must also study the theory of knowledge (TOK) and write an extended essay. They are required to engage in creativity, activity, service (CAS): creativity is usually an arts challenge, activity is often sport and service means what we normally call community service.
- The National Baccalaureate Trust is an organisation that promotes the idea of making all pupils face assessments in non-GCSE areas such as sport, community service and creative subjects – just like the IB.
- Schools can offer subjects that are available as examined GCSE and A-level qualifications, but which are less common, such as history of art, natural history or astronomy.
- Schools can also offer subjects that are not run by exam boards but are run by the school (for examples of this, see the websites of schools such as Bedales, Sevenoaks or St Edward's, Oxford). In most cases, the school gets an independent body to validate their alternative qualification; in all cases, the schools communicate with universities to encourage them to accept this alternative.

All good schools wish to go beyond examinations and the national curriculum. This happens in numerous ways, such as:

- The Extended Project Qualification for sixth formers.
- Extra-curricular sport, music and drama.

- Societies, clubs, cadet force, community service, Duke of Edinburgh Award, Young Enterprise, etc.

At Winchester and Eton, there is a long tradition of pupils being assigned in groups to tutors who teach subjects that are believed to be important for all young people, such as history of art, music or philosophy. The Winchester website says:

> In years 9–11, [we provide] pupils with an introduction to the broad sweep of Western history, from classical times to the Early Modern period. It also encompasses English literature and language, the history of science and art, religious studies and PSHEE.
>
> In the sixth form, each tutor determines the programme. The material selected for inclusion is equally likely to be artistic, literary, philosophical, political, sociological, art-historical, ethical, religious or musical.

These extra-curricular activities are often the basis of lifelong interests and can be an important part of a CV. As a beginner teacher, you are well placed to contribute.

Sequencing

Whatever the level you teach at and the subject you specialise in, you have to decide the order in which things will be taught.

In 'linear' subjects, where one lesson can build on a previous lesson, you will teach the most fundamental and straightforward topics first. Each lesson will, in some way, refer back to a previous lesson. In a 'non-linear' subject such as geography, you could decide to teach two contrasting regions one after the other to enable you to make the contrast clear. In design and technology, you may want to build knowledge of a variety of materials by making something from wood, then plastic, then metal.

It's an obvious point: teach topics in the best possible order.

Displaying your subject knowledge

The reason that qualified teachers in England have to have a degree is because we want them to have very good subject knowledge. Last year I had a trainee who gave her pupils plenty of handouts to fill in and her lessons were full of activity. But she never simply delivered a talk about the period of history she was teaching; perhaps she didn't know enough to be confident. But a teacher of any subject could have delivered the lessons she taught, and that is wrong. Display your subject knowledge.

Primary subject teaching

Language and literacy

The relevant sections in the national curriculum are:

- Spoken language
- Reading
- Writing
- Spelling, vocabulary, grammar and punctuation

Reading

From EYFS onwards, reading is the most important thing you can teach. In our youngest children this starts with language comprehension, so when you read a story make sure to check the pupils understand what's happening by asking them lots of questions. Have some labels around the room and tell them what they say so they start to understand that print has meaning and represents words for things.

Some schools introduce the teaching of phonics in the nursery class, but it will definitely be in place from the reception class onwards. If you are required to teach phonics, you are likely to be given training in the phonics scheme the school uses.

Home reading

Some schools give their pupils books to take home as soon as they start learning phonics. These could be phonics practice books (related to the level of phonics they are learning) or unrelated books from the school or class library.

Here are some important aspects of home reading to be aware of:

- Changing books regularly. Often parents want to help with reading and may become frustrated if the same books are used for too long.
- Communicate with parents about changing books so that they are aware of expectations.
- Have a system for who changes the books and when.
- Have an adult or older pupil help pupils choose an appropriate level of book.
- Remember that not all parents can or will want to help their children with reading at home. It's important that you know who these pupils are and give them extra help.
- Give the parents some pointers for how to read with their children.
- Model how to read with children to the parents. You could send home videos or invite them in for a session on bedtime reading.

Phonics

Systematic synthetic phonics (SSP) is a way to teach pupils to recognise letters (graphemes) and the sounds associated with them (phonemes). It involves breaking the word down into the smallest units of sound; for example, the word 'pink' would be broken down into the three parts of 'p', 'i' and 'nk'.

The teaching of phonics is systematic, as we teachers follow a specific order. Typically, we will begin with frequent single letters, teaching frequent sounds with more than one letter (such as 'sh', 'th' and 'ee'). Phonics teaching initially covers the most common relationships between letters and sounds as they can be used to read many new words, then it covers some of the less common relationships.

How phonics is taught is up to each individual school or trust; however, there are certain phonics schemes that are recommended by the DfE, and schools select from these options.

Early reading

Ofsted visits give an important weighting to early reading (which includes the teaching of phonics), and they will look for the following signs to see that early reading is being taught well:

- Direct, focused phonics is taught every day in Reception and KS1.
- There is fidelity to the chosen programme.
- Children read from books (including the books they take home) with the sounds they know while they are learning to read.
- Teachers and teaching assistants provide extra practice, often on a one-to-one basis throughout each day for the children who make the slowest progress (the lowest 20%).
- All children in Year 3 and above can read age-appropriate books.
- Teachers instil in children a love of literature – the best stories and poems.
- The school creates a 'language-rich' environment.
- The school provides targeted help for identified pupils from an extra adult during the phonics lesson.
- Pupils are organised into groups for phonics lessons according to the grapheme-phoneme correspondences they know.
- Pupils are regularly reassessed so they are placed in a group where they can make the best progress.

Reading after phonics

After learning phonics, children need to be given well-chosen reading material to help them develop reading fluency, confidence and enjoyment. We used to call this the transition from 'learning to read' to 'reading to learn'. Some schools will move their pupils onto reading schemes at this point; some will provide quality texts, though many schools will use a combination of both. Either way, opportunities for quality reading should permeate the curriculum so children are reading across a variety of contexts every day.

More recently, research has shown us that there are some aspects involved with the teaching of reading that have not had sufficient focus. These are fluency, prosody and vocabulary.

Fluency

> *Scientific research has consistently recognized the critical nature of fluency as a bridge between effortful decoding and comprehension. A fluent reader is one who can accurately and automatically decode words.*

(Rasinski, EEF blog, 2022)

To encourage and nurture the development of fluency, pupils need to:

- Be engaged with assisted reading. Pupils read a text while listening to a fluent reading of the same text.
- Be given opportunities for repeated reading. Pupils practice reading texts repeatedly until they can read the text in a fluent manner. This should happen after phonics teaching, not just within it.
- Be read to aloud. This allows the pupils to hear fluent reading modelled for them.

Prosody

Prosody is the aspects of speech that are involved with rhythmic and melodic delivery. This involves reading with good expression, articulacy, intonation, pitch, tone, volume and emphasis on certain words. Fluent readers chunk words together in appropriate, meaningful phrases and use their voice to convey and enhance the meaning of the text, and they know how to pause appropriately at the end of sentences. Reading aloud to pupils is vital, as it models all aspects of prosody.

Vocabulary

We need to ensure our pupils develop powerful word knowledge and understanding over time, as this enables them to access teaching and the spoken word at a higher level. We used to assume pupils would learn the meanings of words though context, but this is now not thought to be the case for all children, so they need to be intentionally taught words.

Read through a text before introducing it to your pupils. Are there some words they may not understand? If so, you should create opportunities to pre-teach the words to them beforehand. This can be done through playing word games, changing the context or getting them to act out words.

Here are some other things to remember about teaching reading:

- Hear the pupils read frequently – it should not always be your support staff, but you who also needs to read with them regularly.
- Discuss the pupils' reading with them, and ensure they comprehend what they are reading. Ask them lots of questions.
- Take all opportunities during the school day for the pupils to read to someone.

There are some common misconceptions in the teaching of reading:

Learning to read is natural	Reading is a complex process that is not natural. It requires explicit instruction.
Children will eventually learn to read if given enough time	This is not necessarily true. Here I like to think of Vygotsky's 'zone of proximal development' – children can only learn the thing that is closest to their current ability. Dyslexic learners may need other interventions, not just time.
Reading is a solo activity	As we've established, reading needs to be modelled and practiced. Reading with partners and having books read to you are very powerful aspects of reading.
Children have books at home	Not all of them do, therefore we cannot assume. We have to provide the reading material in school in case there is none at home.
'My child hates reading'	It's more likely that the reading material given to them is too hard, easy or boring, or there is pressure around reading at home that is stressful for the child. If this is the case, advise the parents how to do this well, or ask them to pause reading at home until the child reaches a certain stage.
Context is the key to learning to lift words from the page	Context can help, but sometimes intentional teaching of vocabulary is needed. Imagine reading 'the rain was falling hard and the petrichor was strong'. You will need to have pre-taught the meaning of the word petrichor in order for the pupils to understand the text.

The 'reading rope' is a metaphor that elaborates on essential reading skills: word recognition and language comprehension (Scarborough, 2001). The rope is further broken down, offering sub-strands of word recognition and language comprehension that make the rope strong:

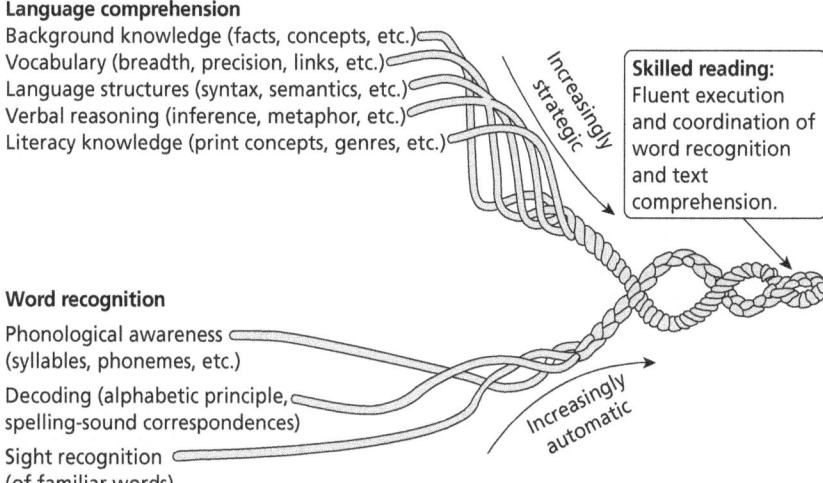

Language comprehension
Background knowledge (facts, concepts, etc.)
Vocabulary (breadth, precision, links, etc.)
Language structures (syntax, semantics, etc.)
Verbal reasoning (inference, metaphor, etc.)
Literacy knowledge (print concepts, genres, etc.)

Increasingly strategic

Skilled reading:
Fluent execution and coordination of word recognition and text comprehension.

Word recognition
Phonological awareness
(syllables, phonemes, etc.)

Decoding (alphabetic principle, spelling-sound correspondences)

Sight recognition
(of familiar words)

Increasingly automatic

Writing

In September 2024 the government identified that writing is not taught as well as it should be in primary schools, in particular handwriting and sentence construction. This was unsurprising, as there had been so much focus on the teaching of reading, early reading and phonics prior to this. Some MATs and local authorities had already identified the issue; Oxfordshire, for example, were rolling out INSET training based on the 'Hampshire writing model', which uses a combination of high-quality texts and opportunities for writing based on them.

According to the model, a school's writing journey may follow this sequence:

● Stimulate and generate.
● Capture, sift and sort.
● Create, refine and evaluate.

Stimulate and generate – read as a reader

In this phase, pupils are introduced to new stimuli and will complete complementary activities to enable them to engage and understand it. There will be the opportunity for pupils to write at length through 'apprentice writes', which provides chances for the pupils to write in a style they have used recently but using the new stimuli.

Capture, sift and sort – read as a writer

In this phase, pupils are taught and provided with opportunities to use new punctuation and grammar techniques. This part of the journey begins by looking at a WAGOLL ('what a good one looks like'). There are opportunities for children to write at length through 'site of application writes', which provides chances for the pupils to apply their newly taught punctuation and grammar in a writing style that will support them with their final write.

Create, refine and evaluate – write as a writer

In this phase, the pupils will write their final piece of work. This will begin with a planning session where the pupils are encouraged to think about the purpose, audience, viewpoint and form of the piece. The rest of this stage provides opportunity for them to write at length, including time devoted to editing. The pupils will evaluate their work once they have published their final piece.

Of course, there are other useful writing models that schools will use, so my advice would be to familiarise yourself fully with your school's approach to writing.

Spelling, punctuation, grammar (SPaG) and vocabulary

SPaG will be taught according to your own style and policy. Some trainee teachers that we have worked with have expressed concern with their own SPaG knowledge, as the national curriculum may have different expectations to the ones they were taught. In England, pupils are informally tested on SPaG throughout school, and there are also optional and compulsory national tests. Do spend some time brushing up your own knowledge in this area before teaching an element of SPaG that you may be unfamiliar or less confident with.

Maths

Don't be frightened of teaching maths. Maths doesn't always come easy to all of us, and for this reason – if you struggled with maths yourself – it's likely to make you a good maths teacher as you will remember the concepts that you found most difficult, which will help you explain things more clearly. Also, most schools have maths schemes that will help with your lesson planning – the White Rose Hub is a scheme many schools now subscribe to, and it gives you all that you need.

The best advice I can give you is to practice before you teach. When I first taught Year 6 maths I had forgotten everything I had learned in my O-level, so I spent every evening reacquainting myself with the maths I would be teaching the following day. I did the sums, learned the methods and made sure I understood all the concepts involved, along with the various methods of calculation. I also practiced Year 6 SATs papers. Only by doing things like this can you discover what the pupils will find difficult.

Calculation policy

Most schools will have a calculation policy (which is accessible on their website), so you can prepare by reading through it and ensuring you know what's expected. The policy will outline the methods and ways in which the various methods of calculation are taught in your school, and is likely to specify what you need to know to teach in each year group.

The Singapore method

Some years ago, we realised in the UK that we were falling far behind some of our Southeast Asian counterparts and their pupils were gaining much higher standards in maths. Following research, it was decided that the Singapore method of teaching maths was the most effective in the world; subsequently, our maths teaching and schemes started to follow this model. The three main aims of the national curriculum for maths are problem solving, reasoning and fluency, and this fits within the Singaporean maths philosophy.

Some key features of Singapore maths include:

- The use of concrete objects for all pupils of all ages. This starts with objects such as blocks and cards, then moves on to pictorial representations and finally to abstract equations. When understanding is secure, pupils can then work abstractly with numbers on paper.
- Pupils learn mental maths strategies to help them develop number sense and flexibility in thinking about numbers.
- Pupils use pictorial models to represent and solve problems, which helps them make sense of known and unknown quantities.
- Pupils learn to think mathematically, as opposed to reciting formulas they don't understand.
- Pupils are taught mental strategies to solve problems, such as drawing a bar model (see below).
- Teachers assess students' understanding throughout a lesson to determine what kind of support they need.
- Teaching doesn't move on from a topic until the pupils have mastered it.

CPA (concrete-pictorial-abstract)

CPA is based on an idea from the American psychologist Jerome Bruner, who also proposed the 'spiral curriculum' approach that we use in the national curriculum.

In Bruner's design, key concepts are presented repeatedly throughout the curriculum but with deepening layers of complexity or in different applications.

Bruner's CPA approach looks something like this:

Concrete	Pictorial	Abstract

You can see how these fit together, moving from the concrete object through to the pictorial representation and finally to the abstract concept. The abstract 3+1, or even the pictorial form, are sometimes shown as cherries or as a bar model, as given in these examples below:

There are common mistakes and misconceptions made by children:

- Younger children may think a bigger object has more value.
- The larger the coin, the higher the value. However, 2p is larger than 20p, so this needs to be taught.
- Multiplication by zero, e.g. $7 \times 0 = 7$.
- Not remembering place holders, e.g. one hundred and one = 1001.
- Thinking there are no numbers lower than 0 before learning negative numbers.
- Misunderstanding the denominator in fractions, e.g. thinking that ¼ is larger than ½.
- Multiplying by 10 is 'adding a zero' e.g. $10.5 \times 10 = 10.50$.

Science

Some teachers are afraid of teaching science to primary pupils; they are afraid they may not understand concepts themselves, the preparation is too difficult or that letting pupils do 'hands-on' work will create chaos. Here are some useful pointers:

- Be prepared well in advance of the lesson; if you are teaching magnets, for example, check to see that they work before class. Similarly with electricity – batteries may have gone flat over time, so you need to check equipment ahead of your lesson as some things may need to be ordered from the school office.

● Make sure your routines for the pupils stopping and listening to you are strong and firm; this way, you don't need to worry about practical activities.

● Make sure you know, firmly and without doubt, what the objective of the lesson is.

● Prepare your learning intention and the connecting cause-and-effect sentences between dependent and independent variables that you want the pupils to learn, such as:

  ● The higher the sun, the shorter the shadow.
  ● The thinner the string, the higher the sound.

● Develop pupils' scientific vocabulary and explicitly teach new vocabulary and its meaning, creating opportunities for repeated engagement and use over time.

● Encourage pupils to explain their thinking, verbally or in written form, creating opportunities and a collaborative learning environment that can capitalise on the power of dialogue.

● Guide pupils to work scientifically, using reasoning and justification, and teach them how to recognise fair testing through control of variables.

● Relate new learning to relevant, real-world contexts. For example, exploring the school grounds and local environment can provide meaningful, real-world contexts that help children connect scientific concepts to everyday life.

● Knowledge organisers can be very useful in helping pupils recap learning, scientific concepts and vocabulary (see the mini-beasts example in Chapter 5).

Example of a primary science lesson

Year 3: How shadows are formed
Working scientifically in Year 3: • Asking relevant questions and using scientific enquiries to answer them. • Setting up simple practical enquiries, comparative and fair tests. • Making systematic and careful observations. • Gathering, recording, classifying and presenting data in a variety of ways. • Recording findings using simple scientific language, drawings, labelled diagrams, keys, bar charts and tables. • Reporting on findings from enquiries, including oral and written explanations, using results to draw simple conclusions and make predictions. • Identifying differences, similarities or changes related to simple scientific ideas and processes. • Using straightforward scientific evidence to answer questions or to support findings.
Learning Intention: I can understand how shadows are formed and change with light sources.

Year 3: How shadows are formed
Key words and phrases: • Shadow, source of light, opaque. • An object that does not allow light to pass through it creates shadows. • The further away the light source, the longer the shadow.
By the end of the lesson, you need them to learn: • Shadows are formed when light is blocked by opaque objects. • The position of a shadow is determined by the light source. • Shadows change shape and size depending on the light source and object position. • Light can come from natural and artificial sources.
Ensure you are aware of possible/likely misconceptions: • Shadows can only occur outside. • A shadow is a reflection. • Shadows are only visible during the day.
Review previous learning: How does light travel? 1. In circles? In straight lines? In zigzag patterns? 2. What is an opaque object? An object that allows light through? An object that blocks light? An object that emits light?
Starter – stimulation: Share a video clip of shadow length as the sun moves across the sky.
Teacher explanation: • Shadows are formed when light is blocked by an opaque object. • Describe how light travels in straight lines. • Model this by using examples of different light sources, both natural like the sun and artificial like lamps and torches. • Illustrate that the shape of the shadow is similar to the object blocking the light. • Discuss how the position of the light source affects the shadow's position.
Let them investigate: • What happens to the length of the shadow if we move the light source closer? • How can we get rid of the shadow? • How can we make the shadow bigger/longer?
Recording results: Drawing their results, or measuring, or both.
Check for understanding: • What creates a shadow? • Where will a shadow appear if the light is on the right of the object?
What have we found out? Model answers if necessary. **Do the pupils understand:** • The further away the light source is, the longer the shadow. • Shadows appear when light is blocked by an opaque object.

Research reviews

As mentioned previously, the Ofsted research reviews in all subjects are worth reading, particularly those that provide specific advice for the teaching of science. Some of their recommendations for science education are that schools should:

● Ensure the curriculum is specific about the knowledge that should be taught and learned in Reception about understanding the world. This knowledge should connect with what pupils go on to learn in Year 1 science.

● Ensure sufficient time is built into the curriculum for pupils to learn and remember key subject knowledge, and that they are also helped to see how this knowledge connects with what they already know about science so they build upon prior learning.

● Ensure the curriculum identifies and sequences the disciplinary knowledge (the knowledge underpinning pupils' understanding of working scientifically) that pupils need to work scientifically. This should include developing pupils' knowledge of all areas of working scientifically, including different types of scientific enquiry, such as pattern seeking, and concepts such as evidence and accuracy.

● Ensure all pupils have enough opportunities to take part in high-quality practical work that has a clear purpose in relation to the curriculum.

● Ensure the science curriculum is planned to take account of what pupils learn in other subjects, particularly in mathematics and reading.

Common mistakes and misconceptions

The Primary Science Teaching Trust has a useful set of common misconceptions for all areas of the primary science teaching curriculum; it's worth checking these before teaching a science topic. These are comprehensive, and therefore there is no need to list them all below as you can find them online. An example is:

Teaching about light

● Sight is purely an active human process – 'I am looking at something, which is why I can see it' – or that eyes give out a form of light to enable us to see.

● Reflective surfaces emit light.

● Only shiny surfaces or water reflect light.

● Opaque objects do not reflect light.

We need to ensure we teach science well. High-quality primary science teaching helps to build pupils' natural curiosity and critical thinking; it helps them to link ideas and concepts together into a coherent understanding of the world around them. From a social mobility point of view, teaching children about things they may not be learning at home and opening their minds to the opportunities they could pursue in later life is important.

When you plan science lessons, you need to consider your role as the modeller of investigations, recording results and explaining your findings. Quality of the dialogue you have with your pupils during science lessons is important; you can see how, in the lesson example on pages 97–8, the role of the teacher is key. You are guiding discussion, stimulating thinking and asking open-ended questions, drawing out and upon the pupil's existing knowledge and understanding. You need to identify and clarify misconceptions and walk the pupils through the learning, thinking and reasoning about what they have observed until they become the scientific 'experts'.

Here's a summary of the recommendations to support you in your science teaching:

- Build scientific vocabulary.
- Encourage pupils to explain their thinking.
- Guide pupils to work scientifically.
- Always relate new learning to relevant, real-world contexts.
- Use assessment to support learning and responsive teaching.
- Always ensure you are well prepared, not only with resources but in knowing exactly what it is you want them to learn in each lesson.

Geography

Geography is a subject packed with excitement and dynamism that synthesises aspects of the world and helps us to better understand its people, places and environments and the interactions between them. Geography also helps us understand how and why places are changing, and to better imagine, predict and work towards likely and preferred futures. Underpinning all of this is a strong spatial component that deepens our understanding of what places are like, why and how they are connected and the importance of location.

Teaching geography to pupils of any age can be a richly rewarding opportunity to increase knowledge and understanding of the world, build cultural capital and develop their understanding of cultures, peoples and places.

If you stopped learning geography before you took your GCSEs, it may feel a little daunting at first. But there are so many ways that you can find support for teaching your geography lessons:

- Start with the school scheme of work, if there is one.
- Ask colleagues.

- Go to BBC Education, where you can find lots of short films.
- Use YouTube videos to explore other countries, terrains, climates, landscape features, etc.
- Consider doing a subject knowledge enhancement (SKE) course.
- Look at websites such as the Royal Geographical Society, Geographical Association or National Geographic Kids.
- Read the Ofsted research review.

We recommend getting a subscription to the Ordnance Survey's Digimap for Schools, which is suitable for children aged 5–16. Aligned with the national curricula for Geography of the four nations of the UK, it aims to support pupils in the following ways:

- Developing knowledge of the location of globally significant places – both terrestrial and marine – through the use of Ordnance Survey data.
- International maps, including the Collins Bartholomew World Panorama reference map, that show definitive international boundaries and territories for all countries in the world.
- Aerial mapping and historical maps of Great Britain aid the teaching and understanding of change, such as how new or changed physical and human geographical features came about, their interdependencies, spatial variation and change over time.

There are some aspects of geography that you really need to know and understand; these are some of the slightly more scientific areas, such as weather, climate zones and compass points. But remember, it's not all meteorological facts and maps; geography enhances understanding of why people are living in particular locations, why they grow the crops in their countries and issues around the Earth's resources and sustainability.

The Ofsted research review is a great resource, as it tells us what types of substantive and disciplinary knowledge pupils need to be taught. Looking at each form of substantive knowledge in turn demonstrates both the substance of each and the relationships between them, as illustrated in the graphic on page 100.

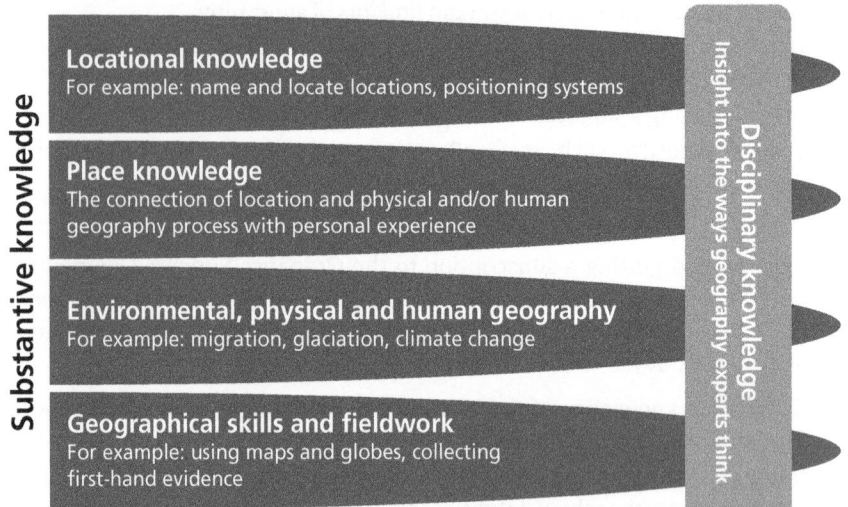

The diagram shows "Substantive knowledge" on the left, with the following categories:

Locational knowledge
For example: name and locate locations, positioning systems

Place knowledge
The connection of location and physical and/or human geography process with personal experience

Environmental, physical and human geography
For example: migration, glaciation, climate change

Geographical skills and fieldwork
For example: using maps and globes, collecting first-hand evidence

On the right: **Disciplinary knowledge** — Insight into the ways geography experts think

Ofsted research review: Geography

Geography is concerned with the local and the global, and how local, regional and national decisions have global impacts. This means that we need to build an understanding of the relationships between regions and countries, for example, in exploring trade and their interdependence. When we plan curriculum content, it's important that pupils consider scale and have the ability to 'zoom in' and 'zoom out' in order to view processes and their impact from local, regional, national and international perspectives.

One school I worked in planned a new geography curriculum based on these principles. It began in the early years and KS1 with studying the local area, then the UK in lower KS2 before moving into world comparisons by upper KS2. Throughout, pupils are constantly engaged with zooming in and out.

If you are following the national curriculum and need to teach about specific regions in the UK, Europe or America, try to pick regions you know about and are interested in, such as Amazonia or Southern Italy. Research these regions well before you start teaching them.

In geography lessons, it's essential to have a globe and a set of atlases. You also need to access Ordnance Survey map extracts for KS2.

Geography trips and activities

You will want to take your pupils outside the classroom to observe the world and record data. For example, obtain some digital thermometers and anemometers and measure temperature and wind speed around your school. You could also take daily weather readings throughout the year.

Geographical vocabulary

In all subjects, it's imperative that we provide our pupils with a rich vocabulary and an accurate understanding of what each word and concept means. Sometimes we need to pre-teach vocabulary before the lesson; this is very true for geography. You will need to ensure you understand the meaning of the words before teaching them to your pupils. Examples are too plentiful to list, but in teaching earthquakes and volcanos in Year 3, for example, you would need to teach them the meaning of these words:

- Crater
- Earthquake
- Dormant volcano
- Eruption
- Extinct volcano
- Lava
- Plate boundary

History

Teaching history can be a joy, but don't be tempted to go down the road of just teaching pupils the gory details – even though this would delight them. They need to know how the past has shaped the present and learn the substantive and disciplinary knowledge that can be built upon year after year.

The Ofsted research review for history is very comprehensive and highlights many things that are of importance. Some of the vocabulary referred to may be new to some of us, so I will try to explain and simplify some of the language and ideas.

Disciplinary and substantive knowledge

Understanding and utilising disciplinary and substantive knowledge in combination is what gives pupils the ability to construct historical arguments or meaningfully analyse sources.

Disciplinary knowledge is concerned with historical enquiry and how historians make sense of the past. The acquisition of disciplinary knowledge is meaningful to pupils when it can be related to particular historical problems where they have already gained sufficient knowledge of the period, setting and topic. This in turn enables the pupils to reason and make inferences about the past.

Disciplinary concepts are sometimes referred to as 'second-order' concepts, and they lead to a shared language related to disciplinary knowledge. The main second-order concepts referred to in the national curriculum that are in common use when we teach history are:

- Cause
- Consequence
- Change and continuity
- Similarity and difference
- Historical significance
- Sources and evidence
- Historical interpretations

It's important that we aim for our pupils to have a secure grasp of these concepts as they occur repeatedly in the history curriculum.

Substantive knowledge refers to the substance, or the subject matter, that pupils are learning about. Disciplinary knowledge is highly dependent on the depth and security of the pupils' substantive knowledge of the period or events being analysed. Examples of substantive concepts we need to ensure our pupils know are:

- Chronology
- Invasion
- Settlement
- Empire

The Ofsted history research review recommends that teachers and pupils should be aware of:

- **Generative knowledge and content emphasis** – the prioritisation of knowledge that will have the greatest impact in supporting pupils to learn more in the future. This is often referred to as 'core' knowledge; it's important to have this stored in the long-term memory.
- **Chronological knowledge** – understanding historical periods, the broad characteristics of them and their relationship to one another provides more context to what pupils learn and can therefore increase their familiarity with new learning. This is sometimes referred to as 'developing pupils' mental timeline'.
- **Enquiry questions** – many schools teach history through the use of enquiry questions, a useful device for shaping curriculum content.

- **Fingertip knowledge** – knowledge that is particularly important for pupils to know in order to reduce working memory space. They will need to be able to access this knowledge readily – to have it at their 'fingertips'.

Ofsted's summary of ideas about quality history education is:

- Learning through meaningful examples.
- Memorisation and security of knowledge.
- Repeated encounters with concepts to increase the security of pupils' knowledge.
- Clear exposition that considers pupils' prior knowledge.
- Developing narrative and story.
- Developing pupils' knowledge of historical contexts.
- Securing pupils' chronological knowledge.

Music

Music is fundamental to a well-functioning society. A baby bouncing to music in time with someone else has been shown to be more settled and cooperative immediately afterward.

Koenig, J, (2021). The Musical Child

Most of us love music, though of course taste varies widely. Yet many teachers are worried about teaching music, believing they don't have the required skills and knowledge. There have been a number of studies that have found that musical experiences in childhood can actually accelerate brain development, particularly in the areas of language acquisition and reading skills, and that learning to play an instrument can improve mathematical learning and even increase SAT scores.

Yet despite this, *The Guardian* reported that:

Music provision in schools, statutory until the age of 14, is under pressure. Last year [2019], work for the all-party parliamentary group for music education found that – due in large part to the government insistence on maths and English testing, and the 2010 introduction of the Ebacc – more than 50% of primary schools were not meeting their curriculum obligations.

The Guardian (2020). Music Education, State of the Nation

The report also found that: 'Intriguingly, a failing Bradford school suddenly improved after providing up to six weekly hours of music.' (*Guardian*, 2020)

So, in March 2021, the DfE, in an attempt to raise the quality of music teaching, published the 'Model Music Curriculum: Key Stages 1 to 2 Non-statutory guidance for the national curriculum in England'. In the same year, they published the Ofsted research review for Music. Both are well worth looking at.

Music, feelings and the human brain

In 2014, Habibi and Damasio published an important and well-respected piece of research into the effects of music on the brain and learning. They found that not only did music enhance academic achievement, but also – and perhaps more importantly – music ignites all areas of child development and skills for school readiness, including intellectual, social-emotional, motor, language and overall literacy, helping the body and the mind to work together. These findings indicate that exposing children to music during early development helps them learn the sounds and meanings of words. Furthermore, dancing to music helps children build motor skills while allowing them to practice self-expression. For children and adults, music helps strengthen memory skills and promotes overall wellbeing.

I'm a musician and have often been the music leader in schools. Here is my simplistic guide to the important things you need to know if you are a non-specialist.

The national curriculum states that pupils in KS1 and KS2 need to be able to:

Understand and explore how music is created, produced and communicated, including through the inter-related dimensions:

- Pitch
- Duration
- Dynamics
- Tempo
- Rhythm
- Timbre
- Texture
- Structure
- Appropriate musical notations

Here are the other musical elements that will need to be taught so that pupils become familiar with the words:

KS1 and KS2:

· Using voice: sing, chant, speak

· Play solo, ensemble

· Improvise and compose

· Listen .

And then these additional elements at KS2:

· Use and understand staff /stave and other musical notations

· Appreciate and understand a wide range of high-quality live and recorded music drawn from different traditions and from great composers and musicians

· Develop an understanding of the history of music.

Ideas for using voice: sing, chant, speak:

· Sing nursery rhymes, body songs e.g. Heads shoulders knees and toes, body percussion songs

· Chants – hand-clapping games

· Play games with rhythm, beat, singing, chanting, ensemble playing, percussion such as Patty cake, Miss Mary Mack, progress onto Cups (Anna Kendrick) – When I'm Gone (Pitch Perfect) as pupils get older.

Listening activities

A good starter activity is to display an image such as the below example and ask the pupils to name any instruments they recognise.

© *Trodler/Shutterstock.com*

BBC 10 Pieces provides full lesson plan ideas along with pieces of music to listen to. Some famous pieces of music are great to listen to with children; the following examples represent certain things such as animals, planets and people:

- Peter and the Wolf, by Sergei Prokofiev
- Carnival of the Animals, by Camille Saint-Saëns
- The Planets, by Gustav Holst

Ask the pupils questions about the music, such as how it makes them feel. Ask what the music makes them see and get them to draw or paint what they can hear.

Composition

If you have tablets, then you can use composition software such as Garage Band (for key stage 2). If you use instruments, you can get the pupils to score their music with simple annotations. Class composition can be either vocal, body or using percussion instruments.

The following approaches will help to prevent the pupils from getting over-excited:

- Stick to the behaviour policy and plan.
- Use non-verbal messages.
- Build in quiet moments.
- Praise the pupils who are doing as you've asked.

Remember, you want the pupils to get excited; it's about having fun, but you don't want to be shouting over them. You can teach them some simple routines for using instruments without getting too noisy. For example:

- When you say 'one', they tiptoe to the instruments.
- When you say 'two', they pick one up and tiptoe back to their place.
- When you say 'three', they put their instrument down in front of them.

Using schemes

If all else fails, you can use published music schemes such as Charanga. These schemes provide full lesson plans and explain how to teach each part of the lesson.

A final word

Your school may use a music specialist teacher. If you are in a school that does this, do take opportunities to observe their lessons. Play some nice, relaxing classical music as they enter the room, as they are writing, working or playing or during art lessons, for example. Discuss what they are listening to – can they describe it? How does it make them feel? Does it help them to concentrate? If you have neurodivergent pupils in your class, they may not like hearing certain types of music, so let them use ear defenders, or choose what they are listening to. Remember the power of music and its importance in our everyday lives and share it with your pupils.

Computing

The Ofsted research review for computing makes it very clear that we should be teaching about declarative and procedural knowledge.

Declarative knowledge can be described as 'knowing that' and is sometimes referred to as conceptual knowledge. This is concerned with facts, rules and principles and the relationships between them. **Procedural knowledge** can be described as 'knowing how' and involves teaching knowledge of methods or processes that can be performed.

So, we could say that:

- **Declarative** = 'By the end of the unit, the students will know that...'
- **Procedural** = 'By the end of the unit, the students will know how to...'

Here's an example of declarative and procedural knowledge:

Year 2 unit: Coding	
Declarative – by the end of the unit pupils will know that:	In computing, a set of instructions is known as an algorithm. Steps in an algorithm must be followed in order to achieve the intended outcome.
Procedural – by the end of the unit pupils will know how to:	• Follow a written algorithm in a plan and interpret it. • Identify events, objects and actions in a plan of an algorithm. • Predict what will happen if the planned algorithm was converted to code. • Use the correct code to implement the algorithm, which includes event 'when clicked', objects and actions.

The national curriculum's purpose of study

A high-quality computing education equips pupils to use computational thinking and creativity to understand and change the world. It's a great subject for creating links across the curriculum, as computing has natural links with maths, science and design and technology, and provides insights into both natural and artificial systems.

The syllabus is divided into three themes:

- **Computer science** – pupils are taught the principles of information and computation, how digital systems work and how to put this knowledge to use through programming.
- **Information technology** – pupils are taught to create programs, systems and a range of content.
- **Digital literacy** – pupils are able to use and express themselves and develop their ideas through information and communication technology at a level suitable for the future workplace and as active participants in a digital world.

The national curriculum for computing aims to ensure that all pupils:

- Can understand and apply the fundamental principles and concepts of computer science, including abstraction, logic, algorithms and data representation.
- Can analyse problems in computational terms, and have repeated practical experience of writing computer programs in order to solve such problems.

- Can evaluate and apply information technology, including new or unfamiliar technologies, analytically to solve problems.
- Are responsible, competent, confident and creative users of information and communication technology.

Teaching computing at EYFS

In the 'Understanding the world' area of learning, children are guided to explore how technology can be used safely and responsibly within the world around them, both at school and at home. Within safe digital environments, children can create and capture their ideas.

In the 'Being imaginative' unit, children use what they have learned about media and materials in original ways, thinking about uses and purposes. They represent their own ideas, thoughts and feelings through design and technology, art, music, dance, role-play and stories.

Teaching ideas at EYFS include:

- Roamers and bee-bots (early programming).
- Using voice and video recorders.
- Taking photos with a tablet.
- Doodling on a tablet.
- Including an old keyboard in the role play area.

Teaching ideas at KS1 include:

- Technology around us.
- Digital art.
- Developing mouse skills and keyboard skills.
- How to keep safe and healthy when using technology in and beyond the home.
- Using bee-bots for programming.
- Creating algorithms.
- Using digital equipment.
- Organising information.
- Keeping safe online.
- Raspberry Pi.

Teaching ideas at KS2 include:

- Using Scratch for creating algorithms and moving images.
- Music technology (e.g. Garage Band).
- Digimap.

- Google Earth.
- Input and output.
- Using micro:bit.
- Data handling.
- Exploring search engines.
- Keeping safe online.
- Stop motion animation.

Common misconceptions in computing include thinking that:

- It's ok to use WhatsApp if you are of primary age.
- Apps and online games don't have age ratings (they all do).
- Everything you read online is true.
- The internet and computer programming are recent technological inventions.
- The first search result is the best.
- Your internet search doesn't shape your online experience.
- Everyone online is your friend.

Search engines

It's important to teach your pupils critical thinking when using internet search engines, including the following principles:

- Whatever we click on will trigger an algorithm to guide other searches.
- Sometimes the top-ranked search result has money behind it to promote it to the top of the page.
- AI generated results are not necessarily accurate.
- We should not believe everything we read.
- Words matter, and the words and phrases you use in an internet search may bias the results we see.

The Ofsted research review

The research review is comprehensive in its coverage of practices and literature involved in the teaching of computing. It makes the following recommendations for quality computing education.

- The planned curriculum includes a breadth of knowledge relating to computer science, information technology and digital literacy.
- Declarative knowledge ('knowing that') and procedural knowledge ('knowing how') are identified, sequenced and connected in the curriculum.

- The curriculum is rich in computer science knowledge, enabling pupils to make sense of the entire computing curriculum.
- Pupils learn important programming knowledge to enable them to become skilful programmers.
- Programming languages are chosen to meet curriculum goals.
- Development of problem solving is underpinned by domain-specific knowledge that is identified and sequenced in the curriculum.
- Pupils' schemata of computing contexts is built through new and repeated encounters with contexts to build a breadth and depth of knowledge.
- The curriculum carefully sequences knowledge related to e-safety to ensure subject content is appropriate for pupils at each stage of their education.
- Decisions to teach the subject in a discrete or cross-curricular way are based on how best to teach the intended curriculum.
- Teachers consider pupils' expertise and prior knowledge when selecting teaching approaches, with novices requiring more explicit instruction.
- Teachers use worked examples appropriately to help pupils solve problems.
- Formative assessment is used to identify misconceptions early.

Useful online resources for teaching computing include:

- National Centre for Computing Education (teachcomputing.org)
- Primary computing resource collections (stem.org.uk)
- Primary computing teaching resources (bbc.co.uk/teach)

Design and technology

The argument for design and technology is declared in the national curriculum's purpose statement:

> *Design and technology is an inspiring, rigorous and practical subject. Using creativity and imagination, pupils design and make products that solve real and relevant problems within a variety of contexts, considering their own and others' needs, wants and values. They acquire a broad range of subject knowledge and draw on disciplines such as mathematics, science, engineering, computing and art. Pupils learn how to take risks, becoming resourceful, innovative, enterprising and capable citizens. Through the evaluation of past and present design and technology, they develop a critical understanding of its impact on daily life and the wider world. High-quality design and technology education makes an essential contribution to the creativity, culture, wealth and wellbeing of the nation.*

National Curriculum (2013)

Design and technology is separated into four interrelated sections (with cooking and nutrition as an additional element):

- Design
- Make
- Evaluate
- Technical knowledge

Design and technology is not simply making and creating things; for example, pupils may choose whether to replace a pair of trainers bought last winter with this winter's new fashion, or they may debate the location of alternative energy in the local environment. If taught well, design and technology can enable the pupils to have an informed view about the principles upon which their design decision making rests.

The following case study follows John, one of my former students who became a teacher, and the resulting impact he had on his school's teaching of design and technology after a series of lectures he had during his teacher training year.

John's school had always taught design and technology. Every year towards Christmas, each class was expected to design and make a Christmas stocking. It was always made out of red felt and stitched by the pupils, and they could choose the design and patterns to cover their stockings with. However, John realised that while the 'design, make, evaluate' process was being fulfilled, the technical knowledge aspect was not. At KS2, where John was teaching, the technical knowledge requirements for pupils were:

- Apply their understanding of how to strengthen, stiffen and reinforce more complex structures.

- Understand and use mechanical systems in their products (e.g. gears, pulleys, cams, levers and linkages).

- Understand and use electrical systems in their products (e.g. series circuits incorporating switches, bulbs, buzzers and motors).

- Apply their understanding of computing to program, monitor and control their products.

> With this in mind, John changed the way his pupils made their stockings and linked their technical knowledge to science. Firstly, they tested materials for strength and durability. Then they tested them for flexibility and pliability. They worked out that the heel and toe parts needed strengthening. They could then choose from a range of suitable materials, and this time the stockings looked different.

This is a small example, but one that hopefully demonstrates that design and technology is more than simply making a product. Looking at the work of famous designers can also add further richness to teaching in this area. Do look at the Design and Technology Association website (designtechnology.org.uk) for further lesson ideas.

Art and design

The summary from the Ofsted research review for art and design suggests that best practice includes:

- The purpose of art and design:
  - Art ideally should be both 'intellectually challenging and creatively demanding'.
  - Art is both practical and theoretical, informed by studio practices and academic disciplines.

- EYFS and primary
  - High-quality EYFS practice develops children's interest and imagination, providing the foundations to be successful in the future.
  - The report has found a recent decline in the quantity and quality of art education at primary, which may be linked to declining levels of funding, subject knowledge and more focus being placed on other subjects.

- The national curriculum
  - Pupils can develop their **practical knowledge** of how to create art by learning the methods and techniques used by artists, craft-makers and designers.
  - Pupils can learn the **theoretical knowledge** of the tools, materials and history of the subject.
  - Pupils can learn the **disciplinary knowledge** of art, such as the ways in which it is judged, valued and evaluated.

Pupils make progress in art when they build all three types of knowledge and make connections between them. I have always had to find art and design lessons online, take advice from colleagues and use resources from art websites. My favourite is the National Gallery Online and their 'Take One Picture' idea, where every year the gallery takes one picture from their collection 'to inspire cross-curricular work in primary classrooms'.

Take One Picture

As I live near Oxford, I would choose a painting from Ashmolean Museum, so that after studying the picture our class could see it for real. After studying it in depth, the children referred to it as 'our picture' and responded with excited gasps as they told the curator all about the picture.

The 'Take One Picture' resources can be used for:

- **Painting links** – work links back to the focus painting.
- **Investigative approach** – projects are shaped by child-led research.
- **Process** – children have the opportunity to learn a new process inspired by the painting.
- **Cross-curricular learning** – projects make meaningful links across the curriculum, particularly in history and geography.
- **Community** – learning involves people or places in the local community.

Physical education

In EYFS, physical development (PD) is not limited to physical education lessons but can include all sorts of activities that can help children gain early skills such as throwing and catching, climbing and motor skills. Some ideas include, but are certainly not limited to:

- Dancing
- Climbing
- Jumping
- Riding a bike
- Skipping
- Throwing, catching and bouncing balls and bean bags
- Walking
- Games
- Musical hide-and-seek
- Obstacle courses
- Parachute games

The Ofsted research review

Similar to other reviews, the advice for physical education is to look at knowledge through the lens of declarative (knowing what) and procedural (knowing how) knowledge.

Declarative knowledge in physical education is the factual knowledge concerning movement, rules, tactics, strategies, health and participation, which is explicitly linked to the content being taught and can be communicated through verbal or written means.

Procedural knowledge is the 'know-how' to apply declarative facts, such as applying the tactics to a practice or game situation, and is put into practice through physical demonstration or physical participation.

The following is some best practice advice:

● Teachers know that physical education includes clearly defined knowledge that is both declarative and procedural and these are usually inextricably linked.

● Teachers know that physical education is not necessarily synonymous with physical activity or sport; they share similarities and differences.

● A strong foundation of fundamental movement skills (FMS) is developed, starting in the early years and developmentally sequenced through the progression of skills.

● Teachers make sure that pupils' movement is context-related, intelligent, efficient and effective, with pupils gaining knowledge of rules, strategies and tactics related to games and other types of physical activity, such as athletics.

● Health, participation and physical activity are taught systematically, and increase in complexity throughout the curriculum.

Languages

Teaching languages at KS2 may involve any modern or ancient foreign language and should focus on enabling pupils to make substantial progress in one language. Languages are generally taught at primary by following one of these three models:

● A specialist teacher is brought into the school to teach languages.

● A teacher in school takes responsibility for its organisation and delivery.

● A member of staff who is a native speaker is asked to lead the subject.

Ofsted make the distinction between intentional and incidental learning in languages, stating that in the classroom it's useful to think of learning as being either one or the other.

Intentional learning happens when the learner is aware of the need to learn. They invest effort in it and knowingly gain explicit knowledge. **Incidental learning** happens when a learner is not aware that they may learn something, but they do. It happens as a by-product of another activity, such as learning to count to ten in French by singing a song.

Some schools prefer to begin teaching a second language at KS1 or even at EYFS; the school decides which language they will teach. Some schools will focus on the language that the school they feed into focuses on, while others may select a language because they believe it to be important or because it may suit the population they serve, or simply because they may have a teacher who specialises in or speaks a given language.

Other advice given in the Ofsted research review includes:

- Use of the target language should be carefully planned within the scheme of work.
- Teaching should support and complement the scheme of work and build systematically on learners' prior knowledge, reinforced by English when needed.
- Activities that are led in the target language, if appropriately planned, are likely to help embed knowledge in the long-term memory, support practice and recall and help pupils to respond to language in meaningful ways.
- As learners progress from novice to more proficient in the language, teachers can alter their use of the target language accordingly.
- The earlier learners are in language learning, the greater the care teachers need to take to ensure that learners are not confused or overwhelmed by teachers' use of overly complex language. A concrete example is the planned use of target language for classroom routines that are clearly understood by learners, as opposed to an attempt to describe more complex grammatical concepts to learners using the target language.

WoLLow

In many schools in the UK, over half of pupils speak a language other than English at home, something we have completely ignored for the past 50 years. Do they need to learn French or Spanish?

You may prefer the World of Languages, Languages of the World (WoLLow) KS2–3 curriculum, which takes a broader approach to language acquisition and attempts to address the fact that so many of our pupils already speak two languages.

Latin

If your school is interested in teaching Latin, do take a look at the Classics for All website (classicsforall.org.uk).

Religious education

Schools in England must teach religious education, but parents can withdraw their children for all or part of the lessons. Local councils are responsible for deciding the religious education syllabus in maintained schools, but faith schools and academies can set their own. In most cases, your school will need to follow the locally agreed syllabus for your county or diocese.

Religious education is a great subject to teach; it can help students develop their beliefs and values and learn about the beliefs and practices of others, and can also help students understand the role of religion in the modern world and promote respect and empathy. It can encourage reflection, allowing students time to think about what they've learned and how it applies to their lives, and help students find meaning in their lives and respond to questions about the purpose of human existence.

Most locally agreed syllabi determine that primary schools should teach Christianity along with two other world religions, although lots of schools choose to focus on other religions too, often through the use of religious festivals or significant events.

Some pupils like to share their own religion with the class while others don't, so always make sure you ask first. Other pupils may have parents who offer to come in, but if this is the case, do make sure you chat to them first about what they wish to talk about or share. While you are an ECT, ask your mentor or a member of the senior leadership team (SLT) for advice as it can be a very sensitive area.

PSHE and RSE

The legislation around both PSHE (personal, social, health and economic education) and RSE (relationships and sex education) are in constant flux due to changing policy and governments, so it's always best to check the current advice. Your school will also have its own policy regarding both subjects.

Despite these challenges, PSHE and RSE can be very rewarding to teach, because being pastoral subjects, they both give opportunities to build closer relationships with your pupils, whether that's through circle time activities or more structured lessons. More and more, there is an emphasis on pupils learning how to look after their own physical and mental health and keep themselves safe online and in real life situations.

Here is some advice for teaching PSHE and RSE:

- Join the PSHE Association and use their resources.
- Don't assume your pupils know anything much.
- Never feel embarrassed answering a question, but do not permit questions that are only asked to goad you.

References and evidence base

Coe, R., Aloisi, C., Higgins, S., and Major, L. E., 2014, What makes great teaching. Review of the underpinning research. Durham University: UK. Available at: Coe_WhatMakesGreatTeaching.pdf

DfE, 2021, Model Music Curriculum: Key Stages 1 to 2 Non-statutory guidance for the national curriculum in England.

Education Endowment Foundation, 2018, Improving Secondary Science Guidance Report. Online at: EEF_ImprovingSecondaryScienceGuidanceReport.pdf

Education Endowment Foundation, 2021, Education Endowment Foundation Teaching and Learning Toolkit, Mastery Learning. Online at: https://educationendowmentfoundation.org.uk/education-evidence/teaching-learning-toolkit

Education Endowment Foundation, 2021, Education Endowment Foundation Teaching and Learning Toolkit, Phonics. Online at: https://educationendowmentfoundation.org.uk/education-evidence/teaching-learning-toolkit

Habibi, A., & Damasio, A., 2014, Music, Feelings, and the Human Brain. Psychomusicology: Music, Mind, and Brain, 24(1), 92–102.

Hirsch, E. D., 1987, Cultural Literacy: What Every American Needs to Know, Houghton Mifflin.

Jensen, E., 2009, Teaching with Poverty in Mind: What Being Poor Does to Kids' Brains and What Schools Can Do About It, ASCD.

Koenig, J., 2021, The Musical Child: Using the Power of Music to Raise Children Who Are Happy, Healthy, and Whole, Harper Collins, London.

Ofsted Research Review Series, DfE. Online.

Rasinski, T., 2022, Education Endowment Foundation, Why focus on reading fluency? Online at: https://educationendowmentfoundation.org.uk/news/why-focus-on-reading-fluency

Rosenshine, B., 2012, Principles of instruction: Research-based strategies that all teachers should know. American Educator, 12–20. Available at: Rosenshine_PrinciplesOfInstruction.pdf

Scarborough, H. S., 2001, Connecting early language and literacy to later reading (dis)abilities: Evidence, theory, and practice. In S. Neuman and D. Dickinson (Eds.), *Handbook for Research in Early Literacy*. New York: Guilford Press.

Take One Picture. The National Gallery. Online.

Chapter 7
Plan and teach well-structured lessons

ITTECF syllabus

Classroom practice (Standard 4 – Plan and teach well structured lessons)

Learn that...	Learn how to...
1. Effective teaching can transform pupils' knowledge, capabilities and beliefs about learning. 2. Effective teachers introduce new material in steps, explicitly linking new ideas to what has been previously studied and learned. 3. Modelling helps pupils understand new processes and ideas; good models make abstract ideas concrete and accessible. 4. Guides, scaffolds and worked examples can help pupils apply new ideas, but should be gradually removed as pupil expertise increases. 5. Explicitly teaching pupils metacognitive strategies linked to subject knowledge, including how to plan, monitor and evaluate, supports independence and academic success. 6. Questioning is an essential tool for teachers; questions can be used for many purposes, including to check pupils' prior knowledge, assess understanding and break down problems. 7. High quality classroom talk (sometimes referred to as oracy), can support pupils to articulate key ideas, consolidate understanding and extend their vocabulary.	**Plan effective lessons, by:** a) Using modelling, explanations and scaffolds, acknowledging that novices need more structure early in a domain. b) Enabling critical thinking and problem solving by first teaching the necessary foundational content knowledge. c) Removing scaffolding only when pupils are achieving a high degree of success in applying previously taught material. d) Using evidence of prior learning to provide sufficient opportunity for pupils to consolidate and practise applying new knowledge and skills. e) Breaking tasks down into constituent components when first setting up independent practice (e.g. using tasks that scaffold pupils through meta-cognitive and procedural processes). **Make good use of expositions, by:** f) Starting expositions at the point of current pupil understanding. g) Combining a verbal explanation with a relevant graphical representation of the same concept or process, where appropriate. h) Using concrete representation of abstract ideas (e.g. making use of analogies, metaphors, manipulatives for counting, examples and non-examples).

Learn that...	Learn how to...
8. Practice is an integral part of effective teaching; ensuring pupils have repeated opportunities to practise, with appropriate guidance and support, increases success. 9. Paired and group activities can increase pupil success, but to work together effectively pupils need guidance, support and practice. 10. How pupils are grouped is also important; care should be taken to monitor the impact of groupings on pupil attainment, behaviour and motivation. 11. Homework can improve pupil outcomes, particularly for older pupils, but it is likely that the quality of homework and its relevance to main class teaching is more important than the amount set.	**Model effectively, by:** i) Narrating thought processes when modelling to make explicit how experts think (e.g. asking questions aloud that pupils should consider when working independently and drawing pupils' attention to links with prior knowledge). j) Making the steps in a process memorable and ensuring pupils can recall them (e.g. naming them, developing mnemonics, or linking to memorable stories). k) Exposing potential pitfalls and explaining how to avoid them. **Stimulate pupil thinking and check for understanding, by:** l) Planning activities around what you want pupils to think hard about. m) Including a range of types of questions in class discussions to extend and challenge pupils (e.g. by modelling new vocabulary or asking pupils to justify answers). Elaborate on and query pupil contributions to support pupils' oral language skills, and knowledge development. n) Providing appropriate wait time between question and response where more developed responses are required. o) Considering the factors that will support effective collaborative or paired work (e.g. familiarity with routines, whether pupils have the necessary prior knowledge and how pupils are grouped). p) Providing scaffolds for pupil talk to increase the focus and rigour of dialogue.

What does a good lesson look like?

In 2012, Barak Rosenshine, a professor at the University of Illinois, produced 'research-based principles of instruction' for teachers. He concluded that top teachers:

1. **Review the last lesson.** A review helps remind pupils what they have learned and allows the teacher to make connections to what comes next.
2. **Present new material in small steps.** Because our working memory is small, never present too much information in one go.
3. **Give very clear and detailed instructions and explanations.**
4. **Ask a large number of questions and engage the pupils in discussion.** This helps the pupils practise and provides useful feedback to the teacher.
5. **Give a large amount of active practice for all students.** Guide pupils as they begin to practise. It's not enough to simply present the pupils with new material, because the material will be forgotten unless there is sufficient rehearsal. Pupils must spend time rephrasing or summarising new material or answering questions in order to store the information in their long-term memory.
6. **Provide models and worked examples.** Pupils need support to help them solve problems. The teacher should provide worked examples, thinking aloud while writing.
7. **Ask pupils to explain what they have learned to the class.**
8. **Check the responses of all pupils.** The most effective teachers in the research frequently checked to see if all the pupils were learning the new material.
9. **Provide systematic feedback and corrections to both oral and written answers.** Make sure the pupils respond to the feedback by repeating the correct answer if the first attempt was not right.
10. **Provide scaffolds for difficult tasks.** A scaffold is a temporary support that is used to assist a student. These scaffolds are gradually withdrawn as pupils become more competent. Scaffolding includes the teacher 'thinking aloud' as they solve a problem.
11. **Require and monitor independent practice.** Guided practice is followed by independent practice, where pupils work alone and practise the new material. Circulate round the room and check progress.
12. **Have a weekly and monthly review.** Pupils need extensive reading and practice in order to develop well-connected networks of ideas (schemas) in their long-term memory. Review the previous week's work every week and the previous month's work every fourth week or so.

What does a good secondary lesson look like?

What a good lesson looks like depends a great deal on the subject being taught; for example, there will be a big difference between an art lesson and a history lesson. The main thing is that at the end of the lesson the pupils all know and understand things they did not know at the start.

Before the lesson

- Have any equipment the pupils are going to use as ready as you can.
- Have your lesson plan and notes ready.
- Have your class list ready.
- Know if there is anything you need to collect in when the pupils arrive, such as homework.
- Be ready to speak to any pupil who missed the last lesson about catching up.

The very beginning of the lesson

- Have an entry-to-the-classroom routine.
- Ensure pupils all know what to bring to lessons and that they get the right things out on the desk without you needing to say anything.
- Start by explaining why the subject matter of the lesson is important.
- Start by giving the pupils work to do; make sure it's neither too hard nor too easy.
- If pupils need to be given things such as a mini whiteboard, pens or marked homework, have a system for handing these things out in silence.
- Carry out a registration while the pupils are working – note who is missing. If they are still missing at the end of the lesson, make a note to see them the next time they are in (and maybe pass on homework).
- If a pupil is late, quietly ask them to see you at the end.
- If a pupil doesn't have the correct materials, quietly provide them and ask them to see you at the end.

After this...

- You could remind the pupils of the last lesson if it's relevant, ideally through quick questions.
- If homework has been set, go through the answers, drawing out common errors and showing the pupils a good piece of work.

Teach the lesson

Teach material by direct instruction; for example, talk, explain, draw and write. Get the pupils to make notes, or at some point give them notes or knowledge organisers for their files. You could give them workbooks where they have to fill in blanks, but they need a record of the lesson.

Ask the pupils to think and give answers. This is most obviously the case in maths teaching, where you will always want to know what the pupils have grasped before moving on. Use formative assessment (pages 190–91), where you ask questions of the pupils to assess whether they have understood what you are teaching and adapt your teaching in response.

Here are some other things to bear in mind while teaching the lesson:

- When setting work, always explain what a good answer will look like, for example, the length of a written answer or the vocabulary you need the pupils to use.
- Teach in small chunks. After each section, ask the pupils to do something, such as writing down an answer on their mini whiteboards. Check all the pupils for understanding, and provide feedback.
- Don't be afraid of silence. It's not a problem if someone is observing your lesson, as the pupils are just working in silence.
- You are responsible for going at the right speed – neither too fast nor too slow. Inject a sense of pace and fun where you can.
- Ask many questions using cold calling.
- Model good answers on the board then get the pupils to try. Get them to explain their answers.
- Aim to generate success, for this is what creates motivation.

Practical work

If you are teaching art, design and technology, physical education, science, drama, dance or any subject with a practical element, there are four things to remember:

- You need to set up much of the equipment before the lesson begins. We don't want to lose teaching time.
- Give the clearest possible instructions and exercise close control. If a pupil will not behave, they should not do the practical.
- Make sure the pupils understand why the practical is worth doing.
- Leave time at the end of the lesson to clear up.

At the end

- Convince yourself they have all learned something by asking questions.
- Set homework with very specific instructions including the minimum which should be written.
- See any pupil who arrived late, did not bring the necessary pens, books, etc, failed to produce homework, etc. Have a quiet word about the problem and warn them of the consequences if it happens again.

What does a good primary lesson look like?

All of the points made in the previous section about secondary lessons are relevant. A good lesson is, indeed, one in which pupils learn something that they either didn't know or couldn't do beforehand.

I have used Rosenshine's principles as a guide for most of my inexperienced teachers or ECTs to use as a lesson planning format. When you are teaching observed, there are some key elements that your observer would like to see, and this is turn can provide you with some guiding principles to use when thinking about your lesson.

Be prepared

- Check that you have the necessary resources and ensure these are readily to hand.
- Give out exercise books in advance.
- Ensure all equipment is in working order, pencils are sharp and whiteboard pens have ink.
- Check that your whiteboard teaching resources are online and ready to go.
- Does your teaching assistant and other support staff know what is expected of them?
- What could go wrong during the lesson? Think about possible problems and eliminate them.
- What scaffolding do you need to have in place for some learners?
- What stretch and challenge activities or questions will you use for more able, greater depth learners?

Good routines for moving into the classroom

- Set your expectations at the start of term.
- Should the pupils be entering the lesson silently?

- Do you want them sitting at desks or on the carpet? Make this clear before or as they enter.
- Should they sit down and immediately start working or wait for your input first? Again, make this clear before or as they enter the room.

Start the lesson

- Explain the context, e.g. 'We are learning this because...'
- Check prior learning, i.e. what the pupils should have learned in the previous lesson or lessons in this unit of work.

Learning intentions and objectives

- Do you need to share this with the pupils? Is it written on the board? Is it already written or stuck into their books?
- Do a vocabulary check. Do all the pupils understand all of the words and meanings in your lesson intention or objective?
- Share the success criteria, so the pupils will know whether they are achieving it or not as they are working.

Start at the end

- Start with the end of the lesson in mind.
- Tell the pupils what the outcome with be and how they will get there.
- Establish their starting points before you start teaching.

This is important. Many trainee teachers do what I used to do as a teacher; that is, being so focused on the activity that you lose focus of what you are intending the pupils to learn. All pupils need to make progress within every lesson; they need to have learned something new. So, focus on the *objective* rather than the activity, and make sure that, with your support, they *all* learn it.

Check that the pupils have all learned the objective before they leave the lesson. In the old days, I taught as though I was firing arrows without worrying whether they hit the target or not. Later in my career, I realised it was *all* about hitting the target, for every pupil. For more on this, see the excellent work by Griffith and Burns: Outstanding Teaching: Teaching Backwards (2014).

Teach

- Use strong explicit instruction to introduce the lesson.
- Model, model, model – model the task and model the thinking involved using your own 'think-aloud'.
- Check for understanding.
- Stop the lesson at various points to clarify and check, then move up to the next level (you are chunking the learning).
- Ask questions and allow thinking time for answers.

Independent and group practice

- Check the learning throughout the lesson.
- Are they on task?
- Do they understand the incremental steps?

Ensure they make good progress

- Ask questions.
- Check work in progress.
- Give feedback.
- Assess and use lots of assessment for learning (AfL).

Plenary tasks

- Summarise the lesson.
- Review and misconceptions.
- Check for understanding and progress.
- Don't let the pupils leave the room unless they know or can do more than they could before the lesson.

Using AI to plan and deliver lessons

Artificial intelligence (AI) is not mentioned in the Teachers' Standards or Core Content Framework, but most teachers are using it, and the proportion will rise. Because the technology is moving ahead fast, we cannot know where we will be in 5–10 years' time.

Here's what some teachers are finding useful now:

1. If you want to teach a topic and there is some element you are unsure about, look it up on an AI site like ChatGPT. Summarize.tech provides summaries of films on YouTube, while DALL-E is good for different artistic styles.

2. If you want a whole lesson mapped out with content including exercises for pupils, ask for it on platforms such as ChatGPT, DeepSeek, TeacherGenAIToolkit or AILA. You can get ready-made slideshows from tome.app.

3. Tests and other assessments for specific topics can be found on magicschool. ai and other sites. Some teachers use Google Forms to create assessments that can be marked. If you have EAL (English as an additional language) or SEND pupils who need a test written in simpler language, ChatGPT can do that.

4. In the future all exams, even a subjective subject like English, will be marked by AI. ChatGPT can mark as well as generate answers to questions.

5. If a pupil needs to research a topic (for an extended project qualification, for example), they could start with elicit.com for a summary of prior research in the topic. Once the pupil has a list of research authors and papers, they know where to look for more information.

6. ChatGPT can create character cards for roles in debates and will even write a speech. This is a useful support for teachers who are trying to promote oracy.

In summary, AI can generate lesson plans, create assignments and assessment materials. Some AI-powered platforms create interactive slide decks for teachers that include open-ended questions; this can help to save teachers valuable lesson preparation time. However, it is important to double-check what the AI has generated, as it can often have incorrect information.

Being organised

A good teacher is organised in the following ways:

- They will have a file with their teaching notes for each class.
- They will have a box for each class in which they keep their exercise books and other resources they need.
- They keep a record of which pupils have missed lessons and when.
- They set and mark work regularly to build up a decent number of marks in their hard copy or online mark book.
- They never forget to set or collect homework.

Keep an A4 week-to-view diary or a planner and write in every lesson you will be teaching, noting those lessons that will be lost to internal exams and school events. This diary or planner will be invaluable. For example, if a pupil is missing from a lesson, make a note of it in the diary and remind yourself to see that pupil in the next lesson. This is the difference between an organised teacher and one who has no idea who missed which lessons when.

The clock

An organised teacher will aim to start a lesson on time and end it on time. This means, for example, that they will start setting homework at least five minutes before a lesson ends. If they know that they have to speak to a few pupils at the end of the lesson, they will leave an extra five minutes to do that. It helps greatly to have a clock on the wall at the back of the room behind the pupils so you, the teacher, can see it without turning round and you don't have to look at your watch, which will trigger some pupils to become impatient.

What about homework?

Your school must have a policy about homework that details when homework is to be done by each class you teach and how long it should take. When you know which evening the work is to be done, you can work out which lesson you are going to set the work and which lesson you are going to collect it in (usually the first lesson you have after the night the work is done) or the time by which the work is uploaded on a platform.

There are three problems with homework. Firstly, many teachers don't spend enough time working out what a useful homework activity could be, so they set something that is boring and of limited value. Secondly, homework is the first thing that falls by the wayside if a teacher feels overworked. Either the teacher 'forgets' to set it, or they set something inadequate. Thirdly, in the primary school, if you set homework that is too hard to be done independently, some pupils may not be able to receive help from their parents, which can widen the 'disadvantage gap'.

In your diary or planner, you will have written in every lesson you will be teaching. Now write in every time you need to set homework and every lesson you need to collect it. There is nothing worse than a teacher who sets homework but fails to collect it.

You need to test your pupils from time to time, especially in a secondary school. So, good homework is 'learn everything on topic x' or 'learn everything we have studied in the past two weeks for a test in class'. In the subsequent lesson, you can spend 25 minutes on a test, 10 minutes marking, five minutes collecting in the marks then five minutes dealing with any pupils who need a specific reward for a great mark or dealing with pupils who did badly.

Setting good homework takes preparation. It's good if the pupils have a textbook, because homework can be set with reference to the book ('do the questions on page x' or 'make notes on pages x to y'). Mark and return work as soon as possible after it is collected; pupils appreciate this, which is part of the message you are sending – that homework matters.

Returning homework

You need to do the following when you return homework:

- Deal with any pupils who failed to produce the homework, but without disrupting the whole lesson too much.
- Deal with any pupils whose work was poor. The aim is not punishment but getting them to improve. Your school should have specific responses to poor homework.
- Go over common mistakes with the whole class.
- Ask them to write out spelling errors that you have indicated in your marking (either write out the correct spelling on their work or write 'Sp' by the word).
- Reward those who did well using your school's methods for doing so.

Is homework really needed?

Homework is not necessarily needed for younger children, but most good schools require homework to be set and, for older pupils, this takes up time needed for revision, making notes and writing essays.

It's difficult to set homework in creative subjects like art and design and technology if pupils are in the middle of making a piece in school, so try to provide times when pupils can come in and spend extra time on their work, for example, during lunch or after school.

Direct instruction

Direct instruction is a teacher-led teaching method where the teacher stands in front of a classroom and presents the information. The teachers give explicit instructions to the students. This doesn't mean the teacher just lectures; they will ask all pupils questions, use good resources like websites and make the lessons fun.

So, what is not direct instruction? The alternative is where pupils are left to do projects by themselves, or 'discovery learning' where they are encouraged to find out things for themselves or do group work.

The merits of direct instruction are that there is less differentiation within the class and, although this may risk leaving struggling pupils behind, on balance it has the effect of pulling them up to a better standard. This method is a faster way of conveying knowledge and teaching pupils than any alternative method.

Common aspects of good direct instruction include:

- Teaching skills and concepts in small steps.
- Using examples.
- Using clear and unambiguous language.
- Anticipating and planning for common misconceptions.
- Highlighting essential content and removing distracting information.
- Using formative assessment (questioning) to guide you.

Where are you going to stand in the classroom when you are speaking? Standing at the front or to the side of the front may enable you to see the most pupils, and it helps greatly if they can all see you. But sometimes you will be right by the board or the visualiser because you are using it, and at times you will walk around the room to check work when pupils are silently writing.

Research evidence for direct instruction

Tabarrok, A. (2022) *Direct Instruction produces large gains in learning*, **Marginal Revolution website**

This paper is a summary of research carried out in Kenya with Bridge International schools and 10,000 pupils. Primary pupils who were given direct instruction gained 0.89 extra years of learning over two years more than those pupils not receiving direct instruction. Direct instruction teachers were sometimes given scripts, which ensured that struggling teachers still got good results.

Kirschner, P., Sweller, J and Clark, R, 2006, Why minimal guidance during instruction does not work: an analysis of the failure of constructivist, discovery, problem-based, experiential and inquiry-based teaching, Educational Psychology 41

This study found that minimally guided teaching approaches, where pupils are expected to discover concepts, don't work; direct instruction, where the teacher fully explains the concepts, does. One reason is that discovery methods rely on the working memory, which is limited and the information there is quickly forgotten.

How to ask pupils questions

Asking pupils questions is a key part of effective teaching. Research has shown that the most effective questioning has certain characteristics:

- Leave enough time for the pupil to answer your question. The single most effective action you can take after asking a question is to keep quiet. Research suggests that teachers average less than one second of silence before repeating or emphasising material or asking a second question.

- Before leaping in with an answer yourself, ask pupils to discuss the questions in pairs. Some kind of answer is usually forthcoming.
- Be clear about what your question is aiming to do. Are you simply trying to see if pupils can recall a piece of information, or are you providing an opportunity for them to clarify their own understanding?
- Ask a friendly colleague to observe and give feedback on how many and what type of questions you use in a lesson. Are your questions largely closed, requiring a simple recall answer, or are they expansive and open, stimulating thought and discussion?
- Encourage deeper responses from pupils by using 'echoing'. When the pupil has given their answer, repeat back to them a section of what they have said ('So you are arguing that...). Then leave a silence.
- Never belittle a question or answer from a pupil that may seem irrelevant, silly or ignorant. Mistakes are a useful way of learning and pupils need to feel that their contributions will not be laughed at.
- Be a good listener. Hear what the pupil's response is and use further questions to pinpoint areas where understanding is poor.
- Some pupils are quiet in a large group situation. Pick them to answer or provide the opportunity for them to speak by using pairs and small group interaction.
- Students don't listen when others are answering a question. So, after an answer has been given, you should ask another pupil whether they agree with the answer. The pupils will then start to listen.

Lesson plans – a valuable tool or a straight-jacket?

A lesson plan is a short account of what you are going to do over the course of one lesson. It includes what the aims are, how many minutes you plan to spend on each section, the resources you need and any special arrangements for individual pupils. The normal problem with lesson plans is that they are too ambitious and therefore the teacher runs out of time. Timing is something that comes with experience.

Lesson plans are something new teachers and teachers being inspected are asked to write. They are helpful to anyone watching your lesson because they tell them what you are trying to achieve. They enable you to demonstrate that you know some pupils need special attention, such as those who work slowly.

Keep a file of your teaching notes for each topic or subject you teach. Start with the knowledge you wish to convey, and add in resources you want to use such as diagrams, links to film clips, good questions to ask, tips you have picked up and past exam papers. Gradually this becomes your sequence of lesson plans but without the time constraints of a one-lesson lesson plan, and you can refine your teaching notes year by year.

In 2022, Jason Anderson from the University of Warwick published an analysis of the characteristics of the best teachers. The top characteristics were the ability to think on your feet, display flexibility, adapt to the needs of pupils and improvise when pupils had difficulties. Some of the best teachers, he found, don't plan lessons at all, but they do reflect on what is happening as the lesson proceeds. And they certainly know what they are going to teach when they walk into the classroom; this comes with experience – and a good set of teaching notes.

Planning a whole term or year

At some point you will be required to plan lessons across a whole term or year. There are several elements here:

- The curriculum or syllabus that has to be covered in this time. For example, you may be expected to teach a whole history A-level paper in one term. You can see that there are 12 teaching weeks in that term, so you divide the relevant syllabus into that time (some parts of the syllabus may only take one week while other parts may take three weeks). The problem you have as a beginner teacher is not knowing how long it takes to teach any given topic – this comes from experience.
- One thing you will certainly find is that many weeks are disrupted, and teaching time is lost due to things such as school exams or Christmas events. So, the time available is often shorter than you think. Ask your mentor for advice and plot every week out in a diary.
- If your class has GCSEs or A-levels at the end of the year, lessons will be disrupted by early exams and study leave. So, you must finish the syllabus by the end of the Easter term (March), leaving a short period available to you in the summer term for revision. If your class has internal school exams at any point in the year, you must leave at least one week before that to revise with them.
- You will quickly see that the autumn term is longer than the spring or summer terms, so you will need to cover much more than one third of the work in the autumn.
- If you are teaching a subject that involves coursework, start teaching it early on as coursework often takes longer than you may expect. Always try to get coursework completed by March of the year in which exams are to be taken – your pupils won't thank you if they are having to do coursework in the summer when they have a wide range of exams to prepare for.
- You need to teach things in the right order (this is known as sequencing).

You never have enough time

No teacher ever has enough time. You are teaching perhaps 100 pupils, and they all have different needs. You may be teaching a course that notionally lasts two years but there are actually only 65 usable weeks, which may only be 130 lessons – that is not enough.

Here's a checklist to help you make the most of the time you have:

- I will plan out the year (or even two years) so I know what has to be achieved each term.
- I will do my lesson preparation before the term begins.
- I will plan my marking workload intelligently.
- I will start every lesson promptly and move through the lesson with pace and urgency.
- I won't lose five minutes in every lesson to petty matters, because this will soon add up to hours.
- I won't read out the homework task (it's there on the school intranet).

Planning your teaching in primary

The quality of any primary lesson plan (or sequence of planning) is influenced by:

- The expertise of the planner.
- The amount of time available for planning.
- Collaboration, as the things we teach are often largely similar across many classrooms and schools.

Planning together saves time and enables collaborative thinking. For example, if there are three of you planning together and you work collaboratively, it can be done in one third of the time and be three times as effective.

When we set things up in ways that encourage teachers to plan their own lessons, we are essentially pushing ourselves to re-invent the wheel. Planning as a team, on the other hand, may result in being more effective for learning, more equitable for pupils and lead to less workload for teachers. By sharing our time, expertise and effort, we can produce more in shorter timescales.

Long-term planning

Long-term plans will often include and incorporate subject aims, vision, curriculum journey from nursery, unit-of-work leading questions, key enquiry questions and key vocabulary progression. These allow for:

- Teachers, subject leaders, children, parents, governors and visitors to understand each subject's journey and direction.
- Subject leaders to analyse and adjust the curriculum intent easily.
- Key enquiry questions to guide teaching and learning, lesson progression, knowledge organisers and assessment.

The starting point for long-term planning is normally the curriculum intent or the intent for each subject. These are often based on the school's values, vision and mission. They also allow for progression over time within a subject.

Medium-term planning

For medium-term planning, think of 'units of work'. These may typically last for the duration of a long or short term or a shorter, three-week unit, for example. Schools may 'buy in' to schemes of work for medium-term planning, and there are, of course, pros and cons when using these.

Pros	Cons (and how to counter them)
Most of the thinking has been done for you.	You have not done the thinking that may be necessary for your own pupils, their ability and their context. It's therefore imperative that you refine a set scheme to suit your own class.
Progression has already been built in.	You may have to move at the speed that is most appropriate for your own pupils.
Learning materials may have already been provided for you (as in the case of White Rose Hub, for example).	You may need to tweak the resources to make them appropriate for your own pupils and context.
You will be given the correct concepts, skills, key learning, vocabulary and subject knowledge that is appropriate for the age and stage.	The schemes may contain vocabulary that is unfamiliar to your pupils; if this is the case, you will need to pre-teach it to make the learning accessible.
Omissions are avoided. Key learning is provided in a sequence with nothing missed out.	You need to check the scheme is accurate in terms of the national curriculum.
They will save you time.	Make sure you have made the necessary adjustments for your own pupils.

Short-term (lesson) planning

Here are some more generic tips for planning a lesson:

- **Set objectives** – clearly define the learning objectives and success criteria for the lesson.

- **Consider your pupils** – understand your pupils' learning needs and build on what they already know.
- **Prepare materials** – gather the resources you'll need before the lesson (this includes any resources you will need for scaffolding).
- **Plan carefully** – ensure support staff know what they will be doing.
- **Create activities** – design engaging activities and content.
- **Chunk the learning** – organise what to do now, next, then afterwards.
- **Model how best to do these** – show the class how to answer a question on the board (don't forget the 'think-alouds').
- **Plan assessment** – decide how you'll assess your pupils' knowledge.
- **Consider time** – think about how much time each part of the lesson will take.
- **Plan for backup** – have backup activities in case they are needed.
- **Allow for review** – set aside time for review of pupil work and feedback.
- **Adapt** – be ready to adapt and modify your lesson based on your pupils' needs.
- **Use formative assessment** – determine what your pupils know and what they need to learn next.
- **Use lesson plans as a reference** – lesson plans can be a useful document to refer back to when planning future lessons.

Common mistakes made in planning

These are some pitfalls to avoid during the planning process:

- **Time management** – teachers may underestimate or overestimate how long activities will take, which can lead to rushed lessons or extra time at the end.
- **Activities that waste time or don't contribute to the lesson objective** – pupil activities should directly contribute to the lesson's objective, not just keep the pupils busy.
- **Lack of variety** – lesson plans should include variety.
- **No plan B** – teachers should have a plan B in case the lesson doesn't go as planned.
- **Not trying out the task first** – teachers should try the task before using it in the lesson.
- **Too much complexity** – keep it simple by not making the lessons too complex.
- **Too much technology** – modelling of lessons should avoid relying on too much technology.
- **Not planning for diverse learning needs** – some of your pupils will require things to be done differently, either to have some scaffolding materials close

at hand, be given extra time or have instructions repeated (see Chapter 8: Adapt teaching to respond to the strengths and needs of pupils).

● **Planning for the teaching assistant to work with the pupils who require the most support** – remember, *you* are the expert in the room, and therefore you should be the person supporting these pupils most of the time.

Sticking to the lesson plan

If the plan is not working, forget it and do something else instead. This can be difficult for an ECT as it takes a certain amount of confidence to admit the plan is not working, but put it down and follow your instinct instead. Some of the best lessons I have taught and observed have been those that have somehow gone awry and then either myself or the teacher I'm observing has let instinct take over. This requires thinking in the moment and a good deal of 'going with the flow', but it will work out better for you than following a lesson plan that is failing.

Routines in the classroom

You will want to have set routines in the classroom. Some schools will have very clear rules about this, which you should be trained to follow. Examples of routines are:

● How pupils enter the classroom. For example, if it's a room with dangerous machinery or chemicals, the pupils should line up outside until they are told to come in.

● Pupils are welcomed by the teacher as they enter. Clayton Cook, a professor in the Institute of Translational Research in Children's Mental Health at the University of Minnesota, assessed the effects of greeting students at the door on behaviour in a small-scale study of 203 pupils in sixth to eighth grades (UK years 7, 8 and 9) (Cook et al., 2018). Teachers taking part in the study's intervention group were provided with training sessions on the technique of greeting pupils at the door, while control classes were not. The study found that, over two months, teachers' ratings of pupils' behaviour positively increased in the intervention group, while those for the control group remained constant.

● Pupils sit according to a seating plan.

● The teacher has a starter activity on the board, and the pupils get out the relevant books without being instructed to and begin the starter without being told to.

● The teacher asks to collect homework or exercise books, and the pupils know to pass it down the rows and the pupil at the end of the row passes it to the front.

- The teacher raises their hand or counts down 5-4-3-2-1 and pupils know that this means they must be silent. 'Pencils down and eyes on me 5-4-3-2-1.'
- Use a standard format for written work that makes it easier to check and mark.
- End each class with a few questions to see if they have remembered the key points (known as an 'exit ticket'). When a pupil has given a good answer, they may leave.

Doug Lemov: *Teach Like a Champion*

Doug Lemov developed his teaching methods by observing the best teachers in schools with disadvantaged pupils in cities in the US. His book (and website), *Teach Like a Champion*, explains his methods, which have been successfully adopted across the world. Think about reading his books and watching the film clips of the following successful teaching methods that accompany them:

- Use a warm-up activity that the pupils can do without instruction.
- Start the lesson with a hook to get them interested.
- In a subject like maths, give them the steps they need to take to solve the problem and go through an example of how to do it on the board (modelling).
- Warn them of common misconceptions.
- Get the pupils to give as many of the answers as possible (rather than you).
- Give them a paper copy of what they need to recall from the lesson (i.e. some notes).
- But also teach the pupils how to make notes.
- Move round the classroom to engage and check on the pupils.
- Repetition matters – the best way to get there is repeated practice.
- Regularly check for understanding.

Generate pace – it's all a giant act

Lemov recommends a number of devices to generate a sense of urgency and pace. For example, when pupils are asked to do work, a time-limit is given and a timer appears on the document projector – 'you have three minutes to answer this question. Ready? Go!'

Other suggestions include:

- Get pupils to repeat sentences after you – this generates energy in the room.
- Ask them lots of fast-paced random questions.

Pace is a characteristic of many good lessons.

Make 'em think

'Ratio' is the term Lemov uses to describe the proportion of cognitive work done by the pupils as opposed to you. You want the ratio to be as high as possible; you can build the ratio through questioning, writing and discussion.

Ideas to build this ratio include:

- When a pupil makes an error, give them more information to allow them to have another go.
- Scaffold – start with easy questions and get harder.
- Force pupils to use the correct academic vocabulary.

Good writing

You can teach good writing skills to pupils using the following methods:

- Ask the pupils to reflect in writing before they discuss with the class.
- Ask them to synthesise a complex idea in one sentence.
- Publicly showcase and revise pupil writing. Take one pupil's work and project it up on the wall with a document camera; the class can suggest revisions.
- Build stamina with long writing pieces.

Linking to real-life experience

Children learn better if new knowledge is linked to their prior knowledge – much of which will come from their life experience. So, it's a good idea to link new knowledge to things the pupils already know. For example, in learning vocabulary, don't offer single words but a sentence in which the new word is inserted. Chemistry lessons should always explain the relevance of what can seem a very abstract science.

An example from primary schools: Forest School

Many primary schools nowadays will have a member of staff who is trained in the delivery of 'Forest School'. Forest School in the UK is based on a rich heritage of outdoor learning. Kurt Hahn (who founded Gordonstoun) began the movement based on his philosophy of learning in the natural environment and, in doing so, laid the foundations for what we today call Forest School. Forest School takes place either in the grounds of the school or a rich natural environment such as nearby woodland. Forest School is often a feature of early years education, but it can also be offered to older pupils as a nurturing intervention.

Forest School supports play, exploration and supported risk taking. It develops confidence and self-esteem for pupils through inspired, hands-on experiences in a natural setting. It helps them develop socially, emotionally, spiritually, physically and intellectually.

Some of the key features of Forest School are:

- It should be run by level 3 practitioners who are qualified as Forest School teachers.
- It's a long-term process with regular contact with a local wooded environment (preferably over the seasons).
- It follows a child-centred pedagogy where pupils learn about and manage risk.
- It has a high adult-child ratio.
- Observations of the pupils are key to enabling scaffolding of the learning.
- Care for the natural world is an important element.

You can access the Forest School Association website at theforestschool.com.

Drill

'Drill' means repeating tasks until they are committed to memory and become second nature. This is the form of teaching Winston Churchill (who went on to win the Nobel Prize for literature) received when he was a pupil at Harrow School:

> *[Mr Somervell] took a fairly long sentence and broke it up into its components by means of black, red, blue and green inks. Subject, verb, object: each had its colour and its bracket. It was a kind of drill. We did it almost daily. As I remained in the bottom form three times as long as anyone else, I had three times as much of it. I learned it thoroughly [...] Thus I got into my bones the essential structure of the ordinary British sentence.*

Winston Churchill, My Early Life, 1930

Nick Gibb, Schools' Minister, said in a speech in July 2016:

> *One English educationist, now residing at an American university, appeared in the TES in December arguing she would "ban" times table tests, and told the Telegraph that they have nothing to do with mathematics. Earlier last year, Conrad Wolfram wrote in the Financial Times that calculation is an "obsolete skill", thanks to technological advances of the 21st century. That last comment reminded me of an influential pamphlet about the future of mathematics entitled 'I do, and I understand'. This pamphlet suggests that in the age of the computer and the "simple calculating machine", mental arithmetic has become a thing of the past.*

It was written in 1967. Such a romantic view was wrong then, and I believe it is wrong today. Five decades of research into cognitive science, as reviewed by the American psychologists James Royer and Loel Tronsky, shows that there is a positive relationship between computational automaticity and complex mathematical problem-solving skills.

'Drill' is a dirty word outside the army, and 'computational automaticity' is not much better, but drill is effective and can be enjoyable in the right hands. The crucial thing is to pitch drill at the right level – not so hard as to be impossible, nor so easy as to be simplistic. Drill needs to give pupils the satisfying feeling of conquering a tricky problem, which is one of the reasons why it will be much more useful for a primary maths teacher than an A-level English teacher.

In *Cleverlands* (2016), Lucy Crehan explains clearly why drill helps East Asian pupils become creative thinkers and intuitive mathematicians. Drill does not stifle imagination or critical thinking; it just means that the mechanical processes that Western children labour with are automatic to East Asian children, freeing them up to grasp more advanced concepts.

Why are so many people worried about drill? Because it doesn't allow pupils to think for themselves, it doesn't encourage independent learning, it prevents debate and it doesn't do all those things education should do, like develop good character and conduct. All this is true, which is why drill can only ever be part of your pedagogy.

Using computers and digital media

Do computer-based lessons make for effective learning? Research suggests they are not better than the conventional teacher-in-a-classroom approach. The experience of online teaching during the Covid-19 pandemic told us that younger children cannot concentrate long enough on a screen, older children were often distracted by other things they could find on the computer and all children found working from home on computers to be dull and socially isolating (Howard, Khan and Lockyer, 2021).

When children first use a computer for learning it's motivating because it is a new experience, but this does not last long. More and more parents and schools in England are becoming concerned about the amount of time children are spending in front of screens of any sort. Some schools, like the Heritage School in Cambridge, have become popular because the school will not allow computers or smartphones. They have found that pupils concentrate better without these devices, and once they banned screens their GCSE results shot up.

On the other hand, there are plenty of good teachers who use tech well. Sometimes this simply involves doing something in a digital format that may otherwise be done by hand, such as typing notes or presenting using slides. Digital-based techniques can improve teaching quality, such as using multimedia in a lesson or interactive stories to boost understanding. Platforms like Zoom can be used to connect with children and speakers across the world, and Google Earth is of tremendous value to geographers, as is AI for simply finding out about things. Get to know a few digital tools well and use them regularly to good effect.

There are many AI lesson planning resources available to you. Aila, a resource available from the Oak National Academy, allows you to tailor suggestions that it makes for a lesson and then gives you a set of downloadable lesson resources.

As you can see, it's pretty comprehensive, and I have to say the learning outcomes and key learning points were just as good as any I could have come up with myself.

Besides lesson planning, AI can be used to generate a variety of other resources for lessons, such as individual work plans, word lists, lists of particular phrases, facts and even writing models, as long as you specify which year groups you are looking for resources for.

AI has the potential to reduce the amount of time teachers spend doing administrative tasks in general, and teachers should consider the best ways in which they can utilise AI so they can focus on what they do best – teaching and supporting their pupils.

Research evidence for digital teaching

Richard Clark and Dave Felton, 2014, *Cambridge Handbook of Multimedia Learning* **(2nd ed).**

Clark and Felton identify the many problems with digital learning. They found that pupils don't concentrate but flutter from one piece of seemingly interesting information to another when working on digital devices. There's no evidence for increased motivation; just because pupils are 'engaged' it does not mean they are learning anything.

Textbooks

In England, 10% of 10-year-olds are issued textbooks; in South Korea, this number is 99%. In secondary science, 8% of pupils in England are issued with textbooks compared to 88% in South Korea and 92% in Taiwan.

Why are English schools not using textbooks? Cost is a factor, but just as important is the growing use of copied worksheets and handouts. Worksheets have certain advantages, such as being tailored to the class and pupils having to focus on that one piece of paper, but some disadvantages, such as the worksheets being easily lost and rarely organised in the pupils' files.

Textbooks are dying out because more materials are now available online alongside the emphasis in schools on differentiated learning discouraging the notion of 'one resource for all'. The demise of textbooks is a downward spiral – if schools don't buy textbooks, publishers can't afford to produce them. In the past, a small number of outstanding teachers earned a good living producing wonderful, captivating textbooks, and these people are now being lost to the system.

So, what's so good about textbooks? Textbooks are better than online resources or paper handouts in several ways:

- They are easier to issue (two minutes at the start of the year) and much easier to refer back to ('let's return to page X, which we did last October').
- They are a big part of the solution for the pupil who joins a course late or misses a large piece of work.
- They are a resource that parents can use to help their children.
- The best textbooks contain exercises, questions and worked examples, making them perfect for setting homework and testing understanding.
- For sixth formers especially, making notes from text is a vital skill they will need at university. With the advent of handouts, fewer and fewer students are learning to make notes.
- Textbooks are far better for revision than handouts, many of which will have been lost.
- Textbooks *can* be used for differentiated learning – all pupils use the same book but work through it at different rates.
- The best textbooks, like those used for maths in Singapore and Shanghai, lead the pupil and teacher through the syllabus in ways that are extremely effective. They save the teacher hours of lesson preparation time as all the essential materials have been written for you by experienced teachers.

If you ask people aged 40 and above if they can remember textbooks they used at school, the answer is usually 'yes'. But more than just the title of the book, they can remember individual pages and diagrams in the text. Will today's children be able to say the same of handouts?

Textbooks of the past had a huge impact on education. They not only reflected exam board syllabuses – they influenced them. The best textbooks were the curriculum; they determined the level to which the stronger pupils worked. The materials supplied by exam boards, especially at A-level, don't pin down the exact level of detail and depth of what a student needs to know – textbooks do this. A good example of successful textbooks would be Robert Peal's Key stage 3 history series: in-depth coverage written in a completely accessible way.

Libraries and textbooks should be regarded as vital resources in all schools. Good books go into depth; they elaborate on and clarify what has been taught in schools. They lodge in your mind. Oates (2014) looked at over 200 teacher textbooks, teacher guides and student workbooks from Hong Kong, Singapore, Finland, Massachusetts (in the US), England and Alberta (in Canada). Maths was the main focus, but the range of subjects included geography, physics, chemistry, biology, history, literature and first language learning. Oates shows that textbook use has declined in the UK compared to higher performing jurisdictions.

The quality of UK textbooks has also declined, as they have increasingly become revision guides. This has happened because this is what the market demanded – schools are under pressure to get their pupils good grades, so all the focus tends to be on exam preparation. What's more, many of these books are 'endorsed' by individual exam boards, meaning it's extremely hard for a school to ignore a text written by a chief examiner and endorsed in this way.

Oates explains that part of the problem is that in England there is a great deal of hostility towards the notion of government-approved or government-recommended textbooks. In other high-performing countries, it's commonplace for the government to ensure that textbooks are written well, by experienced teachers, and stretch pupils.

Use of pen and ink

Scientists have established that handwriting trumps typing as a boost for the brain, and urge teachers to ensure that penmanship remains a core part of teaching even as the use of tablets and laptops becomes more commonplace in the classroom.

A study by researchers at the Norwegian University of Science and Technology (Van der Weel and Van der Meer, 2024) showed that the skill and concentration required to form the shapes of letters while writing with a pen or pencil sparks a far greater range and complexity of connections within the brain than simply tapping the correct keys on a keyboard. The researchers fitted 36 university students with electroencephalogram brain sensors to measure brain activity, and the students were asked to write words in cursive using a digital pen on a touchscreen. They were then asked to type the same words with a single finger on a keyboard.

The findings suggest that visual and movement information obtained through precisely controlled hand movements when using a pen contribute extensively to the brain's connectivity patterns that promote learning. This also explains why children who have learned to read and write on a tablet can have difficulty differentiating between letters that are mirror images of each other, such as 'b' and 'd' – they literally haven't felt with their hands what it feels like to produce those letters.

The study concluded by stating: 'We urge that children, from an early age, be exposed to handwriting activities in school to establish the neuronal connectivity patterns that provide the brain with optimal conditions for learning.'

University students may find it is better to take notes by hand while learning but may wish to switch to a computer when composing longer pieces of work. There is evidence that pupils learn more and remember better when taking handwritten lecture notes, while using a computer with a keyboard may be more practical when writing a long text or essay.

Mueller and Oppenheimer (2014) found that students required to use computers to make notes in a lecture were less effective than those using pen and paper. Students who wrote their notes by hand tended to understand and remember the lecture better than those who had typed.

Cover

Occasionally, either you will need to ask for another teacher to cover a lesson or you will be asked to cover other teachers yourself. Your cover teacher may not be a specialist in your subject, so your cover notes need to be adapted accordingly, meaning they must be detailed and clear. If you are ill and not able to arrange cover, your head of department will no doubt help.

If possible, warn your class in advance that they will have a cover teacher. Thank them for behaving and making the most of the work they will be set. Plan your lesson so there is continuation from the previous lesson and pupils do not see it as a time-filler. If you maintain a file for each class with your teaching notes, organising cover will be so much easier.

The ideal is to create tasks for your pupils, for example reading some text and then answering questions on it. Set work that will be collected and marked so pupils realise that you will be checking up on them. Make sure you set enough work because the cover teacher may struggle if your pupils finish well before the end of the lesson.

Things that don't work so well

'Learning styles'

Learning styles was an idea that grew out of Howard Gardner's work on multiple intelligences. Gardner wrote that different people have different types of intelligence, such as:

- **Verbal-linguistic intelligence** – well-developed verbal skills and sensitivity to the sounds, meanings and rhythms of words.
- **Logical-mathematical intelligence** – the ability to think conceptually and abstractly, and capacity to discern logical and numerical patterns.
- **Spatial-visual intelligence** – the capacity to think in images and pictures, to visualise accurately and abstractly.
- **Bodily-kinesthetic intelligence** – the ability to control one's body movements and to handle objects skilfully.
- **Musical intelligences** – the ability to produce and appreciate rhythm, pitch and timber.
- **Interpersonal intelligence** – the capacity to detect and respond appropriately to the moods, motivations and desires of others.
- **Intrapersonal intelligence** – the capacity to be self-aware and in tune with inner feelings, values, beliefs and thinking processes.

This theory was taken up by others to suggest that all pupils have different learning styles and would benefit from being taught in different ways. However, more recent studies (Pashler et al., 2008) have debunked this theory as an effective way of teaching and highlighted it as a 'neuromyth'. The Educational Endowment Foundation (EEF) concluded that learning styles teaching is 'low impact and based on limited evidence'.

Group work in secondary schools

This sounds like a good idea but often doesn't work because:

- It creates a great deal of noise in the classroom.
- Very often some pupils misbehave or switch off.
- Groups leave one pupil to do all the work. This is why you need to assign everyone in the group a job, such as the pupil in charge of resources, the team leader, the pupil who records any discussion and reports back and the pupil who clears up.

Differentiation

Differentiation means treating different pupils in one class differently according to their ability. If you have a class with a wide range of ability, including SEND pupils, you may need to differentiate the tasks you set them. But there are two big problems with differentiation to be aware of:

- The amount of work required of the teacher is huge if they are having to plan different work for different children in the class.
- Differentiation implies that teacher-led teaching (with the teacher standing at the front and instructing the whole class together) can't happen. But research shows that teacher-led instruction is often the most effective way of teaching a class for maximum impact in the shortest amount of time.

Praise for achievement

Psychological research has shown that praising a pupil for their ability can cause them to stop trying their best and taking risks. Carol Dweck is an American psychologist who devised the theory of growth mindset. She argued that children often have one of two mindsets:

- In a **fixed mindset**, pupils believe their basic abilities, intelligence and talents are just fixed traits. 'I'm no good at maths' would be an example. They dread failure.
- In a **growth mindset**, pupils don't mind or fear failure as much because they believe their performance can be improved by effort.

Dweck found that pupils who receive excessive praise for their intelligence tend to develop a fixed mindset and become risk averse. They avoid challenges and prefer tasks where they can maintain their reputation for being intelligent. What's more, overuse of praise could diminish a child's perceived autonomy – they become more reliant on external validation and less self-directed.

In a series of studies by Dweck, children were given a non-verbal IQ test that consisted of 10 moderately challenging problems. Most of the children performed well on the first 10 problems. One group were given intelligence praise; they were told, 'Wow, you got eight right, that's a really good score. You must be very smart.' Another group were given effort praise: 'Wow, you got eight right, that's a really good score. You must have tried really hard.'

The students were then asked, 'What do you want to work on now? I have some easier things here that you could work on, or I have some challenging problems. They're hard, and you'll make mistakes, but you'll learn some important things.' Most of the students who were praised for intelligence chose the easy task because they simply wanted to look clever – they didn't want tasks that they could fail. But most of the students praised for their effort wanted the challenging task; they wanted something they could learn from and they weren't worried about making mistakes.

The conclusion is that it can be more effective to praise pupils for their *effort* rather than their ability.

Sitting in circles in science labs

Quite often, science labs are designed with practical work areas (such as the sink or gas taps) and seats around the work area. This means that a quarter of the pupils are facing the board and the teacher, half are sitting side-on, and a quarter have their backs to the teacher, unless they turn round.

Given the importance of teacher-led instruction, this is far from ideal. So, the best classrooms have an area where the pupils can sit facing the teacher and a separate area for the practical work.

Discovery-based and inquiry-led learning

This is a 'progressive' method of teaching, where the pupils are expected to research a topic, perhaps from the internet, and work out the answers for themselves. Proponents of this method suggest that it encourages autonomy and is a more effective way of learning (after all, young children learn most of what they know from playful discovery).

The problem is that discovery-based learning doesn't work well. School-age children do not have the prior knowledge to pick up things in this way, and it's also a very slow way of learning.

Cross-curricula work

Many primary schools and some secondary schools like cross-curricular work. For example, there may be a few weeks devoted to the topic of 'migration' taught by geographers, historians and religious studies teachers. Beware – Ofsted research reports tell us that cross-curricular work is often rather weak because a proportion of the teachers don't have the necessary subject knowledge.

Hands up

When asking questions of the class, avoid asking pupils to put their hands up. You should be more interested in those who have not put their hand up.

Self-report

Don't ask pupils if they have understood something, as few pupils will admit they have not understood.

Teaching 'skills' like critical thinking

Some schools brag that they are going to ignore traditional school subjects in favour of teaching 'twenty-first-century skills' like teamwork or critical thinking, but teamwork should be a useful by-product of an activity, like sport, not the main objective. You can't think critically about a subject if you don't know a lot about it; critical thinking skills in one subject don't transfer to critical thinking skills in another.

All good teachers want to teach 'skills' like critical thinking. But research suggests that teaching generic skills is less effective than teaching skills within the context of an actual subject, and that teaching so-called facts is a necessary prelude to teaching the skill. You may want to teach critical thinking in history, for example, but you can't teach critical thinking in history unless the pupil knows some history to be critical about.

Dan Willingham, Professor of Cognitive Psychology at the University of Virginia, writes that:

> Data from the last 40 years lead to a conclusion that is not scientifically challengeable: thinking well requires knowing facts, and that's true not simply because you need something to think about. The very processes that teachers care about most – critical thinking processes such as reasoning and problem solving – are intimately intertwined with factual knowledge that is stored in long-term memory (not just found in the environment).

Willingham, D., 2021

So, focus on teaching knowledge, and the skills will emerge.

Slideshows

Teachers often use slideshows in lessons because they look great and they act as aide memoires for the teacher. However, if every teacher uses slideshows, they become very dull for students – and reading what you have written on a slide is very boring.

Using Swiss rolls to teach fractions

In his excellent book, *How I Wish I'd Taught Maths*, Craig Barton makes the point that using Swiss rolls to teach fractions achieves nothing – the pupils just remember Swiss rolls, not the fractions. The pupils are engaged by the Swiss rolls, but being 'engaged' doesn't mean you are learning anything. This is a good message – gimmicks can get in the way of real understanding.

Making a poster

Don't waste time asking pupils to make a poster. They learn little and it's really measuring artistic ability, not knowledge of the subject.

Double desks

Double desks save space, but they also allow children to copy from each other. For this reason, they are best avoided.

Flipped classrooms

The idea of the flipped classroom is that pupils read about a topic before they come to the lesson with the teacher. This would be a great idea were it not for the fact that some pupils are far better than others at reading about and understanding a topic while sitting at home.

Teaching online

The experience of the Covid-19 pandemic taught us that trying to teach online has several limitations:

- Some pupils don't have a computer or internet access at home.
- Many pupils didn't attend classes, blaming the technology.
- Many pupils can't concentrate during online lessons.
- Going to school is partly a social activity – most pupils hated sitting at home on their own, preferring the company of others, including a teacher in the room.

What do I look for in a good lesson?

When I observe a lesson, this is what I look for:

- The pupils learn something worthwhile.
- They seem motivated.
- They don't waste time on trivial things such as finding a pen.
- There is pace and energy in the teaching.
- The pupils who struggle are known by the teacher and involved.
- The lesson gives a feeling of being very organised.
- There is good, attentive behaviour.
- There is some display of good subject knowledge.

For secondary schools:

- Attention is given to the need to have revision notes.
- Work is marked and the pupils have to respond to feedback.
- Attention is given to good spelling, vocabulary and the use of subject terminology.
- Pupils are encouraged or forced to speak up, using full sentences and academic language oracy.

Revision

Can you remember what these classroom techniques are and why they work? See this chapter and Chapter 5. Can you recall the names of any researchers who advocate these methods?

- Modelling
- Scaffolding
- Worked examples
- Chunking
- Dual coding
- Formative questioning
- Wait time
- Cold calling

References

Anderson, J. and Taner, G., 2023, Building the expert teacher prototype: A metasummary of teacher expertise studies in primary and secondary education, Educational Research Review.

Barton, C., 2018, *How I Wish I'd Taught Maths*, John Catt.

Churchill, W., 1930, *My Early Life*, Charles Scribner's Sons.

Clark, R., and Felton, D., 2014, *Cambridge Handbook of Multimedia Learning*, 2nd edition, Cambridge University Press.

Coe, R., Aloisi, C., Higgins, S., and Major, L. E., 2024, What makes great teaching. Review of the underpinning research, Durham University: UK.

Cook, C. R., Fiat, A., Larson, M., Daikos, C., Slemrod, T., Holland, E. A., Thayer, A. J., and Renshaw, T., 2018, Positive greetings at the door. Evaluation of a low-cost, high-yield proactive classroom management strategy, Journal of Positive Behavior Interventions, 20(3), 149–159.

Cree, J. and McCree, M., 2012, A brief history of forest school in the UK – Part 2, Horizon Magazine, 62 (Summer), 32–35.

Cree, J. and McCree, M., 2012, A brief history of the roots of forest school in the UK, Horizon Magazine, 60 (Winter), 32–34.

Dweck, C. S., 2006, *Mindset: The New Psychology of Success*. Random House.

Gardner, H., 2013, Frequently asked questions—Multiple intelligences and related educational topics.

Griffith, A., and Burns, M., 2014, *Outstanding Teaching, Teaching Backwards*, Crown Publishing, London.

Howard, E., Khan, A. and Lockyer, C., 2021, *Learning during the pandemic: review of research from England*, Ofqual.

Kirschner, P. and Hendrick, C., 2022, *How Teaching Happens: Seminal Works in Teaching and Teacher Effectiveness and What They Mean in Practice*, Routledge.

Knight, S., 2024, Forest School Forward, Horizon Magazine, May 2024, pp 14–16.

Mueller, P. and Oppenheimer, D., 2014, The pen is mightier than the keyboard: Advantages of longhand over laptop note taking, Psychological Science, 25(6), 1159–1168.

Oates, T., 2014, *Why Textbooks Count*, Cambridge Assessment.

Pashler, H., McDaniel, M., Rohrer, D., and Bjork, R., 2008, Learning styles: Concepts and evidence. Psychological Science in the Public Interest, 9(3), 105-119.

Rosenshine, B., 2012, Principles of Instruction: Research-Based Strategies That All Teachers Should Know, American Educator, 36(1).

Van der Weel, F. and Van der Meer, A., 2024, Handwriting but not typewriting leads to widespread brain connectivity: A high-density EEG study with implications for the classroom, Frontiers in Psychology, 14.

Willingham, D., 2021, *Why Don't Pupils Like School*, 2nd edition, Jossey-Bass.

Chapter 8
Adapt teaching to respond to the strengths and needs of pupils

ITTECF syllabus

Adaptive teaching (Standard 5 – Adapt teaching)

Learn that...	Learn how to...
1. Adapting teaching in a responsive way, including by providing targeted support to pupils who are struggling, is likely to increase pupil success.	**Develop an understanding of different pupil needs, by:**
2. Pupils are likely to learn at different rates and to require different levels and types of support from teachers to succeed.	a) Identifying pupils who need new content further broken down.
	b) Making use of formative assessment.
3. Seeking to understand pupils' differences, including their different levels of prior knowledge and potential barriers to learning, is an essential part of teaching.	c) Working closely with the Special Educational Needs Co-ordinator (SENCO) and other SEND specialists or expert colleagues.
	d) Working closely with the Designated Safeguarding Lead.
4. Adaptive teaching is less likely to be valuable if it causes the teacher to artificially create distinct tasks for different groups of pupils or to set lower expectations for particular pupils.	e) Supporting pupils with a range of additional needs and using the SEND Code of Practice: 0 to 25 years, which provides guidance on effective school systems and approaches for identifying and supporting the special educational needs of pupils with SEND.
5. Flexibly grouping pupils within a class to provide more tailored support can support learning, but care should be taken to monitor its impact on attainment, behaviour, engagement and motivation, particularly for low attaining pupils.	f) Utilising existing opportunities to engage with parents and carers to better understand pupils' individual needs (e.g. meetings with parents).
	Provide opportunity for all pupils to experience success, by:
	g) Adapting lessons, while maintaining high expectations for all, so that all pupils have the opportunity to meet expectations.
6. There is a common misconception that pupils have distinct and identifiable learning styles. This is not supported by evidence and attempting to tailor lessons to learning styles is unlikely to be beneficial.	h) Balancing input of new content with the revisiting of prior learning so that pupils master important concepts.

Learn that...	Learn how to...
7. Pupils with SEND are likely to require additional or adapted support; working closely with colleagues, parents/carers and pupils to understand barriers to learning and identify effective strategies is essential. 8. High quality teaching for all pupils, including those with SEND, is based on strategies which are often already practised by teachers, and which can be developed through training and support. 9. Technology, including educational software and assistive technology, can support teaching and learning for pupils with SEND.	i) Making effective use of teaching assistants and other adults in the classroom. j) Making effective and judicious use of specialist technology to support pupils with SEND. **Meet individual needs without creating unnecessary workload, by:** k) Making use of well-designed resources (e.g. textbooks, manipulatives). l) Planning to connect new content with pupils' existing knowledge or providing additional pre-teaching if pupils lack critical knowledge. m) Building in additional practice or removing unnecessary expositions. n) Reframing questions to provide greater scaffolding or greater stretch. o) Considering carefully whether intervening within lessons with individuals and small groups would be more efficient and effective than planning different lessons for different groups of pupils. **Group pupils effectively, by:** p) Applying high expectations to all groups, and ensuring all pupils have access to a rich curriculum. q) Intentionally grouping in relation to a specific learning outcome, regularly reviewing those groupings, taking care to monitor their impact and avoiding the perception that groups are fixed.

All children and teenagers are different. Some are naturally clever; some are diligent, while others are not. Some like your subject, while others hate it; some are ambitious and want to please you, while others don't. For teachers, this is a formidable problem because you may be facing a class of 20–30 pupils, all of whom are different. But you cannot teach them all individually.

We know that computers and artificial intelligence (AI) allow us to offer more individualised, personalised instruction. In many (though not all) subjects, computers can teach a topic, test the learning and then repeat the topic or move on to further topics depending on the test results. But we also know that learning from a computer can be dull compared to a teacher-led lesson.

So, you must try to strike a balance between not treating your classroom as a factory, turning out pupils as if they are all the same, and the enormous strain that comes from treating every pupil as an individual with different learning requirements.

Differentiation

Most classes contain pupils with a range of abilities. Differentiation means adapting your teaching to take this variation into account.

For much of the past 50 years, there has been a debate about the relative merits of mixed ability classes and setting by ability. There is no clear answer. Setting has the great advantage of the teacher being able to pitch the lesson at a level that suits the majority of pupils in the set. But it has the disadvantage of potentially making the lower sets feel discouraged, and they don't benefit from the example given by more able or harder working pupils. A bottom set full of unfocused, poorly behaved pupils may be a high price to pay for setting.

Setting seems to be more necessary in secondary maths and languages but less so in other subjects. Schools therefore often have some subjects that are setted but others that are of mixed ability. AI can help to quickly generate lesson plans, content and tests that are adapted to pupils of different levels of ability and needs (see pages 132 and 147).

In primary schools, differentiation still exists but is less common. There is now more of a philosophy of 'teaching to the top', where teachers scaffold for pupils who may find learning more difficult. With previous forms of task differentiation, stigmatisation and self-esteem could easily become affected. Not long ago, I was visiting a Year 3 classroom in a primary school and one of the pupils told me, 'That table does the difficult work in maths, but we're not so clever.' I still have a friend from my primary school who will say to me, 'Of course you can do this, you were on the top table.' Such inflexible labelling of pupils can affect them for the rest of their lives.

Whether you are teaching a mixed-ability class or a setted class, you will have some range of ability. How do you adjust your teaching? Firstly, you have to avoid low expectations. You must work on the assumption that every pupil can do well. So, pupils who are unfocused or learn slowly will require more of your attention than others. They need to be encouraged and praised where possible but also compelled to try harder.

You can't give pupils in your class very different work to do much of the time. After all, direct instruction – teaching the whole class from the front – is probably the quickest and most effective way to make progress. But while the slowest pupils are struggling to write answers, the quicker pupils (who have finished the work you set) should be given more challenging questions to try or be asked to write something interesting about the topic that is not part of the initial questions you had set. This requires careful preparation of extension questions on your part.

If different pupils in one class are going to be treated differently in this way, you need to try and create a strong class culture. The pupils must all accept that this is going to happen from time to time for the benefit of everyone.

Able pupils can be enthusiastic or difficult. It's vital to keep them interested and feed their intellectual curiosity; this is one of the greatest challenges for teachers. Talk to able pupils about their potential, high tariff universities and setting their sights high.

Mastery maths in primary

Extension questions are often used in the primary classroom, as is the mastery approach, which is sometimes referred to as 'greater depth' teaching and learning. This is a teaching model that involves breaking down complex concepts into smaller learning objectives. The goal is to help students develop a deep, long-term understanding of the subject and ensure that all learners meet expectations. If your school uses the White Rose scheme for the teaching of mathematics, the mastery approach is built into the order that the scheme should be delivered in and contains mastery elements in all the lesson modules.

The National Centre for Excellence in the Teaching of Mathematics (NCETM) uses the Singapore and Shanghai approach to mastery maths. They have further codified it for their maths hubs to include five big ideas in teaching for mastery:

1. **Coherence** – The progression of teaching and learning is designed to enable coherent learning progression, providing access for all pupils to develop a deep and connected understanding of maths that they can apply and communicate in a range of contexts.
2. **Representation and structure** – This is all about mental images and the CPA (concrete, pictorial, abstract) approach. This refers to the representations of maths that teachers select to expose mathematical structure, which are intended to support pupils in 'seeing' the maths rather than using the representations as tools to 'do' the mathematics.
3. **Mathematical thinking** – This is central to how pupils learn maths and includes looking for patterns and relationships, making

connections, estimating, reasoning and generalising. Pupils should be encouraged to discuss and communicate their ideas using accurate mathematical vocabulary.

4. **Fluency** – Rapid and accurate recall of key number facts and procedures is essential for fluency, freeing space in the working memory and enabling pupils to think deeply about concepts and problems. It also involves recognising relationships and making connections. Knowing number facts (for example, 6 x 8 is 48 and number bonds to 10 and 100) without having to think about the calculations are key elements of fluency.

5. **Variation** – This element is all about focusing on a key element of a mathematical concept or structure through keeping one concept or structure constant and varying others. Variation in maths teaching can help pupils understand concepts by showing them different representations of the same idea. Here are some examples of variation in maths teaching:

   - **Conceptual variation** involves showing pupils different representations of the same concept to deepen their understanding of it. Below, for example, you can see that alongside the fraction ¾ there are three visual representations.

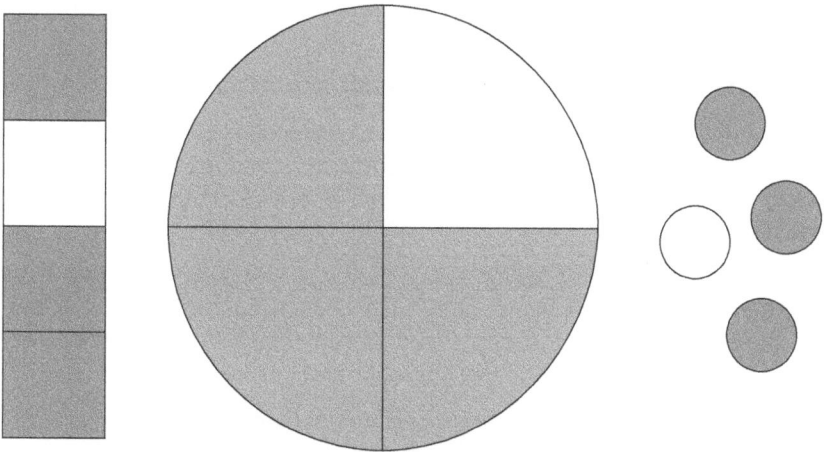

   - **Procedural variation** involves slightly varying the concept that is being taught from one question to the next while keeping everything else the same. In this way, pupils build on previous understanding in steps. Understanding what is the same and what has changed helps to exercise the understanding of the target concept. It provides the opportunity to focus on relationships, not just the procedure, and to make connections between problems using one problem to work out the next. For example:

4 x 10 = ?	What do you notice?
40 x 10 = ?	What is the same?
400 x 10 = ?	What is different?

These ideas are interconnected and work together to support pupils' mathematical development. They help to develop a mathematical toolkit of conceptual understanding, flexibility, mental structures and deep knowledge.

The sequence in teaching for mastery looks like this:

1. Diagnostic pre-assessment with pre-teaching where necessary.
2. High-quality, group-based initial instruction.
3. Monitoring progress through regular formative assessment.
4. High-quality corrective instruction when needed.
5. Enrichment or extension activities.

Special educational needs and disabilities (SEND)

In 2025 in England, 5.3% of children have an education, health and care plan (EHCP). A pupil has an EHCP when a formal assessment has been made. A document is in place that sets out the child's needs and the extra help they should receive.

Another 13.1% of children have special educational needs support (SEN). Extra or different help is provided as part of the school's usual curriculum. The class teacher and special educational needs coordinator (SENCO) may receive advice or support from outside specialists. The pupil does not have an EHCP.

In total, 1.7 million pupils were receiving additional support in England in 2024.

The most common type of need among pupils with an EHCP is autistic spectrum disorder (ASD). In 2024, one in three pupils with an EHCP were identified with a primary need of ASD. The most common type of need among pupils with SEN support are speech, language and communication needs. This is followed by social, emotional and mental health needs and moderate learning difficulty.

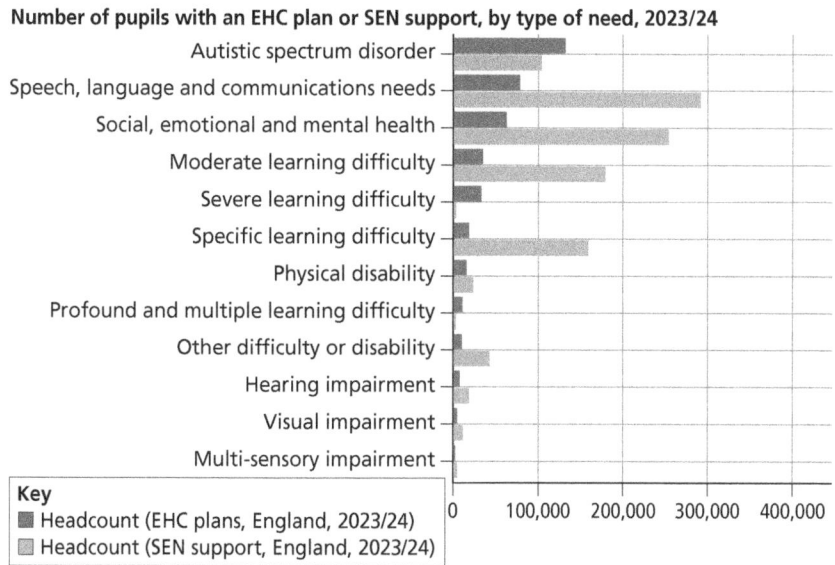

Number of pupils with an EHC plan or SEN support, by type of need, 2023/24

DfE, Special educational needs in England, 2023-24.

The percentage of pupils who have SEN support increases during primary school, reaching a peak of 16.3% of pupils at age nine. This then steadily declines through secondary ages, to 12.9% at age 15. The proportion continues to decrease after that. SEN continues to be more prevalent in boys than girls. 72% of pupils with an EHCP are boys, and 62% of pupils with SEN support are boys.

Pupils with an EHCP or SEN are more likely to be eligible for free school meals. 42% of pupils with an EHCP and 38% of pupils with SEN support were eligible for free school meals in 2024. This compares to 21% of pupils who are on free school meals but are not classified as having a special need.

Your school will have a SENCO, who will tell you which of your pupils has SEN, how they might be helped by a special needs assistant in or out of your classroom and what you could do to help as well. You need to know about these special needs and be able to talk to parents about the actions being taken to help the individual child.

Just because a pupil has a special need, it doesn't mean they are unintelligent and can't do well in school. Therefore, when planning lessons, generally aim high and provide support for pupils who need it. Many children with special needs will have social, emotional and mental health problems as well, and they will need a school environment that is safe, structured and where they experience consistency.

You will be given information about pupils with SEN in your class. This will help you in your planning and behaviour management. But you should not view the SEN label as an excuse for pupils not to work hard and try to do well – they may just take more time to get there.

Whole School SEND (wholeschoolsend.org.uk) provides access to a broad range of materials and support services across the range of SEN. The National Children's Bureau (ncb.org.uk) provides a range of information materials to families and professionals.

Please also refer to:

● wholeschoolsend.org.uk/itt–resources
● wholeschoolsend.org.uk/teacher–handbook

The SEND code of practice (DfE, 2015) clearly establishes that SEND is everybody's responsibility, and this principle is commonly phrased as 'every teacher is a teacher of SEND'. This is a move away from SEND being purely within the remit of the SENCO or SENDCO to also being the class teacher's responsibility. It is expected that class teachers will work in tandem with school SENCOs to prevent SEND pupils from falling behind their peers and flexibly alter teaching practices in the moment in order to further support pupils as necessary.

In the 2019 ITTCCF standard 5, 'Learn that...' section, point 1 has been amended from:

> Pupils are likely to learn at different rates and require different levels and types of support from teachers to succeed.

to:

> Adapting teaching in a responsive way, including by providing targeted support to pupils who are struggling, is likely to increase pupil success.

The main difference between the two statements is the removal of 'require different levels'. The 2019 version introduced the notion of 'adaptive teaching' as a more effective form of supporting different needs in the classroom.

Articles and research published in the interim years by the Education Endowment Foundation (EEF) have reiterated the need to move from models of differentiation to models of flexible grouping and adaptations made either at the planning stage or in the moment. Useful blogs published by the EEF can be found at the end of this chapter (see page 182).

Adaptive teaching

Adaptive teaching is a high-quality teaching strategy for pupils with SEND. It is firmly based on the idea that there are particular strategies that are likely to already be within the repertoire of every mainstream teacher or can be relatively easily added to it. Effective teaching for pupils with SEND requires:

- A climate and classroom culture of healthy relationships leading to positive interactions between teachers and pupils and among peers.
- Additional teaching, such as teaching well-structured steps towards an ultimate learning goal.
- The use of different strategies, such as the use of word mats, graphic organisers, mnemonics, sentence starters or other learning scaffolds.
- Different interventions, such as supporting fluency in reading.

In short, the idea is that adaptive teaching requires nothing that is outside of a trained teacher's competence.

The use of the phrase 'different interventions' above does not necessarily refer to an old-style intervention group outside of the classroom being taught by a teaching assistant. Instead, such interventions are more likely to include:

- Pre-teaching or post-teaching (also referred to as catch-up teaching).
- Flexibly designated groups working for longer periods of time with the teacher during a lesson.
- Support from a teaching assistant or another pupil (peer support).
- The use of a range of scaffolding techniques and resources.

So, what is adaptive teaching if it's not differentiating?

The table below shows two very different examples of two of my lessons. The first is an example from 2008, when I was teaching years 5 and 6 using differentiation. The second is from 2021, when I was teaching the same age group but *without* differentiation and *with* adaptive teaching. Notice the elements highlighted in the second column, as we will be discussing these elements later.

2008: Differentiating for high-, middle- and low-attaining pupils	2021: Adaptive teaching for all pupils
Assembly – all pupils	Assembly – pre-teaching some maths for **some EAL and SEND** pupils
No retrieval practice	Retrieval practice – flashback four
Lesson starter – all pupils, teaching assistant watching	Lesson starter **explicit instruction** – all pupils, teaching assistant sitting with a whiteboard and a **group of three pupils**

2008: Differentiating for high-, middle- and low-attaining pupils	2021: Adaptive teaching for all pupils
Teacher modelling – pupils watching and hands-up	Teacher modelling – 'I do, we do', pupils responding on whiteboards, **AfL happening, misconceptions being addressed, methods discussed for effectiveness**
Independent work – less able pupils on a table or outside the classroom with teaching assistant, three levels of differentiated worksheets	Independent work – teacher keeping **a small group** on the carpet to ensure understanding, others completing the same exercises
Teacher checking all pupils are working	Teacher mini-plenaries – to **check understanding** and **move on the lesson** in another small step
Going through three worksheets to give answers for pupil self-marking	Going through answers as a class and **addressing misconceptions**

Five-a-day

The EEF's 5-a-day approach (2022) to supporting SEND pupils in the classroom is a really useful document for inclusive classroom practice. It identifies and explains five elements of everyday practice that can support SEND learners in all lessons.

1. Explicit instruction

One of the most important principles of effective teaching is explicit instruction, which makes sure that all instructions are clear and comprehendible, are understood and that pupils are given feedback on tasks. The EEF recommends that teachers use explicit instruction effectively by:

● Explicitly teaching knowledge using clear explanations, relatable examples and succinct language.
● Checking pupils' understanding frequently throughout a lesson.
● Helping pupils to organise their thinking by 'chunking' the content and introducing new material in small steps.
● Modelling how to complete a task before expecting pupils to work independently.

2. Cognitive and metacognitive strategies

Metacognition encourages pupils to think about their own thinking and learning strategies and how they can best utilise these in problem solving, critical thinking and decision making. The EEF recommends that teachers use cognitive and metacognitive instruction effectively by:

- Being careful not to overload working memory.
- Supporting pupils to recall previously learned content before moving on to new content.
- Supporting pupils to plan, monitor and evaluate their own learning.
- Modelling 'think-alouds' so pupils can demonstrate their own thinking process when approaching a piece of work.
- Modelling the selection of metacognitive strategies, for example by using checklists to monitor their progress.

3. Scaffolding

In scaffolding, learning is broken down into digestible chunks of learning, and tools or support structures such as a word mat, writing frame or sentence starters are provided for each 'chunk' of learning to help the learner access and complete the task. The EEF recommends that teachers use scaffolding effectively by:

- Providing scaffolds (visual, verbal and written) that allow all pupils to access the learning.
- Using scaffolding in a way that reduces pupils' reliance on adult support over time.
- Providing scaffolds in a non-stigmatising way, for example by providing them at the whole-class level, enabling students to opt-in to a scaffold for a particular task.
- Reframing questions to allow greater scaffolding or greater stretch.
- Gradually reducing the amount of scaffolding both within and between lessons, although it may at times be necessary to return to increased scaffolding on topics that pupils may find more difficult or where information may have dropped out of their memory.

The idea behind scaffolding is that each child has two levels of development:

- What they can do on their own.
- What they can do with the help of someone else, or an MKO ('more knowledgeable other').

The scaffolding approach is credited to the work of Russian psychologist Lev Vygotsky. Vygotsky argued that teaching should always be aimed at the child's emerging and developing skills, rather than the existing ones (1978). Vygotsky called the space where the child's skills are emerging the 'zone of proximal development', which looks something like this:

Zone of proximal development

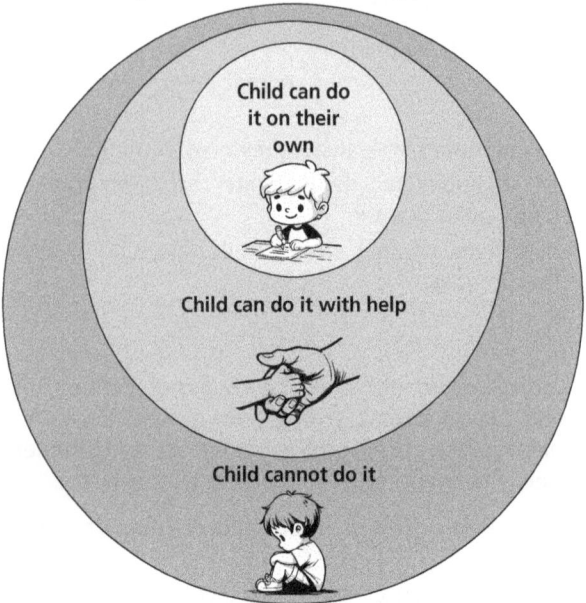

When children are learning to tackle a new challenge, scaffolding is a highly effective approach. It means giving children just enough help to do something that they couldn't do alone. Over time, this help is then gradually decreased until the children are able to do something for themselves.

In the early years, scaffolding is sometimes carried out through shared thinking and is something that happens between two or more people. This will most frequently be between an adult and a child, but it may also be between children if one child is a 'more knowledgeable other' (MKO). The use of the phrase 'work together' underlines the emphasis on scaffolding being an active and creative process where both or all of the parties must contribute to the thinking. An example of how this can be used as a useful cognitive way to solve a problem, clarify a concept, evaluate or elaborate thinking could be the following, where two four-year-olds are painting on an easel.

Teacher: Wow! Look at that pig you have painted! That's a great tail and snout.

Child 1: Yes, I like the tail. But I need pink and there is no pink paint.

Child 2: You could use the red paint?

Teacher: You could use the red paint, but is that the right colour for your pig?

Child 1: Not really, I want it to be pink.

Teacher: I wonder whether you could mix something with the red paint to make pink?

Child 2: Maybe white? Pink looks like lighter red.

In this way, the teacher *and* two children have worked together to solve the problem.

Sentence starters and writing prompts

Sentence starters are words and phrases that can help guide the writer through a text. They can be used to make comparisons, contrast or express order. They are typically used in the primary classroom to introduce the rest of the sentence, and are usually set apart by commas. They introduce what the sentence is about, so the reader knows what to expect. For pupils who need scaffolding with their writing, they give a useful framework to support.

Here are some examples of sentence starters:

- To make comparisons, e.g. 'in the same way', 'likewise', 'again' and 'along those lines'.
- To show contrast, e.g. 'then again', 'on the other hand', 'despite that' and 'nevertheless'.
- Expressing order and time sequences, e.g. 'next', 'then', 'after that' and 'later'.
- For added emphasis, e.g. 'indeed', 'undoubtedly', 'generally speaking' and 'obviously'.
- Expressing uncertainty, e.g. 'it's possible that', 'perhaps', 'although not proven' and 'arguably'.

In the primary classroom, it's not uncommon to see these displayed as word mats or on the working wall so they are easily accessible for the pupils.

Time	Order	Place	Additional information	Comparison
One morning	At first	At the end of	Also	Although
After that	Next	Over the	For example	However
Soon	Then	Next to	Another	Yet
Meanwhile	Finally	Under the wall	Again	Unlike

Sometimes it's necessary to provide further support in the form of a writing frame. These are likely to combine sentence starters with choices for the pupils to start making for themselves. A writing frame can simply be a box with a photograph in it followed by blank ruled lines for the children to write on, but sometimes they can be more scaffolded than this, for example:

We know some facts about the fire of London	because		told us.
	if	Samuel Pepys	wrote a diary.
	when		recorded it.

The fire is thought to have started	because		set fire to a pile of wood in a bakery.
	if	a spark from a fire	was carried to the River Thames.
	when		set fire to some curtains.

and then...			

Reducing scaffolding

Knowing how and when to reduce scaffolding so that your pupils start to learn more independently is a skill the teacher must possess. The time and rate at which scaffolding will be removed will alter from pupil to pupil. Scaffolding should be reduced when pupils can demonstrate that they can complete a task independently and with confidence. If pupils are still given scaffolding when they no longer require it, this will be counter-productive as additional scaffolding can lead to cognitive overload. Remember, scaffolding is a temporary structure designed to be removed when no longer needed.

Here are some strategies for reducing scaffolding:

● **Gradually reduce frequency** – Reduce how often you provide scaffolding such as writing outlines, sentence starters, word mats and writing frames.

● **Transfer the control to your pupils** – You can gradually give your pupils more control over when and how they use scaffolding. Perhaps word mats or multiplication tables are no longer provided on the desk, but they are available in a drawer if a pupil needs to collect them.

● **Remove components** – You can slowly remove parts of scaffolding, such as reducing the size of a template and inviting more of an element of independent work to the task.

● **Use performance assessments** – You can use assessments to identify when students have developed the skills to begin reducing scaffolding.

4. Flexible grouping

Flexible grouping involves adapting tasks and instructions for different groups of learners. It involves groups based on ability, understanding of a particular subject and whether they require support within a particular lesson. Flexible learning allows for groups to flex and change so pupils can learn effectively while still feeling part of the wider class. An example of this would be in a primary maths lesson when the teacher invites pupils to work with them for longer after other pupils have begun independent work.

The EEF recommends that teachers use flexible grouping effectively by:

- Grouping pupils in a way that reduces stigma, ensuring such groups are based on the relative difficulty of curriculum content rather than being fixed and inflexible.
- Promoting peer tutoring by placing pupils in groups in which they learn from one another.
- Pre-lesson pre-teaching, e.g. giving examples during assembly time or before school starts.
- Post-lesson, gap-closing sessions.

5. Using technology

Technology can bring learning to life for pupils, particularly those who learn visually or through interaction, and can also support learning outside of the classroom. The EEF recommends that teachers use technology such as an interactive whiteboard or a visualiser when modelling work for pupils. This affords opportunities to:

- Enhance modelling and explaining.
- Promote inclusion.
- Demonstrate the teacher's thinking.
- Give children clear understanding – 'I do, we do, you do'.
- Set high expectations.
- Assess and give feedback.
- Share children's work.

Using technology can also help pupils to record their learning through speech-to-text software, or help dyslexic pupils who find handwriting and spelling difficult.

Neurodiversity

Neurodiversity describes the different ways that we all think, move, hear, see, understand, process information and communicate with each other. The term 'neurodivergent' refers to someone diverging from the average or socially derived norm.

(Ellis et al., 2023, p. 5; p. 9)

'Neurodiversity' is a general term that refers to the diversity of all people, but it's often used in the context of autism spectrum disorder (ASD) as well as other neurological or developmental conditions such as ADHD or learning disabilities. The neurodiversity movement emerged during the 1990s, aiming to increase acceptance and inclusion of all people while embracing neurological differences. Through online platforms, more and more autistic people were able to connect and form a self-advocacy movement.

There is a need to be mindful of the language we use around neurodiversity as some of the terms imply deficit. We have used the term 'ASD' as an acronym used to describe 'autism spectrum disorder'; however, I prefer to use the term 'ASS' as an acronym for 'autism spectrum syndrome', or simply 'AS' for 'autism spectrum'. It really is a spectrum. At the upper end of the spectrum may be non-verbal with PMLD (profound and multiple learning difficulties), while at the lower end of the spectrum it can be barely noticeable or manifest itself in a variety of ways, such as liking things to be done in a particular way or the need to plan ahead meticulously.

Neurodiversity is not straightforward, as different types of neurodivergent thinking and operating can be combined with others. For example, you may notice that autism may have similarities with obsessive compulsive disorder (OCD). Other types of neurodiversity are commonly found together as coexisting syndromes, such as dyslexia and dyspraxia. For these reasons, I like the definition below:

> *Neurodiversity describes the idea that people experience and interact with the world around them in many different ways; there is no one 'right' way of thinking, learning and behaving, and differences are not viewed as deficits.*

(Baumer and Freuh, 2021)

Here is a list of some of the more common forms of neurodiversity and terms you may come across in the classroom, along with some of the things you can do to help neurodivergent pupils.

Term	Common manifestation	Things you can do to help (environmental)	Things you can do to help (learning)
Attention deficit hyperactivity disorder (ADHD)	ADHD is characterised by inattention and finding difficulty in concentrating for long periods of time. It may manifest as impulsivity and is likely to be observed in early to mid-childhood. The degree of inattention and hyperactivity impulsivity present in a child can significantly interfere with academic functioning. It can lead to sudden mood fluctuations and difficulty in dealing with certain social situations.	• Classroom seating plan, for example seating the pupil near the teacher or next to a good role model. • Keep learning areas light and airy. • Pre-empt tricky times, for example particular times or situations where there are concerns, the start of the lesson, lining up or lunchtimes, and have a member of staff who can meet and greet and adapt transition times. • Use an agreed card to allow them to leave the room or situation.	• Be consistent and use regular rewards systems. • Reward attention by giving special privileges, certificates and prizes. • Give praise in the presence of others. • Set realistic targets by breaking tasks down into small manageable chunks. • Ask for instructions to be repeated back to you to clarify understanding. • Use visual prompts and task lists to tick off work completed where possible. • Have stretch breaks and then refocus on the task. • Develop techniques for getting a child to listen, such as making eye contact. • Teach organisational skills, such as giving rewards for remembering to title work and carrying out planner checks. • Allocate study buddies.

Term	Common manifestation	Things you can do to help (environmental)	Things you can do to help (learning)
Autism spectrum disorder (ASD), or autism spectrum condition (ASC)	ASD, or ASC, is a condition that is characterised by persistent challenges with impulse control and sensory regulation and may also include the inability to initiate or sustain social interaction and communication. It can be characterised by restricted, repetitive and inflexible patterns of behaviour and interests.	Use the same approaches as above, as well as: • Clear and calm routines. • Visual timetables. • 'Now and next' boards. • A clock for timings, with five-minute warnings given for ends of activities. • A clear, uncluttered classroom environment. • Warnings for unexpected events, for example a change of teacher or disruptions to the school day. • A plan for potentially difficult times, e.g. playground noise. • Depending on the wishes of the child, they may like an enclosed personal area to work in. • Classroom seating plan, for example having a child or young person seated near the teacher or next to a good role model. • Keep learning areas light and airy. • Pre-empt tricky times (e.g. the start of the lesson, lining up or lunchtimes) and have a member of staff who can meet and greet and adapt transition times. • Use an agreed card to allow them to leave the room or situation.	• Use a school buddy system to support with friendships. • Enable paired work, which can help improve understanding and self-awareness. • Encourage participation during lunchtime and after school clubs. • Avoid sarcasm and put downs and try to focus on rewarding the positive behaviours. • Label and praise positive social behaviour you would like to see more of. For example, 'Well done, I really like the way you came into the classroom today.'

Term	Common manifestation	Things you can do to help (environmental)	Things you can do to help (learning)
Developmental coordination disorder (DCD), or dyspraxia	DCD, or dyspraxia, is a motor coordination disorder that is characterised by a significant delay in acquiring more complex gross and fine motor skills and usually by impairment in the planning and execution of coordinated motor skills. This can manifest itself as clumsiness, slowness or inaccurate motor performance.	• Provide a distraction-free environment. Reduce social demands while learning and allow time out if the pupil is over-stimulated. • Provide extra opportunities to practice a new skill or task. • Model planning skills. • Provide extra time for exams and coursework to help the pupil organise thoughts and formulate their answers. • Provide a writing slope to help with writing.	• Provide more time and help for learning new tasks and model by talking through your steps out loud. Ask questions about what may come next. • Break down difficult tasks into smaller parts and practise them regularly. • Adapt tasks and make them easier by adding special grips to pens and pencils and allow shoes with Velcro fasteners, for example. • Have a look at the pupil's clothes after physical education and help to ensure they have things on the right way round.
Dyscalculia	Dyscalculia refers to difficulty in understanding numbers, performing mathematical calculations and applying number concepts.	• Offer graphic organisers for organising information. • Offer graph paper to help line up numbers and problems. • Show the pupil how to focus on one problem by covering the others with a piece of paper. • Let the pupil use visual aids or manipulatives. • Let the pupil write out charts or draw sketches to solve problems.	• Use manipulatives, as physical objects can help students with dyscalculia make connections between numbers and mathematical ideas. • Visual aids can help students understand maths concepts. • Explore maths language, as pupils with dyscalculia may have good language skills.

Term	Common manifestation	Things you can do to help (environmental)	Things you can do to help (learning)
		• Allow use of a calculator when computation is not the focus of the lesson. • Limit the amount of information needed to transfer to paper by including tables, graphs or number lines on the worksheet.	• Incorporate multisensory techniques, for example counting physical items can help pupils build basic maths concepts. • Help students see relationships between words by talking through problems or writing them down. • Break tasks down into manageable chunks. • Provide classroom accommodations. For example, pupils with dyscalculia may be entitled to extra time on tests, access to a calculator or a quiet space to work.
Dyslexia	Dyslexia is a learning disorder with impairment in reading and difficulties in learning academic skills related to reading, such as accuracy, fluency and comprehension. It may also affect language cognition in the brain, which manifests itself in difficulties in reading, writing and ordering speech. Working memory is also affected, as is executive functioning.	• Have visual timetables on the walls and read them aloud. • Offer coloured bookmarks so pupils can focus on a line of text. • Provide letter and number guides so pupils know how to write correctly. • Use large font size in handouts. • Use audiobooks and videos in lesson plans and text-to-speech software. • Provide a laptop for typing up work. • Give extra time for tasks and to read text in class.	• Tasks should be broken down into small and manageable steps (short-term memory is associated with dyslexia), with each step clearly written down and placed into a sequence for the pupil to refer to. • Use fonts for dyslexics. Technology offers numerous innovative tools to help those who live with dyslexia, such as Dyslexie.

Term	Common manifestation	Things you can do to help (environmental)	Things you can do to help (learning)
	Having said this, dyslexic children are often able, keen readers, are good at spelling, can write well (albeit in unstructured ways) and sometimes simply require more time.	• Provide study buddies to help dyslexic pupils with reading and writing. • Have multisensory tools in your classroom such as flashcards and puppets to help teach.	• Encourage computer use, as handwriting can be torturous for pupils. This lets the pupil use spellchecker and helps with grammar and punctuation while you can still see the quality of the content. • Boost confidence. Children with dyslexia can lack confidence as they struggle with different things. Praise their hard work, don't ask them to read aloud or copy the text on the board and never criticise their difficulties. • Create a supportive classroom culture by encouraging your pupils to collaborate. • Teach exam strategies, as it's important for dyslexics to know exactly what to expect. • Dyslexia writing strategies include line readers, coloured keyboards, pocket spell checkers and text-to-speech software. • Mark work based on effort and ideas. • Meet regularly with parents to discuss their child's progress.

Term	Common manifestation	Things you can do to help (environmental)
Stimming	Stimming refers to repetitive behaviours or movements that are sometimes used to help cope with emotions. Some examples of stimming include biting your nails when you feel anxious, making repetitive sounds or flapping the hands or arms.	• Reduce textures or lights that may be upsetting. • Soundproof windows and rooms. • Provide a quiet space with sound-blocking headphones. • Provide stress management tools or 'fidget toys', such as a fidget spinner, stress balls or a swing set. • Evaluate the sensory environment. If a student is overstimulated, you can try moving them to a quiet room or focusing on one toy at a time. If they are under-stimulated, you can try giving them more playtime outside or introducing new toys and textures. • Encourage exercise. This can release endorphins, which can reduce the need to stim. • If the stim isn't self-injurious, you can try joining the stim. For example, if the pupil stacks objects, you can buy blocks and stack with them. • You can try teaching an alternate behaviour that meets the same needs; for example, you can try replacing hand flapping with squeezing a stress ball.

Term	Common manifestation	Things you can do to help (environmental)	Things you can do to help (learning)
Tourette's syndrome, or tic disorder	Tourette's syndrome is a condition that causes a person to make involuntary sounds and movements called tics. People with Tourette's syndrome may also have obsessive compulsive disorder (OCD), ADHD or learning difficulties.	• Recognise that tics are involuntary movements and sounds. • Reduce stress and anxiety, as these can increase symptoms. • Identify the skills deficits that may contribute to stress and symptoms, as well as the strategies and support to address these deficits. • Ignore the symptoms that can be ignored. • Be aware of co-occurring conditions, such as OCD or ADHD, which are common for pupils with Tourette's syndrome. • Promote communication with parents or caregivers. Be sure to share the pupil's achievements and strengths. • Use the Tourette's Association's resources.	• Consider whether accommodations are needed for handwriting issues. Handwriting issues are among the most common difficulties for children with Tourette's syndrome. Try the use of a computer, tablet, a scribe or notes. • Be creative with interventions. Teaching life-long strategies and providing support, accommodation and modifications. • Involve the pupil in developing plans and strategies for managing symptoms that can be difficult or impossible to ignore.

The following organisations provide advice, information and training on specific impairments:

- Autism Education Trust
- Speech and Language UK
- The Dyslexia-SpLD Trust
- The National Sensory Impairment Partnership (NatSIP)
- MindEd

Executive functioning

Most types of neurodiversity go hand in hand with difficulties in executive functioning. Some people describe executive function as 'the management system of the brain'; this is because the skills involved let us set goals, plan and get things done. When children struggle with executive function, it impacts them in all areas of life.

Executive function is a set of mental skills. It includes working memory, flexible thinking and self-control. We use these skills every day to learn, work and manage daily life. Trouble with executive function can make it hard to focus, follow directions and handle emotions, among other things.

Let's look at an example of how a pupil with poor executive functioning could find their school day challenging.

Jana is a bright pupil with plenty of friends. Intellectually, she can perform well, but she has some issues with day-to-day tasks that other pupils find easy. Each situation or reaction has a number associated with it, so that you can identify the executive function that is challenging Jana.

On arrival in school, Jana becomes confused when she finds a different teacher in her class (1). Her friend tells her that they were told yesterday that there would be a cover teacher in class this morning (2). Jana has forgotten to bring her homework (3), which upsets her (4).

The cover teacher asks the class to get out their writing books and complete a comprehension task. Jana is good at reading but finds it difficult to frame her answers (5). The teacher then stops the class and asks them a question, but Jana can't put her hand up to answer the question as she wasn't concentrating (6).

At breaktime, the class is asked to put their books away, collect their snack and line up at the door, then wait for the bell to ring before leaving the classroom. This is a lot for Jana to process and remember (7). By the time she gets outside, her friend is playing with someone else and she is upset (8).

When they return to class, the teacher is modelling some writing on the board and asks the class to come up with some ideas to describe a setting, but Jana can't think of any (9). Finally, the teacher asks the class to compose their own piece of writing, but Jana is finding it difficult getting started (10). Once she gets going after some prompts by her teacher, she is writing away but doesn't realise she is running out of time, and the bell interrupts her work (11).

So, what we see here is:

1. Panic when rules or routines change.

2. Forgets things easily.

3. Difficulty with organisation.

4. Difficulty regulating emotion.

5. Difficulty organising thoughts.

6. Difficulty maintaining attention.

7. Trouble following directions or a sequence of steps.

8. Getting overly emotional and fixating on things.

9. Trouble organising thoughts.

10. Trouble starting and completing tasks.

11. Trouble managing time.

Hopefully this example can help you understand how being in a lesson may feel for a pupil with poor executive functioning. Trouble with executive function isn't a diagnosis or a learning disability, but it is common in people who learn and think differently, and many types of neurodiversity coexist with this. There are things we can do as teachers to help our pupils with these situations, for example:

Panic when rules or routines change	Have a notice ready for when pupils arrive to remind them of changes to the routine.
Forgets things easily	As above, and have a visual timetable for each day.
Difficulty with organisation	Keep to regular routines and ensure Jana is prompted to remember homework.
Difficulty regulating emotion	Helping to keep Jana organised will prevent her from getting upset.
Difficulty organising thoughts	Jana may need prompting by the teacher or to have a work partner.
Difficulty maintaining attention	Key Jana in, make sure she is paying attention and give eye contact.
Trouble following directions or a sequence of steps	Repeat the instructions, ask Jana to repeat them back to you and use task management boards.
Getting overly emotional and fixating on things	Help Jana to understand that these things happen and not to take it personally.
Trouble organising thoughts	Teacher modelling, partially worked examples, prompt sheet, sentence starters and work partners.
Trouble starting and completing tasks	Teacher modelling, partially worked examples, prompt sheet, sentence starters and work partners.
Trouble managing time	Time reminders from the teacher, encourage pupils to use the clock and give warnings e.g. five minutes left.

Teaching neurodivergent pupils

You need to remember that there's not a 'one-size-fits-all' approach, and you will need to spend time getting to know all of your pupils individually. Early meetings with parents can help, as they may have responses in place to help their children with certain challenges and situations. Ask them, 'What else, or what can we do differently that would help?'

One of my pupils gave me a list of things that would help with his autism. It included:

- Giving him extra time with tasks.
- Repeating instructions.
- Sitting at the back of the class.
- Having structure at playtime.
- Having warnings before changes in routine.

Another pupil was frequently given task boards with 'Now' and 'Next' headers so she knew what to expect after completing a task. However, she was still feeling anxious about what lay ahead, so I suggested adding a 'Then' header, which made her feel much better.

Now	Next	Then
PE – throwing and catching	Maths in groups	Lunchtime

You will find that most of the specific things you can do as a teacher to help your neurodiverse pupils will benefit all pupils, both in their learning and their emotional security. Here is a list of some things that are tried and tested by myself, but also many others I have worked with. It is worth trying them all, as it is likely to help your pupils but also make life easier for you too.

● Repeating instructions.
● Giving reminders.
● Providing a visual timetable.
● Mixed ability grouping and work partners.
● Making sure all pupils understand the task.
● Giving sufficient time.
● Scaffolding – providing words for spelling, number lines and squares, planning and writing frames, sentence starters.
● Creating task boards.
● Reading aloud instructions and information.
● Creating a positive atmosphere in your classroom where it's ok to ask for help and make mistakes.

Teenagers, special needs and mental health

There has been a great increase in the number of secondary pupils being diagnosed with ADHD, other types of special needs or mental health problems. Around 20% of pupils are allowed extra time during exams; there are a number of potential reasons behind this number:

● An increase in the scale of mental ill-health, quite possibly linked to use of smartphones and the length of time spent in front of screens.
● The fact that special needs were stigmatised in the past and parents therefore didn't seek a diagnosis. Now there is more awareness of special needs, which has reduced the stigma around them.

The increase in special needs and mental health diagnoses creates two problems:

● Schools can't cope with such numbers, nor can the local children and adolescent mental health services (CAMHS).

- The most severe cases, where urgent care is needed, are not receiving the care because of the pressure on resources.

There are many schools and psychiatrists who are worried about two dangers of overdiagnosis: teenagers being given medication, the long-term consequences of which are uncertain, and the fact that teenagers use the diagnosis as an excuse to stop trying to deal with any problems they may face (Pemberton, 2025). We may be medicalising normal, everyday issues that teenagers experience; the solution in many situations is not drugs but less screen time, especially in the case of ADHD.

References

Aubin, G., 2022, EEF blog: The Five-a-day approach: How the EEF can support a range of resources to support high-quality teaching for all pupils. Online, Education Endowment Foundation.

Baumer, N. and Frueh, J., 2021, What is neurodiversity?, *Harvard Health Blog*. Online.

Cullen, M. A., Lindsay, G., Hastings, R., Denne, L., and Stanford, C., 2020, Special Educational Needs in Mainstream Schools: Evidence Review.

Department for Education, 2015, Special educational needs and disability code of practice: 0 to 25 years, GOV.UK. Online.

Eaton, J., 2022, EEF blog: Moving from 'differentiation' to 'adaptive teaching'. Online, Education Endowment Foundation.

Education Endowment Foundation, 2021, Assess, adjust, adapt – what does adaptive teaching mean to you?

Ellis, P., Kirby, A., and Osbourne, A., 2023, *Neurodiversity and Education*, Corwin, UK.

Honeybourne, V., 2018, *The Neurodiverse Classroom*, Jessica Kingsley Publishers, UK and USA.

McLeskey, J., Billingsley, B., & Lewis, T.J., 2018, *High Leverage Practices for Inclusive Classrooms*, Rouledge.

Mould, K., 2021, EEF blog: Assess, adjust, adapt – what does adaptive teaching mean to you? Online, Education Endowment Foundation.

Pemberton, M., 2025, Labelling is too easy and this over-diagnosis is dangerous to children, *The Times*, January 4 2025.

Vygotsky, L., 1978, *Mind in Society*, London: Harvard University Press.

Chapter 9
Make good use of assessment

ITTECF syllabus

Assessment (Standard 6 – Make accurate and productive use of assessment)

Learn that...	Learn how to...
1. Effective assessment is critical to teaching because it provides teachers with information about pupils' understanding and needs. 2. Good assessment helps teachers avoid being over-influenced by potentially misleading factors, such as how busy pupils appear. 3. Before using any assessment, teachers should be clear about the decision it will be used to support and be able to justify its use. 4. To be of value, teachers use information from assessments to inform the decisions they make; in turn, pupils must be able to act on feedback for it to have an effect. 5. High quality feedback can be written or verbal; it is likely to be accurate and clear, encourage further effort, and provide specific guidance on how to improve. 6. Over time, feedback should support pupils to monitor and regulate their own learning. 7. Working with colleagues to identify efficient approaches to assessment is important; assessment can become onerous and have a disproportionate impact on workload.	**Avoid common assessment pitfalls, by:** a) Planning formative assessment tasks linked to lesson objectives and thinking ahead about what would indicate understanding (e.g. by using hinge questions to pinpoint knowledge gaps). b) Drawing conclusions about what pupils have learned by looking at patterns of performance over a number of assessments (e.g. appreciating that assessments draw inferences about learning from performance). c) Choosing, where possible, externally validated materials, used in controlled conditions when required to make summative assessments. d) Using available evidence to accurately identify what is required for individuals to meet their next steps and use this understanding to guide teaching adjustments for sub-group and individual pupils. **Check prior knowledge and understanding during lessons, by:** e) Using assessments to check for prior knowledge and pre-existing misconceptions. f) Structuring tasks and questions to enable the identification of knowledge gaps and misconceptions (e.g. by using common misconceptions within multiple-choice questions).

Learn that...	Learn how to...
	g) Prompting pupils to elaborate when responding to questioning to check that a correct answer stems from secure understanding.
	h) Monitoring pupil work during lessons, including checking for misconceptions.
	Provide high quality feedback, by:
	i) Focusing on specific actions for pupils and providing time for pupils to respond to feedback.
	j) Appreciating that pupils' responses to feedback can vary depending on a range of social factors (e.g. the message the feedback contains or the age of the child).
	k) Scaffolding self-assessment by sharing model work with pupils, highlighting key details.
	l) Thinking carefully about how to ensure feedback is specific and helpful when using peer- or self-assessment.
	Make feedback manageable and effective, by:
	m) Recording data only when it is useful for improving pupil outcomes.
	n) Working with colleagues to identify efficient approaches to marking and alternative approaches to providing feedback (e.g. using whole class feedback or well-supported peer and self-assessment).
	o) Using verbal feedback during lessons in place of written feedback after lessons where possible.
	p) Understanding that written marking is only one form of feedback.
	q) Reducing the opportunity cost of marking (e.g. by using abbreviations and codes in written feedback).
	r) Prioritising the highlighting of errors related to misunderstandings, rather than careless mistakes when marking.

Assessment is the bridge between teaching and learning. If pupils always learned what we taught them, we wouldn't need assessment. And assessment *drives* learning.

The vast majority of the curriculum is not externally assessed. In primary, nothing apart from English and maths is externally assessed, and in secondary, the KS3 curriculum isn't externally assessed. But you should be assessing your pupils in every lesson.

Most of the time you will be assessing your pupils informally by asking questions that are answered orally or written on a mini whiteboard and held up. Sometimes you will be slightly more formal, where the pupils write answers to questions in an exercise book or a workbook, and you can be more formal still, such as setting a 20-question test where the marks are recorded.

In a primary setting, most of the assessment will be informal. However, there are also opportunities for summative testing or low-stake tests that could take place at the end of a lesson or a unit of work. While questioning is seen as a good means of assessment for all ages, the younger the children are the less they will be able to articulate an answer. Observations of behaviours are therefore crucial in assessing young children, particularly in reception.

Assessment is important for three reasons:

1. You get to know what the pupils know and understand, and can therefore identify common errors and reteach them.
2. You are making the pupils think, which is a powerful way of helping them learn rather than just being passive observers.
3. For secondary subjects especially, if pupils have to memorise work and then recall it, this will help them store that information in the long-term memory, which is what good education is all about.

For Common Entrance, GCSE and A-level, there is little better than setting past papers or question papers you have written and then going over model answers in class. Knowing things is not the same thing as writing it down correctly in an exam, so the pupils must practise this.

The main mistakes that are made with assessment are:

- Assessing before the topic has been carefully taught. High quality initial instruction will reduce the work that assessment needs to do.
- Demotivating the weaker pupils. Kluger and DeNisi (1996) found that feedback increased learning for many of the students they looked at, but for

one third of them, feedback actually decreased learning. So, feedback can sometimes discourage pupils.

- Getting a false impression by allowing pupils to 'cheat', for example by getting their parents to do their coursework for them. If pupils can cheat, they often will.
- Spending hours writing comments on the work that the pupils more or less ignore. The main point of marking is to help the pupil improve. You cannot spend too much of your life marking, and you need to find efficient ways of making your marking have an impact. You want pupils to learn from your feedback, but sometimes all they do is look at the mark – that is not learning.

So, do the following things:

- Always provide clear objectives and success criteria when setting work.
- Make your comments on the pupils' work specific and focused.
- Show exactly what your pupils need to do to improve.
- Go over common mistakes with the whole class.
- Make pupils really think about their errors. For example, some teachers ask pupils to list their main mistakes on a sheet at the front of their files, which can be referred to later. Get them to write out corrections or a better version of the work they have done.
- Correct spelling mistakes and make the pupils learn them by writing them out.
- Analyse the best answers with the whole class using a visualiser.
- Get pupils to mark each other's scripts as a way of making them think about the characteristics of a good answer.

Formative and summative assessment

Formative and summative assessment are very different things. Formative assessment means you are asking pupils questions in order to find out what they know, which helps them and the teacher know what to do next to fill any gaps. This is sometimes called 'assessment *for* learning'. The whole point of formative assessment is that you adapt your teaching in response to the pupils' understanding – it happens throughout the lesson.

('Formative assessment' is actually an unfortunate phrase because most people can only think of exams when they see the word 'assessment'. 'Responsive teaching' is a better term, as it highlights the need to adapt teaching based on the results of the assessment.)

Summative assessment means measuring how much the pupils know and remember. This is often called 'assessment *of* learning'. Summative assessment normally comes at the end of a block of teaching.

Formative and summative assessment can look the same but have different purposes. Formative assessment tends to focus on one small area of knowledge, while summative assessment covers a wider part of the syllabus.

Research evidence

Black, P. and Wiliam, D., 1998, *Inside the Black Box: raising standards through classroom assessment*, King's College London

Black and Wiliam explore the value of formative assessment, especially its effectiveness for lower-performing students. They recommend that teachers:

● Hand work back to pupils with no mark or grade, only comments, so they focus on how to improve rather than what was wrong. Pupils must respond to the marked work in some way.

● Ask questions with plenty of thinking time, and which allow for deeper understanding, not just factual recall.

● Give pupils rubrics, success criteria and exemplar work.

● Get pupils to assess each other's work.

Doug Lemov, *Teach Like a Champion*

Doug Lemov (see page 139), whose methods were developed in America but are used across the world, makes the following suggestions:

● Allow pupils to feel safe about making and discussing mistakes. Welcome errors.

● Be calm and positive about all answers.

● Never allow one pupil to mock another.

● Delay revealing an answer until you've discussed it. If you just give the answer, the pupils stop thinking.

● Praise pupils who are willing to take risks.

● If some pupils can't answer a question, don't disturb the whole class – instead, see them quietly either in the lesson or outside the class.

● Use common pupil errors as teaching tools.

● Have the pupils do corrections so they all have a copy of the correct answer.

Speckesser, S.,Runge, J., Foliano, F., Bursnall, M., Hudson-Sharp, N., Rolfe, H. and Anders, J., *Embedding Formative Assessment: evaluation report and executive summary,* **2018, Education Endowment Foundation**

The Education Endowment Foundation (EEF) commissions research into 'what works' in the classroom. In this piece of research run by the National Institute of Economic and Social Research, teaching in 140 schools was analysed. Some schools used formative assessment, others less so. Students in the formative assessment schools made the equivalent of two additional months' progress, but the research found no evidence that formative assessment improved English or maths results at GCSE. So, the results were mixed and suggested that some teachers were better at using formative assessment than others.

A key point about assessment is this: if a pupil clearly doesn't know enough about a topic, they don't need more feedback – they need more instruction.

Summative assessment tips for secondary

The following can help you provide effective summative assessment in the secondary classroom:

- Keep a record of marks in a paper or digital mark book. Make a note of what the marks were for as well as any weaknesses, which can be useful when writing reports for parents.
- If a pupil owes you a piece of work, chase it. Don't allow failure to produce work to be the final word.
- Generally speaking, it is good to give homework some type of mark as a way of motivating the pupils
- Don't predict exams grades unless you are experienced enough to do so. Ask a more experienced colleague instead.
- Apply to become an exam marker. It's a difficult job, but you'll learn a vast amount.

If you are teaching to GCSE or A-level, you need two things:

1. Past papers and examiners' feedback from the relevant exam board website.
2. Copies of GCSE and A-level scripts written by pupils from your school, which the school can access after each exam series. Get scripts at different levels (e.g. GCSE grades 9, 5 and 3), which tell you about the standard at each grade.

There is no simple read-through from marks to grades at GCSE and A-level – grading is a different process from marking. The national distribution of grades is predetermined by Ofqual and is laid on top of the rank order of marks. So, any given mark may lead to a slightly different grade in different years.

Effective questioning

Teachers spend a lot of time asking questions in lessons. This keeps pupils on their toes and tells the teacher if they are understanding what is being taught. The following are some effective methods of questioning.

Cold calling

This is where you pick a pupil by name to answer a question instead of asking the class to put their hands up. This forces all the pupils to concentrate. All pupils have to formulate an answer in their head before they find out who has been selected to answer.

This can sometimes be adapted into the 'pause-pounce-bounce' approach, when a teacher extends the questioning by 'bouncing' it around a few pupils to take a variety of answers. Teach your pupils to say, 'I agree with what they said, and also...'

Wait time

Make sure to wait a good length of time for an answer. Some teachers have a bad habit of moving on after just a few seconds; pupils often need more thinking time than we tend to give them, particularly if they have poor executive functioning skills (see Chapter 8). They may need time to write an answer on a mini whiteboard or chat to a partner, so they can 'try out' their answer before articulating it in front of the whole class.

Hinge questions

Every 20–30 minutes, you need to check everyone has understood the work and do this quickly so as not to disrupt the teaching too much. So, you need to plan two things in advance:

1. Hinge questions, which will tell you if the pupils understand (e.g. 'Describe three types of plate boundaries').
2. A method by which you can see that everyone has 'got it', such as:
   - Asking a question to the class, either on the board or orally. The emphasis must be on quick responses by the pupils.
   - Where opinion is divided, asking pupils to construct their case to persuade others of their point of view.

Use mini whiteboards

Using mini whiteboards gives pupils the opportunity to spend time thinking about their answer and then writing it out, possibly with the help of a partner.

'Say it again, but better'

Insist on pupils using full sentences and subject-specific vocabulary, as this will help you distinguish between pupils with a deep grasp of the topic from those who only have a superficial understanding.

Avoid self-reporting

If you ask a pupil if they understand something, the chances are that they will say 'yes', even if they don't. Instead, make sure to ask the pupil to give a full answer and explain their reasoning to check their grasp of the topic.

Involve the pupils

A lot of pupils tend not to listen when others are answering a question. So, after an answer has been given, you should ask another pupil whether they agree with the previous pupil's answer. More pupils will then start to listen. You can ask younger pupils for feedback on the answer – do they agree (thumbs up)? Disagree (thumbs down)? Not sure (thumbs sideways)? Do you want to expand on the answer (hands up, for example)?

Be nice

Don't criticise a pupil for getting a question wrong. Move on to the next pupil, and when you have the right answer go back and see whether the pupil who was wrong has now got it. Never belittle a question or answer from a pupil that may seem irrelevant, silly or ignorant. Mistakes are a useful way of learning and pupils need to know that their contributions will not be laughed at.

Clarify the aim of your questioning

Are you simply aiming to see if pupils can recall a piece of information? Are you providing an opportunity for them to clarify their own understanding, or to apply or elaborate that understanding?

Echoing

When a pupil has given their answer, repeat a section of what they have said back to them. For example, 'So you are arguing that...?' Then leave a silence and wait for the pupil to further demonstrate their understanding.

Feedback

Feedback can be part of both formative and summative assessment. It is conventionally thought of as a dialogue between teacher and pupil, but it can take a variety of forms. Peer and self-assessment can be equally valuable, and constructive feedback should be specific, honest and supportive. It is really important, therefore, that the conditions where this takes place within a classroom are right.

Feedback provides information about where a pupil is in relation to their learning goals, meaning they can evaluate progress, identify gaps or misconceptions and take action that results in enhanced performance in the future. Effective feedback shouldn't simply focus on current performance but should also feed forward in an actionable way, so the learner understands what they need to focus on in order to improve.

Teach well before you give feedback, as high-quality initial instruction will reduce the work that feedback needs to do. The best feedback is specific to the learning you are trying to achieve and is given in such a way that the pupil can learn how to improve. Feedback will be counter-productive unless the pupil is in the right frame of mind to act on the feedback – they have to believe they can benefit from the advice you are giving.

Effective peer and self-assessment

Peer and self-assessment are powerful forms of feedback when used well. You can't expect pupils to master the art of effective peer and self-assessment without understanding how to meaningfully respond to feedback themselves and having a clear mental model of what effective peer and self-assessment looks like. It needs to be taught in advance.

When done well, peer and self-assessment can:

- Give pupils the opportunity to think carefully about their own learning and that of their peers.
- Reduce marking for the teacher.
- Allow pupils to develop their mental model of what success looks like in a task and support them to develop transferrable knowledge.
- Support self-regulation and independence.
- Enable pupils to more accurately and clearly reflect on the effectiveness of their own work by assessing the work of their classmates.

When done poorly, however, peer and self-assessment can lead to:

- Poor progress for pupils.
- A waste of lesson time.
- Pupils focusing on the wrong learning points.
- Pupils developing a poor mental model of effective feedback.
- The development of misconceptions.

The Learning Pit

I first discovered the Learning Pit (a form of self-assessed learning) from Burns and Griffith in their fabulous book, *Outstanding Teaching: Teaching Backwards* (2014). The Learning Pit helps students to be more comfortable with challenge, realise that learning is a journey to develop problem-solving strategies and articulate their learning. Created by James Nottingham in the early 2000s, it is now used in thousands of schools around the world. In one of my schools, we used the Learning Pit consistently across all of our classes. It looks something like a version of this:

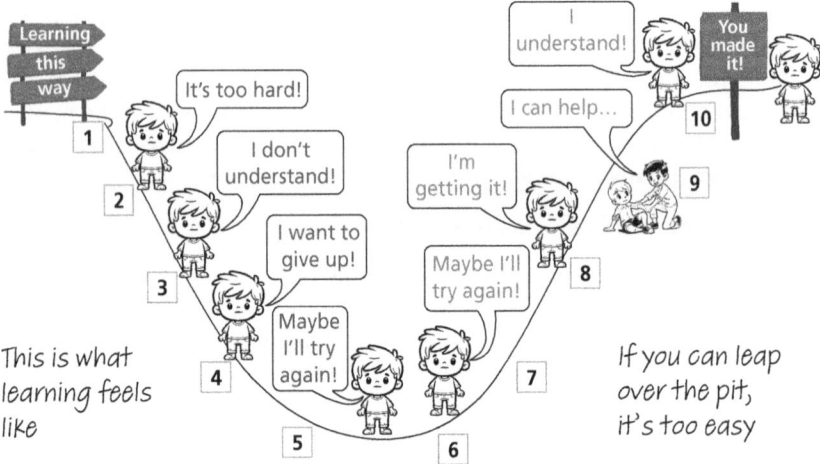

Pupils can experience many benefits by using the Learning Pit, such as:

- Improving attitudes towards challenging situations.
- Developing skills of learning.
- Deepening knowledge and understanding.
- Opportunities to carry out self-assessment.

When we used the Learning Pit for self-assessment in our classrooms, pupils would assess themselves against the learning objective at the beginning of the lesson and then again at the end. Not only did the pupils begin to understand and communicate their progress, but the teacher could see at a glance how they were assessing themselves against success criteria at the beginning and end of the lesson.

The pupils would annotate it like this:

Learning intention: To calculate areas of irregular shapes	Date: Thursday 14th October
Self-assessment: 2 (beginning) 8 (end)	

In this way, the teacher would know the following:

- That the pupils started the lesson with a little understanding.
- That they finished the lesson with a lot more understanding.
- Because they had not scored themselves '10', they needed a little more practice to be secure. They could get to '10' after recall and retrieval in the next lesson.

Common mistakes

Try to avoid the following mistakes when assessing and feeding back to primary pupils:

- Writing comments that they can't understand (particularly for younger pupils).
- For older pupils, making the written feedback too long and making comments unrelated to the task.
- Returning assessing and marking too late. The pupils will have forgotten the task and therefore assessment is then meaningless.
- Not giving pupils time or the opportunity to respond to the feedback. In the moment is much better, for example, than the next day or week.
- Not understanding common misconceptions and using them as a teaching aid.
- Not using WAGOLLs ('what a good one looks like').
- Not focusing on effort.
- Not noticing when too much help is given by peers.
- Not teaching pupils how to peer or self-assess well. They need to see modelling, WAGOLLS, worked examples and checklists.
- Not using end-of-term assessments to understand where pupils are at the start of the subsequent term.
- Not informing parents of progress or gaps in understanding.
- Not getting feedback from a teaching assistant who may have worked with a group.

Using technology in assessment

Technology can aid assessment in the classroom in many ways:

- Using a visualiser to look at examples of good work.
- Providing information in digital format allows cross-referencing of a wide range of examples.
- Use of digital tools makes it easier to give 'in-line feedback' so pupils can see to which section of their work a feedback comment refers. For example, during a writing task, having all pupils working on a Google doc means the teacher can 'live mark', providing in-the-moment feedback.
- Digital tools that support self, peer and group evaluation are all means of actively engaging pupils with success criteria and the process of making academic judgement.
- Using comparative judgement. Many primary schools now use a tool called No More Marking to assess pieces of written work against other pupils nationally. The tool also gives a comparative score for each pupil and each school. Comparative judgement works on the principle that people make better judgements if they compare two items and decide which is better, rather than try to evaluate each piece of work in isolation.

Achieving good public exam results in secondary schools

The ITTECF doesn't provide specific guidance on how teachers should go about getting good exam results for their pupils. The secret of success involves the following factors.

Before you begin...

You should make sure the following resources are available to you:

- The exam board syllabus.
- Past papers with answers and examiners' reports.
- Exam board-approved textbooks.
- Exam scripts done by former pupils that have been marked and returned to you by the exam board, and which show what a script looks like at each grade.

You should also make sure you have done a close study of past papers and know what questions come up, which are likely to come up and the level of answer required (the relationship between the mark awarded for a given question and the type of answer needed).

Then...

- You have to persuade pupils that hard work will pay off and good exam results will reward them in many ways.
- Make sure you test the pupils regularly, so they embed knowledge into the long-term memory. Anyone who does badly must be retested.
- Have formal mock exams twice a year so pupils get used to them.
- Make sure the pupils have good resources (e.g. notes and revision guides) to learn from.
- Finish the syllabus by the end of the spring term, leaving the summer term for revision.
- Tell the pupils' parents they need to be revising in the Easter holidays.
- Do plenty of practice papers and go over model answers.
- Become a public exam marker yourself, so you learn what a high-grade piece of work looks like.

What doesn't work?

- Trusting that pupils understand and learn the work. Many may have switched off and learned little, so you have to test them properly to discover the truth. You gave your pupils excellent notes, but they may do nothing with them.
- Trusting pupils to keep well-organised notes. If their notes are untidy and disorganised, they will find them impossible to learn, so you need to check them regularly.
- Learning by reading or highlighting books or notes.
- All the knowledge is on the screen. In fact, it's often easier to learn from the printed page than a screen.
- Giving the pupils poor marks but doing nothing about it except complaining. If a pupil gets poor marks, you have to get them to repeat the work at a better standard. This is what 'high expectations' actually means.

Coursework

Many subjects have coursework, and it's really important that the teacher is expecting the students to get a high mark. It doesn't matter whether your subject is art, physical education or geography, the rules are the same:

- Know what sorts of coursework themes work best. Study the rubric and speak to experienced teachers.
- Study the mark scheme carefully.
- Provide examples of good coursework to show the pupils. Every year, gather copies of the best work.

- For longer pieces, set short-term targets and mark them. It's no good just setting pupils off and leaving it to them – many will do the wrong thing. So, you need to set and check weekly tasks.
- Each pupil needs a personal supervisor for longer coursework.

Memorisation

We discussed ways in which pupils learn or revise in Chapter 5. As a reminder, the key points are:

- Talk with your class about the best ways to revise. This is metacognition = knowing what works for me.
- Make your teaching memorable, for example using field trips, practicals and images in addition to text (dual coding).
- Make sure your pupils have good notes and revision guides (which you can buy or make yourself).
- Focus on subject vocabulary and terminology that will be needed in most answers.
- Give regular tests and practice papers. Each test covers the past two weeks and all weeks before that.

In terms of the pupils revising, remember the following:

- The best way for your pupils to revise is to make notes from their notes (or revision texts). These notes can be turned into revision cards if they wish. Make sure they aren't passively reading or highlighting notes.
- This should immediately be followed by self-testing. This aids in driving information into the long-term memory and helps the pupils identify things they don't yet know.
- The pupils should convert any long articles into notes.

Grading in public exams

It is important to remember that marks and grades are not the same thing. Marks are of course given by the marker using a marking scheme, while grading is done by the exam boards under the direction of Ofqual.

Grades are determined in two ways:

1. The proportion of pupils getting each grade in each subject is very similar to the pattern of last year. This is called 'comparable outcomes' and is designed to prevent grade inflation. Each subject has a different grade distribution.
2. However, what happens if the students this year are actually better than those last year? This is dealt with in two ways:

- At GCSE, a large number of pupils take an English and maths test in March before the main exams; the questions set are the same every year. If a cohort does better in these tests than the previous cohorts, their grades will be allowed to inflate. These are the national reference tests.
- In all subjects, and especially those with small numbers of pupils, examiner judgement plays a role. If examiners can show that the quality of answers has risen, more pupils will get higher grades than those dictated by the comparable outcomes approach.

Marking quality in exams

Ofqual has done a great deal of research into marking quality. On the whole, they find that the quality is good. Markers mark online and often only mark a limited range of the questions set. Answers that have already been marked by expert markers are seeded into the answers being marked by each marker. If they mark the seed answer wrongly, they are stopped and retrained.

Measuring progress

There are two ways of interpreting summative assessment data:

1. Looking at the **raw results** and how they compare to other pupils in the cohort. The DfE publishes data on results for your school so you can see this (search for 'Compare the performance of schools and colleges in England').
2. Analysing the **progress** made by the pupils over time compared to other pupils who were at a similar level at the beginning of this period. This is sometimes called '**value-added**'. There are two obvious examples of this: the progress made from the KS2 SATs and GCSEs, which is called Progress 8, and the progress made between GCSEs and A-levels. In both cases, every pupil's relative progress is determined by comparing them with every pupil who got the same score at the start of the period (for example, the same SATs results).

One flaw with progress scores is that the result will depend on the validity of the score at the start of the time period. For example, if a secondary school recruits pupils from more disadvantaged primary schools, it is more likely to get better Progress 8 scores because the pupils' SATs results were less good than they might have been.

But progress scores are much better than raw exam results when judging a school. Some schools take many pupils from disadvantaged backgrounds and their raw results may be weak, but their progress scores can be strong.

Many schools use the A-level performance system (Alps), which shows how their A-level results compare with the A-level results of other pupils in the country with similar GCSE results. A school can see which subjects get the best value-added and which pupils achieved the best value-added. It also allows schools to predict A-level results from a pupil's GCSE grades, which in turn allows schools to set target grades for individual students.

Summative assessment in primary schools

Here are the tests that state primary schools are required to administer:

The RBA and EYFSP

Teachers are required to complete the RBA (reception baseline assessment) with pupils within the first six weeks after they enter reception. Assessments must then continue throughout the academic year for any pupils who join reception and have not already participated in the RBA.

The assessment needs to be carried out on a one-to-one basis by a practitioner who is known to the pupil. This is usually the class teacher but doesn't need to be; it could also be a reception teaching assistant or suitably qualified practitioner, such as an early years leader or SENCO.

In the final term of the year in which pupils reach age five (reception), and by 30th June in that term, the EYFSP (Early Years Foundation Stage profile) has to be completed for each child. This is therefore usually undertaken by reception teachers. By completing the RBA and EYFSP, progress across the year can be measured.

Year 1 phonics screening

The phonics screening check is taken individually by all pupils in Year 1, usually in June. It is designed to give teachers and parents information on how a child is progressing in phonics. It will help to identify whether they need additional support at this early stage, so they don't fall behind with early reading skills. It is a standardised test administered ideally in a low-stakes environment on a one-to-one basis, usually with a familiar Year 1 teacher. It is a 40-word test designed to check that the child can:

- Sound out and blend graphemes in order to read simple words.
- Read phonically decodable one- and two-syllable words, e.g. cat, sand or windmill.
- Read a selection of nonsense words that are referred to as pseudo or alien words. These are words that are phonically decodable but aren't actual words with an associated meaning e.g. 'brop' or 'snarb'. These words are included in the check to assess whether a child is able to decode a word using purely phonics skills and not their memory.

KS1 SATs and teacher assessments

Starting from autumn 2024, KS1 SATs have been non-statutory. If they are still used, they are now internally moderated and marked. The optional tests are designed to assess pupils' knowledge and understanding of the KS1 programmes of study. Schools can choose to use these to support the measurement of pupil attainment.

The optional KS1 tests are in reading, English grammar, punctuation and spelling and maths. They are not designed to be strictly timed. It is recommended that teachers use their discretion to decide if pupils need a rest break during any of the tests or whether, if appropriate, to stop a test early.

Schools deciding not to use the optional tests must assess the learning of their KS1 pupils in different ways to ensure there is still assessment against the KS1 programmes of study.

Year 4 MTC

The MTC (multiplication tables check) is statutory for all Year 4 pupils registered at state-funded maintained schools, special schools or academies, including free schools, in England. It is normally administered in the first two weeks of June.

The purpose of the MTC is to determine whether pupils can recall their times tables fluently, which is essential for future success in mathematics. It will help schools to identify pupils who haven't yet mastered their times tables so that additional support can be provided.

KS2 SATs

At some point in the middle of May each year, Year 6 pupils undertake formalised testing, which is reported nationally and used as a measure of the academic success of a state school.

The externally marked KS2 tests consist of:

- English grammar, punctuation and spelling paper 1: questions
- English grammar, punctuation and spelling paper 2: spelling
- English reading
- Mathematics paper 1: arithmetic
- Mathematics paper 2: reasoning
- Mathematics paper 3: reasoning
- English grammar, punctuation and spelling test

Criticism of primary summative tests

Some arguments made against primary summative tests include:

- They are stressful for pupils.
- Focus on 'teaching to the test' can cause the Year 6 curriculum to become too narrow.
- They take one full week to administer, detracting from teaching time.
- The results are often not used by secondary schools, some of which choose to undertake their own baseline tests in Year 7.
- There is too much emphasis on reading ability, even the ability to read the questions in the maths tests.
- The reading test sometimes requires a higher level of cultural capital.

Types of summative assessment in secondary schools

Written exams

Strengths of written exams include:

- They are fair, meaning everyone takes a similar exam and cheating is hard. In a high-stakes system, this matters a lot.
- An exam forces pupils to memorise the subject, which is a fundamental aspect of education.
- The exams include easy and harder questions, which yield a good range of marks. You need a good range of marks, because one purpose of an exam is to differentiate between the best and lower attainment pupils.

Weaknesses of written exams include:

- Written exams create some stress, although there's no evidence that this lowers performance.
- Written exams only sample the syllabus.
- Marking of longer questions is quite subjective. Different markers may give different marks, leading to unreliable grades in subjects that are tested by essays, such as English and history. This is clear from the research undertaken by Ofqual (2018), who compared the marks given by less experienced markers with the marks given by more experienced markers. It is perfectly possible for those marking a given essay to award a mark of 18, 19 or 20 out of 25 and each of those marks to be legitimate and acceptable (this is called 'marking tolerance'). But this tolerance of a range of possible marks means that two pupils with identical answers could end up with different overall grades.

- Of course, written exams are a poor way of assessing some physical or practical skills, such as the ability to dance.
- Written exams are sat in 'unreal' environments, such as the exam hall.

Coursework and portfolios

Strengths of coursework and portfolios include:

- Coursework written over time and outside an exam hall is in some ways a better way of assessing, as it may encourage greater creativity and independence and there is less emphasis on memory.
- Coursework is essential for some creative subjects such as design and technology, art and music.
- The Extended Project Qualification (EPQ) is attempted every year by many of the best sixth formers. It allows pupils to research a subject that is valuable but that they may not be being taught at A-level, and allows sixth formers to develop research skills and universities like it.

Weaknesses of coursework and portfolios include:

- Cheating is common – teachers and parents provide too much help. Ofqual sometimes finds coursework marks are bunched at the top end.
- AI also allows pupils to cheat with coursework. Quite often they cheat because they know that rank orders matter and they fear the other pupils will cheat, pushing them down the ranks.
- Coursework creates a lot of work for teachers.
- Continuous assessment by coursework turns the whole course into an exam.
- Coursework can be formulaic and dull (as was the case with controlled assessments in the period 2005–2015).
- Coursework requires external moderators, which adds to the cost.
- External moderation is impossible for big exams like GCSE English, where there are simply too many pupils to moderate.
- Coursework can't be marked as accurately as a written exam. Different markers give a wide range of different marks.
- Teacher-assessment is certainly biased – it tends to be too generous. We saw this in 2020 and 2021, when exams were not sat and teachers were asked to give grades.

Oral exams

Oral exams are effective because they support speaking as opposed to writing skills. They are quite safe from cheating but are harder to mark consistently and moderate between different schools.

Multiple-choice questions

If you are writing multiple-choice questions (MCQs), here are a few tips:

- Provide 3–4 options. Fewer than three is too easy, whereas more than four takes too long.
- Avoid easy answers.
- Every answer option should be viable, i.e. not obviously wrong.
- Avoid 'none of the above' as an option, as pupils are likely to assume this is the correct answer.
- Target possible misconceptions so you know whether the pupils have 'got it'.

Strengths of MCQs include:

- They are straightforward for most pupils to do.
- They are quick to mark.
- They can be a quick way of detecting levels of knowledge and understanding.

One major weakness of MCQs is that they are better for factual recall than more analytical topics.

Have a look at *Examining exams: Are there credible alternatives to written examinations?* (Richmond and Regan, 2023). They conclude that written exams are still the fairest system:

> *[Written exams] are a relatively low-cost, standardised and impartial way to assess students' knowledge and understanding, with a much lower probability of being affected by malpractice or inconsistent grading than other methods of assessment. The controlled setting in which exams normally take place also means that students, parents, universities, employers and the government can have confidence that the awarded grades are a genuine reflection of a student's attainment.*

The future of Common Entrance

The former Minister of State for Schools, Sir Nick Gibb, said several times that he was jealous of the 13+ Common Entrance (CE) exam because it drove prep school pupils to a much higher level than those in the state sector of the same age. Is this true? And if so, why have some prep schools abandoned the CE?

CE used to be an exam that pupils had to pass to get into good senior schools. This is still the case with some senior schools, but not as many. The reason is that in the 2000s more senior schools followed Eton by introducing 'pre-selection tests' for applicants when they were 10 or 11. This had the advantage that fewer pupils would fail at CE stage, a good thing given that the results emerge in June, only three months before the September entry to the new school.

So, if the sifting of pupils happens at age 11, why bother with 13+ CE at all? I believe there are good reasons for having CE exams, even if the grades achieved may not matter much for entry to senior school.

First and most importantly, CE exams motivate pupils in years 7 and 8 and help to drive their knowledge into the long-term memory. This is because as long as they can be persuaded that they need to do well in CE, even if only for setting purposes in the senior school, pupils will work harder. Material learned at CE will still be in the memory when the pupils get to GCSE, so CE leads to good preparation.

Another big advantage is that if most pupils have taken CE, senior schools know what they know. Senior schools can build on this with that knowledge and avoid the fatal mistake of repeating work that pupils have already done. The CE syllabi have generally been written by prep school teachers and they are constantly updated. They are accessible to most pupils but sufficiently demanding to stretch the more able.

All independent schools live or die by providing what parents want. What most parents want from a prep school is for their children to come out with reasonable written English, pretty good maths, a grasp of a least one modern language and a well-rounded appreciation of science, computing, history, geography, religious studies, art, music and design and technology. They want their children to have enjoyed their time at school, be well-behaved and to have gained confidence across a range of traditional subjects as well as sports and drama.

Pupils at prep schools learn less by the age of 13 than was the case 30 years ago — just look at CE past papers. But they learn more than they would do without this long-standing and valuable set of exams.

References

Black, P. and William, D., 1998, *Inside the Black Box: Raising Standards Through Classroom Assessment*, King's College London, GL Assessment Ltd.

Black, P. and Wiliam, D., 2009, Developing the theory of formative assessment. Educational Assessment, Evaluation and Accountability, 21(1), 5–13.

Burns, M., and Griffith, A., 2014, *Outstanding Teaching: Teaching Backwards*, Crown House Publishing, UK.

Coe, R., 2013, *Improving Education: A Triumph of Hope Over Experience*. Centre for Evaluation and Monitoring.

Education Endowment Foundation, 2021, Teacher Feedback to Improve Pupil Learning Guidance Report. Online.

Kluger, A., and DeNisi, A., 1996, The effects of feedback interventions on performance: a historical review, a meta-analysis and a preliminary feedback intervention theory, Psychological Bulletin, 119(2) 254–284.

McGill, R., 2023, *The Teacher Toolkit Guide to Questioning*, Bloomsbury.

McGill, R., 2024, *The Teacher Toolkit Guide to Feedback*, Bloomsbury.

Ofqual, 2018, *Marking consistency metrics: An update*, Ofqual.

Richmond, T. and Regan, E., 2023, Examining exams: Are there credible alternatives to written examinations? EDSK.

Speckesser, S., Runge, J., Foliano, F., Bursnall, M., Hudson-Sharp, N., Rolfe, H. and Anders, J., 2018, *Embedding Formative Assessment: Evaluation Report and Executive Summary*, Education Endowment Foundation.

Chapter 10
Managing behaviour

ITTECF syllabus

Managing behaviour (Standard 7 – Manage behaviour effectively)

Learn that...	Learn how to...
1. Establishing and reinforcing routines, including through positive reinforcement, can help create an effective learning environment. 2. A predictable and secure environment benefits all pupils, including younger pupils, but is particularly valuable for pupils with special educational needs. 3. The ability to self-regulate one's emotions affects pupils' ability to learn, success in school and future lives. 4. Teachers can influence pupils' resilience and beliefs about their ability to succeed, by ensuring all pupils have the opportunity to experience meaningful success. 5. Building effective relationships is easier when pupils believe that their feelings will be considered and understood. 6. Pupils are motivated by intrinsic factors (related to their identity and values) and extrinsic factors (related to reward). 7. Pupils' investment in learning is also driven by their prior experiences and perceptions of success and failure.	**Develop a positive, predictable and safe environment for pupils, by:** a) Establishing a supportive and inclusive environment with a predictable system of reward and sanction in the classroom. b) Working alongside colleagues as part of a wider system of behaviour management (e.g. recognising responsibilities and understanding the right to assistance and training from senior colleagues particularly where pupils exhibit unacceptable behaviours). c) Giving manageable, specific and sequential instructions. d) Checking pupils' understanding of instructions before a task begins. e) Using consistent language and non-verbal signals for common classroom directions. f) Using early and least-intrusive interventions as an initial response to low level disruption. g) Responding quickly to any behaviour or bullying that threatens physical or emotional safety. **Establish effective routines and expectations, by:** h) Creating and explicitly teaching routines in line with the school ethos that maximise time for learning (e.g. setting and reinforcing expectations about key transition points).

Learn that...	Learn how to...
8. Teaching and modelling a range of social and emotional skills (e.g. how to recognise and understand feelings, manage emotions, and sustain positive relationships) can support pupils' social and emotional development. 9. Teaching typically expected behaviours will reduce the need to manage misbehaviour. 10. Pupils who need a tailored approach to support their behaviour do not necessarily have SEND and pupils with SEND will not necessarily need additional support with their behaviour. 11. A key influence on a pupil's behaviour in school is being the victim of bullying.	i) Practising school and classroom routines at the beginning of the school year. j) Reinforcing established school and classroom routines (e.g. by articulating the link between time on task and success). k) Working with the SENCO, other SEND specialists or expert colleagues if a pupil needs more intensive support with their behaviour to understand how the approach may need to be adapted to their individual needs. **Build trusting relationships, by:** l) Liaising with parents, carers and colleagues to better understand pupils' individual circumstances and how they can be supported to meet high academic and behavioural expectations. m) Consistently applying the school's behaviour policy, including where individual pupils have an agreed tailored approach. **Motivate pupils, by:** n) Supporting pupils to master challenging content, which builds towards long-term goals. o) Providing opportunities for pupils to articulate their long-term goals and helping them to see how these are related to their success in school. p) Helping pupils to journey from needing extrinsic motivation to being motivated to work intrinsically. **Develop pupils' self regulation by:** q) Helping pupils to think through scenarios before they occur and using cues to help them recall agreed upon behaviours. r) Providing new opportunities to exercise self-regulation and for the youngest pupils to practise impulse control.

Without good behaviour, little can be achieved

When it comes to the behaviour of pupils, much depends on the institutional context. Some schools have systems and head teachers who establish good behaviour, making the teacher's task easier, but some don't. Behaviour in your classroom will depend more on your own systems and personality. Some schools have amenable pupils, while others don't.

There are two types of behaviour that we should be concerned about:

1. Messing about and breaking rules.
2. Failure to do work properly, or at all.

In this chapter, we are mainly concerned with the first type.

A Teacher Tapp survey (2024) asked the question, 'What forms of disruption did you experience in the last lesson you taught?' The survey found that in primary classrooms, disruptive fidgeting was the number one disruptive behaviour (61%), whereas in secondary classrooms, inappropriate talking or chatting happened the most frequently (53%).

Behaviour in primary schools

In the primary classroom, low-level disruption involves:

● Fiddling with equipment or fidgeting.
● Talking when the teacher is speaking.
● Calling out answers.
● Being slow to start work or follow instructions.
● Showing a lack of respect for the other pupils and staff.
● Not having the right equipment.
● Being inappropriate, e.g. slurping from a water bottle.

To mitigate for some of these things, certain rules are necessary. Sometimes, these may be covered by general class rules, for example 'ready, respectful and safe'. In other cases, more specific rules may be needed, such as:

● 'We don't speak when others are talking.'
● 'We don't call out.'
● 'We use indoor voices in the classroom.'
● 'We can only drink from our water bottles before the lesson begins.'

Some primary schools use a combination of rewards and sanctions.

Sanctions

Sanctions may include a loss of breaktime or lunchtime for a serious breach in behaviour. However, more subtle mechanisms can be used by the primary teacher for less serious breaches. It may be that basic body language, such as a look in the direction of the interrupting pupil or a pause in the middle of a sentence, is sufficient for the pupil to check themselves and get back on track. It may be that a simple quiet word is needed (note, this is more effective than a reprimand in front of the class). Or it may be a discussion after the lesson has ended, such as the following example:

Teacher: Why did you snatch the pencil from him?

Pupil: Because he wouldn't let me borrow it.

Teacher: Is it acceptable to snatch something from someone's hand?

Pupil: No.

Teacher: What would have been a better thing to do?

Pupil: Ask him for it when he had finished with it?

Teacher: Yes, I think so. Can you remember that next time?

Pupil: Yes, I'll try to remember.

Teacher: Ok, so you try and remember next time. You can go to break now.

Rewards

Rewards can include stars, stickers, class points, a marble placed in the class jar, house points, letters home, dojo points, certificates or post cards. Class rewards may be given, for example extra playtime for the whole class on the completion of a full 'marbles in the jar' or a full recognition board.

Recognition boards are an idea suggested by Paul Dix (2017). They are an effective means of ensuring everyone in the class is successful in relation to a given target. Ordinarily this will be a target or expectation set on a Monday morning, either by the class teacher or another teacher during assembly. An example may be, 'Everyone has to try to use good manners as much as possible this week.'

As an example, Tariq starts off his lesson by asking his teacher, 'Please can you say that again?' The teacher's response will be to place Tariq's name or photograph onto the recognition board. Throughout the remainder of the week, pupils are placed on the board as they demonstrate similar behaviour or attitude to work. By Friday afternoon, anyone who has not made it onto the board will be invited to try to do or say something that will grant them a position on the board, so that by the end of the week everyone has been successful. This is an incredibly powerful tool to use in a primary school as it's simultaneously motivating and rewarding.

Establishing and reinforcing routines

You need to establish routines from the outset. Much of the first few days of the school year should be spent expressing your expectations in terms of behaviour and classroom culture. There is likely to be a school behaviour policy or a relationships and behaviour policy (we know of the importance of getting relationships right in primary), so take your lead from the school policy.

Some teachers like to set up a class charter on the very first day, with expectations listed and displayed in the classroom as constant reminders. Make sure that these are positively framed – you can use the following examples.

Don't use 'don't'	Do use 'do'
'Don't run indoors.'	'Do remember to walk indoors.'
'Don't interrupt others.'	'Do wait until someone has finished speaking.'
'Don't shout in the classroom.'	'Do speak quietly and politely.'
'Don't be unkind to others.'	'Do be kind.'

If you use 'we', for example, 'We remember to walk indoors', then the expectation is that we work collaboratively as a team to make these things happen. You can also use dual coding if your class are younger, so that they can refer to a picture as well as writing, for example:

- Remember to walk
- We speak quietly and politely

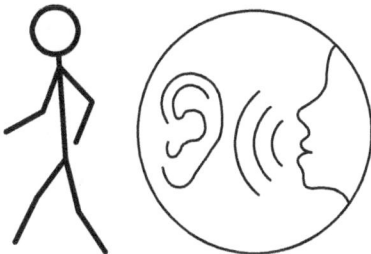

These charters can then be signed by all pupils to show that everyone has agreed to them. One new teacher I observed used to get his pupils to read them aloud at the beginning of every lesson as a reminder. It is easy to forget to establish all your routines and expectations, so consider these examples and tell the pupils what you expect. Think about the following questions and get your pupils to practice regularly.

- How will they come into the classroom? Quietly? Lined up?
- Where will they go in the classroom once they are in? Do you want them on the carpet or in their seats?
- How will they transition from their tables to the carpet and back again?

The most important thing to remember is that no learning will take place if behaviour is poor, so don't be tempted to move on to the learning until the behaviour is right. You can get your class to practise routines over and over again until they are perfect if necessary.

Silent hand signals

We all agree that there must be a stable and positive learning environment in our schools. We know that pupils benefit from calm and consistent behaviour management strategies and their teachers making their expectations very clear. Children feel safer when the environment is relaxed and predictable, so it's worth using the same routines all the time for behaviour management.

One simple and effective way this can be achieved is through agreed silent signals. There are several uses of silent signals that you can try in your classroom.

Team 'stop' signal

The 'stop' method involves the following steps:

1. The teacher raises their hand and doesn't speak.
2. They then smile.
3. A magical domino effect happens, as children return the signal.
4. All the pupils return the signal, looking at the teacher and keeping their hands still.
5. The teacher scans the room to make sure all the pupils have stopped.
6. The teacher drops their hand when the room is silent, and only then starts talking.

The 1, 2, 3 routine

This routine aims to move the children silently from carpet to table in under 15 seconds:

1. The teacher uses the team STOP signal.
2. They hold up one finger for 'children stand'.

3. They hold up two fingers for 'children walk and stand behind your chairs'.
4. They hold up three fingers for 'children sit down and prepare to read or write'.

And in reverse, you can move the children from table to carpet in under 15 seconds:

1. Hold up one finger for 'children stand behind their chairs'.
2. Hold up two fingers for 'children walk to carpet'.
3. Hold up three fingers for 'children sit down beside their partners'.

Turn to your partner (TTYP) signal

Partner work should be used consistently in all lessons:

1. Get the pupils to hold both hands pointing forward as if they are two open gates.
2. Get them to close the gates as soon as you have finished asking the question.
3. Show the pupils how they should turn their heads towards their partners, not their whole body or chair. This can be done without the noise of moving chairs and therefore used often in the lesson.

Practise this signal until children immediately turn to their partners to answer a question. Once children do this automatically, you will no longer need to say the words 'turn to your partner'.

Behaviour in secondary schools

You must decide how strict you are going to be. Normally, you will be strict to start with and then less strict when you feel under control. But don't be afraid of being strict – it is kinder to the majority of pupils if they feel safe and their learning is not disrupted by a minority of other pupils. Sometimes, you need to be strict to be kind.

But being strict doesn't mean being mean and unsmiling. Behaviour in your classroom will be better if you have a good relationship with your pupils, so you can certainly greet pupils by name as they arrive. You should show an interest in their lives and be kind to them. Being kind doesn't mean you can't also be clear and firm about what behaviour you expect.

In the classroom

Setting standards

You must demand good behaviour. You are the adult, and you are in charge. You need to be bold and appear to be sure of yourself – this may just be acting of course, but a good teacher often needs to be a good actor. The good news is that most pupils want you to maintain control, as they don't want their lessons disrupted.

If you tolerate poor behaviour, such as pupils chatting when you are talking, you are encouraging poor behaviour. You must be 100% clear what the rules are, and you must explain them to your pupils in very simple terms. Introduce pupils to the rules and expectations of the classroom in their first lesson of the school year. Give precise directions on what to do, not what *not* to do. Make sure your response to poor behaviour is very predictable.

Remember that some pupils may not know what good behaviour looks like as they come from difficult backgrounds, so they must be taught what good behaviour means and why it matters. They need boundaries, and you need to set them.

Sanctions

You need a system of sanctions that the pupils understand. Normally this system will be determined by the school. There will be a hierarchy of responses (warning, final warning, detention), although for certain offences there will be a fixed punishment, such as a detention for failing to produce homework.

But your aim should be to *not use* the school punishments, but achieve good order without them by using your own methods and the power of your personality. If you have a good relationship with your pupils, good behaviour is more likely (but not certain).

Praise

Praise pupils doing the right thing in order to convey a positive message to the others, for example, 'Well done Maria for making a good start on the work.' This is much better than shouting, 'Come on most of you haven't even started!'

Acknowledging good behaviour encourages repetition and communicates the school's expectations and values to the pupils. In 2024, my nephew got mixed academic end-of-term reports, but then he received a postcard from the head of pastoral praising him for his positivity and his good influence on his boarding house. Reinforcing the positive is just as important as pointing out weaknesses.

But don't feel you should always give rewards for good behaviour. This undermines what you are trying to achieve, which is *intrinsic* motivation, not a system that relies on bribes.

Bad behaviour will make you feel bad

Insults from pupils may make you feel angry, but whatever your feelings may be, you must hide them. Some pupils get a kick out of making teachers angry.

Use the minimum force to achieve the good behaviour you seek

Try not to interrupt a lesson; just shoot a quick look at the two pupils chatting so they know you know – a quiet stare rather than shouting. Telling a pupil to see you at the end of the lesson is often better than a full-scale shaking down in the middle of a lesson.

Be firm but calm. Persistence and consistency are key to developing relationships of trust with pupils, especially vulnerable or highly challenging ones. Pupils want to be valued, and you cannot convey that if you are in a permanent state of opposition with them.

If a pupil is really offensive, you need to de-escalate

Here are some methods for de-escalating if a pupil is very difficult:

- Speak to them quietly.
- Bob down to their level rather than towering over them.
- Focus on the work to be done rather than the offence.
- Use humour and a light touch rather than being angry.

Some infringements of rules should be ignored

Sometimes you should ignore minor misbehaviour in favour of maintaining good relations and preventing disruption during the lesson. For example, with a pupil whose tie is not done up properly, you will still aim to get them to do up their tie, but this is not something that should cause a row in the middle of a lesson. You may overhear a pupil swearing, but you can choose to ignore it.

Never make criticism of a pupil personal

'You are a lazy boy' is much less likely to result in improvement than, 'You *can* produce good work on time and tomorrow you need to do so.'

Never punish a whole class

Punishing a whole class is unfair on those who are keener to learn, who may then respect you less. If anything, it's better to pick on one or two and use them as an example to the rest.

Use support systems

If you feel you are losing control of a class, you need to ask the right senior leader to help you. Don't be too proud to do this – even very experienced teachers face this problem from time to time.

You are on their side

Explain to the pupils that your aim is to get good results for them, and that this is why good behaviour is essential. Demonstrate regularly that they are making good progress.

Trust

Some teenagers are capable of behaving very badly and generally should not be trusted – though you may still like them. So, on a school trip, for example, they shouldn't be given any opportunity to misbehave. Rules must be very clear and enforced properly.

Bad behaviour during break and lunch time is common, so if you're on duty then, be clear what you're supposed to do in any particular situation.

SEND

If a pupil has special needs that affect their behaviour, the school will need to consider what the law requires. Standards of behaviour should still be upheld, but sometimes adaptations are necessary.

Technology

A lot of bad behaviour is associated with smartphones and bullying on social media. All schools will have policies about this, and wise schools ban smartphones.

Make lessons interesting

Good behaviour is much more likely if your lesson has pace and the pupils are given plenty of interesting work to do. You will be better at controlling the lesson if you are confident within yourself, and you will be more likely to be confident if you are on top of what you are going to teach. This involves good teaching notes and you knowing what to do with them.

Dealing with individuals

If a pupil is troublesome, you're going to need to find time to talk to them quietly. Try asking the pupil questions about themselves and listening carefully to their replies. Make the child feel that you care about them. Some children have experienced adverse childhood experiences, and this may lie behind behaviour such as refusing to work, bullying others or running away.

Systems

In his book, *Teach Like a Champion*, Doug Lemov advocates training pupils to respond quickly to two words. This technique drives good behaviour and academic engagement, but it has to be taught first. It is worth seeing the films Doug has made of teachers using these methods successfully: rb.gy/ztwrnn.

The first word the teacher can say is 'star', which stands for:

● Sit up, look interested and stay engaged.
● Track (look at) the speaker to show other people their ideas matter.
● Appreciate your classmates' ideas by nodding and smiling when they speak.
● Rephrase the words of the person who spoke before you, so they know you were listening.

The second word the teacher can say is 'slant', which stands for:

● Sit up.
● Listen.
● Ask and answer questions.
● Nod your head to show engagement.
● Track the speaker.

Many schools have two other systems in place:

● 5-4-3-2-1, which is where you give an instruction and then count down. By the time you get to 1, everyone should have completed the task and then be silent and looking at you.
● The one voice rule, where only one person can be speaking at any moment.

New teachers are often more concerned about behaviour than anything. This is understandable but remember that your main task is to teach them something worthwhile.

Smartphones and social media

In 2024, Jonathan Haidt published his influential book, *The Anxious Generation*, about the impact of smartphones on the mental health of children and young people. Many head teachers have concluded that smartphones are the source of issues in schools, including bullying, anxiety and an inability to concentrate.

Children playing with phones at night get less sleep, and this, too, impacts their mental health and learning.

In 2024, the large Ormiston Academies Trust started to phase out smartphones in school. Parent groups like 'Smartphone Free Childhood' have formed in some schools to work together to not buy their children smartphones. Mobile phones have already been banned from schools in several countries, including France and China.

Research evidence

Ward, A., Duke, K., Gneezy, A., and Boz, M., 2017, *Brain drain: the mere presence of one's own smartphone reduces available cognitive capacity*, Journal of the Association for Consumer Research, 2(2).

These researchers brought college students into a lab and randomly sorted them in three groups: those who left their phone outside the lab, those who kept their phone in a pocket or bag and those who had their phone on the desk next to them. They were then given cognitive tasks to measure memory and intelligence. Those who did best left their phones outside, those who did worst had the phone on the desk, with the group with pocketed phones in the middle.

Bullying and peer-on-peer abuse

For many children and young people, the worst thing that happens to them in school is being bullied by other children. Much of this is analysed in the DfE's 'Keeping children safe in education' guidance. There are many types and levels of bullying, but all can be deeply damaging to the victims. As a teacher, you need to be quick to identify bullying of any sort and never turn a blind eye. When you are at the beginning of your career, you must report any incident or concerns so more senior colleagues will investigate and take action where needed.

Sometimes bullies say, 'I was only joking', and of course this may be true. But adolescents are bad at identifying the fine line between a joke and saying something very hurtful. So, incidents of bullying, including name-calling, often require careful investigation and action by schools. Children and teenagers can be very nasty.

Much is reported in the media about adults who have abused school-age children, but the vast majority of abuse in schools is children bullying other children. It is your job to report any concerns you might have.

Sexual abuse

In 2020, a website called 'Everyone's Invited' was created, which encouraged young people, especially girls, to report cases of abusive sexual behaviour by teenage boys. Thousands of entries were made, and Ofsted was asked to review the situation, publishing the *Review of Sexual Abuse in Schools and Colleges* in 2021. This revealed a very serious problem and has resulted in a rethinking of relationships education for young people in most schools.

Attendance

The worst issue regarding behaviour may be non-attendance, because if the pupil is not there nothing can be learned. Children who attend school regularly are twice as likely to achieve good GCSEs in English and maths as those who are frequently absent.

In the school year 2022–23, 150,000 children in England were recorded as being absent every other day (half of all teaching time). There can be many reasons for non-attendance, ranging from the understandable ('I had a music lesson') to truancy. The increase in parents working from home has led many to be more relaxed about their children missing school, particularly on Fridays, despite parents' legal duty to ensure their attendance. Poor mental health is often cited as being a driver behind school absences.

Whatever the reason, you need to do two things:

1. Report non-attendance using the system used by your school.
2. Make a note of the non-attendance (such as a cross in your mark book) and take action to help the pupil to catch up ('do the homework you missed by next Tuesday', 'copy Samantha's notes by Monday'), and then check these things happened.

All pupils need good notes to revise from, so if a pupil has missed a great deal, you will need to copy notes for them and go over the notes at a time you can both manage. This is one of the ways that absent pupils greatly increase the workload of teachers.

Some children are classified as 'school refusers'. School refusers usually say they want to go to school but they can't because of some distress that makes them angry or tearful. Parents often don't know what to do, so they need help from schools, mental health professionals and local authorities.

Behaviour management in primary schools

If the lesson is pitched right, behaviour will be better. As we mentioned in the planning chapter, don't be afraid to drop your lesson plan if needed. You can restart it if you need to, ensuring it is pitched more accurately for your pupils.

Think about timings – younger pupils need more frequent breaks. Don't expect them to sit on the carpet for too long. Similarly, if they are working at their desks, frequent checking on the learning will help to break up time for them. Get them to stop, turn and look at you, then remind them of objectives, or move them onto the next chunk in their learning. Get them to discuss their work with a partner. Just as important is not to disturb them too often – you will get this right when you get to know your class better.

'The Behaviour You Walk Past is the Behaviour You Accept'

This was a poster that was created in one of the schools I led. It was on the inside of the staffroom door, so all teachers read it as they left the staffroom. As Barnaby says, 'If you tolerate poor behaviour, such as pupils chatting when you are talking, you are encouraging poor behaviour.' It is so important to remember this. If you ignore bad behaviour, the message you are giving to your pupils is that it is acceptable.

You are the boss. You tell them what is acceptable and what is not, ALL THE TIME.

Some pupils will try to push the boundaries. They need to know where the boundaries are, so you have to constantly remind them. They may not have firm boundaries at home, so they need to test things in the classroom, to see whether the rules at school are the same as the ones at home. This is human nature, and children feel much, much safer when they know the boundaries.

The Early Thank You

'Maya, please can you stop talking, thank you.' 'Callum, please remember to walk indoors, thank you.' Your early 'thank you' implies consent and indicates an expectation that the action will be done without question. This works well – another little magic trick for you to try.

Rewards

Some schools have a fixed set of rewards and sanctions. Make sure you know what these are, as it is much easier to follow the school policy and it creates consistency across year groups. Rewards might include things such as:

- Stickers or stars
- Table points, house points

- Genuine, specific praise (let them know what you are praising)
- Certificates, notes or calls home

Whatever your reward system, it needs to be clear and fair. Parents will want to know what these systems are. I always found that group or table points often worked more effectively than individual ones as it engendered a sense of group responsibility. But this will not work if one pupil is constantly spoiling it for others. Pupil voice can be a powerful way of setting rewards and sanctions – Year 6 pupils, for example, may not be too keen on stickers. Ask them what matters to them.

In terms of fairness and consistency, try to avoid over-rewarding the child with challenging behaviour simply for doing the right thing. Others will be doing the right thing consistently and not be noticed or rewarded for doing so.

At one of my schools, once we had established a culture of high expectations and good behaviour, we got rid of the rewards listed above. We decided that, however well we tried, sometimes we were missing pupils' good behaviour. So we eradicated all rewards and instead had this in our Behaviour Policy:

High standards of behaviour are expected at New Marston School, therefore we do not often reward good behaviour. The reward system at New Marston is based predominantly on the class Recognition Board.

Every classroom has a Recognition Board that staff will use to reward a specific characteristic derived from Monday Values Assemblies. Examples include being a good partner, showing excellent manners and asking thoughtful questions. The expectation is that every child will be recognised throughout the week as achieving this in some way. The theme is introduced in the Monday assembly and recapped in the Friday assembly.

Sanctions or restorative approaches?

Many schools have a system of sanctions that can be used if behaviour is not good. These are often stipulated in a behaviour or relationships policy. Below is again, an example from the same school:

Dealing with Negative Behaviour

Although the emphasis is always on encouraging positive behaviour, we have used a formalised system for dealing with instances of disruptive and harmful behaviour. Teachers can deal with disruptive behaviour by using the steps [on page 220].

Steps	
1	Positive reinforcement of other children around them
2	A private conversation with the child
3	Another private conversation followed by a choice and a consequence
4	Time out in a neighbouring/parallel class (or on the edge of the playground during breaktime)
5	Time out with a senior member of staff

Examples of the kind of behaviour that would lead to a child moving towards these steps include:

● Name-calling or rudeness
● Lack of effort
● Refusal to cooperate with staff or fellow students
● Preventing other children from working
● Minor physical acts

Serious Offences

Some serious offences may require a greater or quicker level of action e.g. wilful damage to school property, seriously disrupting the learning of others and violence. On occasions such as this, a senior member of staff or a member of the Inclusion Team will be called, using another child if urgent. In these circumstances the parents will be informed and a record made.

Racist or homophobic incidents are not tolerated and will be recorded on the school safeguarding system. For a first offence, a conversation with the child and teacher plus a member of SLT will be held and recorded. For a second offence a restorative session will be held along with a meeting with parents/carers. For any further offences, exclusions and/or an Individual Behaviour Plan may be considered, along with the involvement of outside agencies.

Restorative approaches

Restorative practices in schools are a way of resolving conflict that focuses on repairing harm and building relationships. They are non-punitive approaches that aim to create a culture of support and challenge and work with people rather than doing things to them.

Some benefits of restorative practices in schools include:

● **Improved conflict resolution** – Restorative practices can reduce disruption to teaching and learning and improve relationships and the school environment.

- **Improved emotional competencies** – Restorative practices can help develop empathy, self-discipline and more responsible decision making.
- **Improved understanding of social responsibility** – Restorative practices can help pupils develop an understanding of social responsibility and the responsibility to make things right.

Restorative practices can include:

- **Restorative conversations** – Even if a formal punishment is given, restorative conversations can help pupils understand how they have affected others.
- **Restorative questions** – Questions can be used to help pupils who have caused harm, reflecting on what happened, what they were thinking and what they can do to make things right.
- **Circle time** – Children sit in a circle and only speak when holding a beanbag or some other object. Everyone can say what they feel and they will be listened to respectfully. Circle time can help pupils build relationships with each other and talk about experiences and feelings.

Case study 1

Before we moved to a restorative approach, J found life difficult. His father was in prison and, being one of many siblings, he wasn't able to get much attention at home. Rules and expectations meant little to him, and he wasn't interested in schoolwork or doing the right thing. Getting attention was his biggest priority, so he would deliberately break rules in order to cause a scene. Soon, his peers thought he was funny, so he played up to that.

We went through the list of sanctions with him, starting with a look, then a verbal reminder, and then a quiet word. J started arguing with teachers, calling out in class and swearing. He wasn't bothered about sanctions, even short-term exclusions, because this meant he could stay at home and play on his computer. The school knew J well as he had to spend lots of time with them and in parallel classes, but still nothing worked.

When we brought in our restorative approach, rather than sanctioning his behaviour or offering him rewards, we would talk to him, either with his peers or anyone he had upset. He was a bright boy, so he quickly came to understand the impact he was having on others and how he was upsetting people, including his friends. Little by little, his behaviour improved until we were hardly noticing him. Much of his negative behaviour was as a result of needing attention, so we started to give him responsibilities around the school so that he felt noticed.

Case study 2

A's behaviour was similar to that of J, but the restorative approach did little to improve her behaviour. She too had problems at home, and though her parents were supportive of the school, the restorative conversations were not making any difference. She found it difficult to empathise with the feelings of others. Soon she found herself having short-term exclusions, and this built up in her a feeling of resentment towards staff, so things spiralled downwards.

We decided to set up a 'nurture room', as we had a spare classroom. This was used for up to six pupils and was manned by two highly skilled members of support staff who were very understanding and experienced in the use of restorative approaches. The aim was to replace missing early childhood experiences around play while simultaneously developing positive relationships with both staff and peers in a supportive environment. We used an assessment tool in order to determine which pupils would need to be in the nurture group based on their social, emotional and mental health needs.

A responded well to the adults in the nurture room. They offered her play-based therapy, drawing and talking interventions and emotion coaching. They introduced her to the vocabulary of emotions. She felt safe with them, but soon she started to miss her friends and her teacher. So, we set up a system whereby she was dropped off in the mornings at the nurture room and eat with the adults and other pupils in there. When both adults thought she was ready, she would go into her regular classroom for the day.

A knew that she had a 'free pass' into the nurture room and could use it anytime she needed to, as long as she told her class teacher where she was going. Lessons were not missed as she would take her work into the nurture room. Soon she wasn't needing it at all but would pop in from time to time to say hello. As she grew older, she became involved in the running of the nurture room, helping out with younger pupils during lunchtimes.

Values-based Education

The development of an emotional or ethical vocabulary is essential in schools so that pupils can communicate their feelings and emotions with others. Values-based Education was set up in the UK by Dr Neil Hawkes, an ex-headteacher. A school will adopt a set of values, and this will become part of the culture of a school. Pupils know that these principles guide their behaviour and interactions with others.

Some schools adopt 22 values to be used once per month over two years; others may adopt three or six and focus on one value per term. Values will be words like integrity, community, kindness, growth, love and flourishing. These values are a really helpful way of guiding pupils and helping to establish a school culture.

Zones of regulation

Set up as a behaviour intervention, zones of regulation (ZoR) can be implemented for use by particular pupils or used as a whole-school approach. The idea is that an emotion or a group of feelings will be equated with a colour (red = angry, blue = sad, yellow = anxious, green = good). Pupils can have the ZoR stuck on their table and move around a counter to express their feelings or have a lanyard with the colours on. If the teacher notices they are feeling anything other than green, they can then be asked what they need to move back to it.

Teacher modelling

When the Adults Change, Everything Changes: Seismic Shifts in School Behaviour is a book written by British educationalist Paul Dix. When I was at the school above, we based our behaviour approaches on his work (he has a website you can visit).

The main idea is teacher modelling. As teachers, we are the models. We set the tone and create the positive atmosphere. The ways that we interact with each other and with pupils provides the model for our pupils to follow. At the above school, this was an important part of our behaviour policy, as we can see with the following example leadership policy:

All adults working or helping in school have a duty to ensure the highest standards of behaviour through their relationships with and expectations of all children and by acting as a great role model. Good behaviour can be promoted by adults by:

- Modelling the standard of behaviour that is expected from the children.
- Ensuring that children are properly supervised at all times.
- Dealing appropriately with breaches of the school rules from all children in all areas of the school.
- Being consistent and fair in their management of behaviour by following the school's behaviour systems.
- Responding rapidly to serious incidents including violence, bullying, homophobia, peer abuse, sexism or racism (these breaches are recorded on safeguarding software).

- Working towards raising the self-esteem of all children.
- Providing opportunities for children to discuss behaviour and express opinions as to what is and what isn't acceptable.
- Demonstrating tidiness and encouraging children to take a pride in their school building and resources.
- Encouraging children to appreciate the work of everyone employed.

Belonging

Children and adults need to have a sense of belonging in their primary school in order to feel emotionally secure so they can learn and thrive. In our current world where some children are experiencing multiple adversities and technological overload, it's becoming more difficult for them to experience emotional safety and a sense of belonging.

This is an excerpt from Paul Dix's website:

> *Children and young people thrive in an environment that is emotionally safe for everyone, inclusive, equitable and driven by high expectations and the highest possible levels of attainment.* When the Adults Change *isn't punishing learners in a different way. It isn't holding doors open for distressed learners for a little longer, or sticking children with complex needs in different boxes.* When the Adults Change *is the foundation, the place from which, regardless of background, ability, circumstance or need, every child has the right to belong, the ability to have a voice and the opportunity to achieve in all the areas of life they need to thrive.*

(Whentheadultschange.com, Paul Dix, 2024)

Useful reading

Chapman, R., Buckley, L., Sheehan, M., and Shochet, I., 2013, School-based programs for increasing connectedness and reducing risk behaviour: A systematic review, Educational Psychology Review, 25(1), 95–114.

Coe, R., Aloisi, C., Higgins, S., and Major, L. E.,2014, What makes great teaching: Review of the underpinning research, Durham University: UK.

Dix, P., 2017, *When the Adults Change, Everything Changes: Seismic Shifts in School Behaviour*, Independent Thinking Press, UK.

Education Endowment Foundation, 2021, Education Endowment Foundation Teaching and Learning Toolkit.

Haidt, J., 2024, *The Anxious Generation: How the great rewiring of childhood is causing an epidemic of mental illness*, Allen Lane.

Institute of Education Sciences, 2008, Reducing Behavior Problems in the Elementary School Classroom.

Lemov, D., 2021, *Teach Like a Champion 3.0*, Jossey-Bass.

Ofsted, 2021, *Review of Sexual Abuse in Schools and Colleges*.

Rogers, B., 2007, *Behaviour Management: A Whole-School Approach*, Sage.

Rogers, B., 2015, *Classroom Behaviour: A Practical Guide to Effective Teaching, Behaviour Management and Colleague Support*, 4th edition, Sage.

Ward, A., Duke, K., Gneezy, A., and Boz, M., 2017, *Brain drain: The mere presence of one's own smartphone reduces available cognitive capacity*, Journal of the Association for Consumer Research, 2(2), 140–154.

Willingham, D. T., 2009, *Why Don't Students Like School?* Jossey Bass.

Chapter 11
Wider professional responsibilities; personal and professional conduct

ITTECF syllabus

Professional behaviours (Standard 8 – Fulfil wider professional responsibilities)

Learn that...	Learn how to...
1. Effective professional development is likely to be sustained over time, building knowledge, motivating staff, developing teaching techniques, and embedding practice.	**Develop as a professional, by:** a) Engaging in professional development focused on developing an area of practice with clear intentions for impact on pupil outcomes, sustained over time with built-in opportunities for practice.
2. Reflective practice, supported by feedback from and observation of experienced colleagues, professional debate, and learning from educational research, is also likely to support improvement.	b) Strengthening pedagogical and subject knowledge by participating in wider networks and as part of the lesson preparation process.
3. Teachers can make valuable contributions to the wider life of the school in a broad range of ways, including by supporting and developing effective professional relationships with colleagues.	c) Seeking challenge, feedback and critique from mentors and other colleagues in an open and trusting working environment.
4. Building effective relationships with parents, carers and families can improve pupils' motivation, behaviour and academic success.	d) Engaging with research evidence by accessing reliable sources, seeking support for how findings can inform practice, and monitoring the impact of applications.
5. Teaching assistants (TAs) can support pupils more effectively when they are prepared for lessons by teachers, and when TAs supplement rather than replace support from teachers.	e) Reflecting on progress made, recognising strengths and weaknesses and identifying next steps for further improvement. **Build effective working relationships, by:** f) Contributing positively to the wider school culture and developing a feeling of shared responsibility for improving the lives of all pupils within the school.

Learn that...	Learn how to...
6. SENCOs, pastoral leaders, careers advisors and leaders and other specialist colleagues also have valuable expertise and can ensure that appropriate support is in place for pupils.	g) Seeking ways to support individual colleagues and working as part of a team.
7. Engaging in high quality professional development can help teachers improve.	h) Communicating with parents and carers proactively and making effective use of parents' evenings to engage parents and carers in their children's schooling.
8. Teacher attitudes towards inclusion and SEND are a key determinant in the school experience of pupils with SEND.	i) Working closely with the SENCO and other professionals supporting pupils with additional needs, making explicit links between interventions delivered outside of lessons with classroom teaching.
9. Research evidence can vary in its level of reliability, which is determined by how the research was conducted and other factors that might introduce bias, such as the level of independence. High quality research communicates methods and limitations transparently.	j) Drawing on guidance from expert colleagues, sharing the intended lesson outcomes with teaching assistants ahead of lessons.
	k) Ensuring that support provided by teaching assistants in lessons is additional to, rather than a replacement for, support from the teacher.
	l) Knowing who to contact with any safeguarding, or any pupil mental health concerns.
	Manage workload and wellbeing, by:
	m) Using and personalising systems and routines to support efficient time and task management.
	n) Understanding the right to support (e.g. to deal with misbehaviour, or support pupils with SEND).
	o) Collaborating with colleagues to share the load of planning and preparation and making use of shared resources (e.g. textbooks).
	p) Protecting time for rest and recovery and being aware of support available to support good mental wellbeing.

The ITTECF account of professional behaviours is perfectly good but quite limited in its perspective. It focuses on two things: the importance of continuing your development as a teacher (CPD) and learning to work well with teaching assistants and special needs specialists (SENCOs). Its advice about managing workload is valuable.

The Teachers' Standard 8 is similar:

Fulfil wider professional responsibilities:
* *Make a positive contribution to the wider life and ethos of the school.*
* *Develop effective professional relationships with colleagues, knowing how and when to draw on advice and specialist support.*
* *Deploy support staff effectively.*
* *Take responsibility for improving teaching through appropriate professional development, responding to advice and feedback from colleagues.*
* *Communicate effectively with parents with regard to pupils' achievements and wellbeing.*

What can I contribute to my school?

When you ask people to recall the most influential experiences of their school days, they often come up with activities that took place outside the classroom. So, you should want to contribute to these things. In your first year as a teacher, you may not have enough time – after all, you're having to plan every lesson for the first time, and if you're training, you need to leave time for writing assignments. So, consult your mentor before agreeing to everything. If you work in a boarding school, you will certainly be expected to have pastoral and co-curricular responsibilities, but try to manage these responsibly.

Examples of worthwhile contributions are:

* In a small primary school, being in charge of a subject.
* Running extra classes during lunchtime and after school.
* Being in charge of a form or, later in your career, a year group or a school house.
* Becoming a combined cadet force officer.
* Assisting with the Duke of Edinburgh Award scheme or community service.
* Helping with plays and musical events.
* Running societies, such as debating.
* Running school competitions such as a spelling bee or general knowledge.
* Editing a school magazine.
* Running a sport or sports team.
* Taking school trips.

These activities can be as important to a young person's development as the academic curriculum. They enable pupils to develop lifelong interests and leadership skills and young teachers to pass on their interests to the next generation. Get involved.

School trips

You may be asked to run or help with school trips during your teacher training year. These trips can involve anything from an away football fixture with your team to accompanying a Duke of Edinburgh Award expedition.

There are key things you need to know when you are involved in a school trip:

1. Your school must have a policy document defining the requirements for a trip. These must include:
   - Getting permission to run a trip.
   - Making a budget and getting it approved.
   - Whether or not parental agreement is needed.
   - Insurance cover.
   - Whether or not parents can be charged and how money is collected. Is financial assistance available?
   - Minimum staff-pupil ratios.
   - The qualifications needed by at least one member of staff if the trip is at all hazardous, such as mountaineering and first aid qualifications for Duke of Edinburgh Award expeditions.
   - Writing a risk assessment. What things can go wrong and what will happen if they do go wrong? What do you do if a pupil is ill?
   - Whether pupils have to wear things like fluorescent jackets (mainly for primary school trips).

2. For some types of trip, you need to go on a reconnaissance trip ('recce'). For example, if you are taking a trip abroad, it can be well worth the money to do a quick recce of the location.

3. How long in advance you inform parents depends on the trip. Anything local requires around 4–8 weeks, while trips abroad typically require more than nine months.

4. For all trips, you need to define the rules before you go. School trips are an opportunity for naughty pupils to go mad. Warn them that breaking the rules will mean they can't go on another trip. You must never take a pupil on a trip if you don't believe they can behave appropriately.

5. You should provide pupils with a list of anything they are required to bring.

6. You must arrange cover for your own teaching.

7. You will always need an experienced teacher with you because they will know what to do if there is a problem.

8. Teenagers need to be regularly reminded of the rules. Both young and older children must carry a piece of paper explaining what they do if they get lost.

9. If you have booked a coach, ring the coach company two weeks in advance to check the booking.

   When using a coach, you need a plastic bag to collect rubbish. Pupils need to be warned that they must wear seat belts and not leave their seat, they must not put rubbish anywhere other than the rubbish bag and they must be reasonably quiet. Troublesome children must sit with or near the teachers. At the end of any journey, you must check the coach is left in a good condition.

10. Do not agree to use your private car for transporting pupils.

11. Do not drive a minibus unless you have had training.

12. You need a list of all the pupils going, their parents' contact phone numbers and the school contact numbers.

13. If your trip takes place during a normal school day, you should arrange activities for any pupils who can't go.

14. Remember that anything can go wrong during trips. Teenagers forget to bring their passports, they damage hotel rooms, they lose their phones and they stay up all night chatting. So, they need clear rules and constant supervision, and you need to remain vigilant.

Paul Dix (Gilbert, 2018) writes in favour of taking misbehaving children on trips on the grounds that many such children derive particular benefit from new experiences – which is true. But on Paul's example of a trip to the theatre, his rowdy pupils made a racket during the performance and kicked the backs of the seats of other members of the audience. When the offended adults tried to find Paul, he hid – he had lost control of the group and was too nervous to speak to the adults. So, if you decide to follow Paul, up the number of adults and don't make the mistake he did of letting the worst behaved boys sit separately from the rest of the party.

Child poverty

Some schools are struggling to cope with demands caused by poverty. We know from experience, as well as studies by organisations such as the Joseph Rowntree Foundation, that staff routinely help parents with housing, visas and benefits problems, as well as providing them with food, clothing and other necessities. Teachers have some responsibility to check that their pupils are eating and sleeping properly, without which learning is much less likely to happen.

Working with SENCOs and support staff

As you already know, SENCOs (special educational needs co-ordinator) or SENDCOs (special educational needs and disabilities co-ordinator) support the education of SEND (special educational needs or disabilities) pupils within a mainstream school. They're also responsible for developing the school's overall approach to special educational needs and helping teachers to support SEND pupils. They work closely with teaching staff at all levels, including the headteacher and senior leadership team. The role is sometimes also called additional support co-ordinator or additional learning needs co-ordinator.

More commonly these days, schools are using the term 'inclusion leader' as the role can be far-reaching and include other aspects of inclusion, such as:

● Provision for disadvantaged, pupil premium children and 'children we care for' (CWCF).
● Provision for service children and families.
● Provision for young carers.
● Support for pupils with extra needs, such as mental health, trauma, neurodiversity, emotional and behavioural needs or bereavement.
● Inclusion leads are often one of the school's DSLs (designated safeguarding leads).

SENCOs and inclusion leaders work in both primary and secondary schools, and they may either focus on working with pupils and staff in a specific school or work across several different schools. SENCOs are usually already qualified teachers or headteachers, which means that SENCOs often also have their own teaching responsibilities and must work to balance the two roles. They also need to have or be working towards gaining a SENCO qualification.

How do SENCOs and inclusion leaders work with teachers?

A SENCO or inclusion leader is there to support other teachers and the headteacher to provide for pupils with additional needs. They tend to work closely with teachers, the headteacher and a child's parents to develop an individual learning plan that fulfils the child's needs. They also support teachers in developing appropriate teaching strategies for children with additional needs and often are required to help to establish strategies for managing behaviour in the classroom.

They are often the line managers for teaching or learning support assistants. Providing additional training for staff on working with children with additional needs is a key responsibility that's also beneficial for the teacher's own professional development. They are also a point of contact for teachers to report any concerns they have or seek out support related to teaching pupils with additional needs. It is important that you seek help from them before approaching the child or child's parents with any concerns you may have.

What do SENCOs or inclusion leaders do for pupils?

SENCOs and inclusion leaders support pupils in several ways. SEND pupils can easily feel isolated or left behind in school, so ensuring they feel supported is essential. Typical duties for SENCOs and inclusion leaders may include the following.

Giving support and guidance on creating inclusive environments

SENCOs and inclusion leaders help to create an inclusive environment and ensure that children with additional needs feel included and welcome at school. They often act as trusted members of staff that SEND pupils can approach when they require support.

One significant responsibility of theirs is to identify children who need additional support. This includes observations and coordinating tests and external support, for example an educational psychologist that will assess the child's academic abilities. Additionally, SENCOs and inclusion leaders sometimes provide mental health support for pupils.

Producing personalised learning plans

SENCOs and inclusion leaders use various strategies to support children who have special educational needs and help them succeed in school. Because pupils have individual needs, the strategies used often differ between the individual children that they support. Alongside developing personalised learning plans in consultation with teachers and parents, SENCOs and inclusion leaders monitor and assess the progress of pupils. This could be through further testing or observing their progress and behaviour in lessons.

Working effectively with parents

The 'SEND code of practice: 0 to 25 years' (DfE, 2014) recognises that parents and carers know their children best and should be involved in decision making regarding their child's education. Views from the home context contribute valuable information and experiences in building a full picture of the child's needs and how they can be supported.

Helping children settle in at new schools, or with transition within a setting

SENCOs and inclusion leaders support children with additional needs who move to a school from elsewhere or move within their own school, helping them settle into the new environment and making sure they get the appropriate educational and pastoral support. If a pupil needs external support for their needs, such as psychological support or support with speech and language, SENCOs and inclusion leaders are responsible for organising this and working collaboratively with outside agencies.

Other common SENCO and inclusion leader responsibilities

Other responsibilities include:

- Developing the school's overall SEND strategy and ensuring that it is properly implemented.
- Developing and implementing interventions that reduce the attainment gap between pupils with SEND and other pupils.
- Giving advice and managing the school's budget for SEND.
- Presenting annual reports on SEND provision to the school's governors.
- Staying up to date with local and national SEND policies and sharing this information with other staff.
- Keeping records on pupils with SEND.
- Providing progress reports and updates for parents.

Working with your SENCO or inclusion leader

SENCOs and inclusion leaders are there to assist and guide you as a new teacher. They will be able to give you advice but won't have the time or the availability to do all the support work themselves. They will be able to advise on the needs of specific pupils and how you can best support them inclusively within your classroom.

Support with parents' meetings

During parental consultation evenings, SENCOs and inclusion leaders are likely to be on hand to support you when meeting with parents of pupils with additional needs. If you are offered this support, do take it as you will find their presence at the meeting helpful and their knowledge about the child will help to focus the conversation with the parents. At other times, they may have organised a meeting with parents during the school day, for example to review a pupil's EHC plan. If this is the case, try to get release time so you can be at the meeting as well.

Experience and advice

Often, your SENCO or inclusion leader will know a child and their needs before you become the teacher of that child. Make sure you read all the information about the child before you begin teaching them, and if you are unsure about anything, seek advice from your SENCO or inclusion leader.

Whole-school training needs

Your SENCO or inclusion leader will continually plan whole-school training needs. At times, they will lead staff training that in some cases may be optional, depending on the type of school you are in.

Working with teaching assistants

Teaching assistants and learning support assistants can make an important contribution both to the development of children and young people and the support of teachers in delivering teaching and learning. They often provide a flexible resource and can be deployed in several ways to support the workforce. SENCOs and inclusion leaders are likely to have worked with other senior leaders to review the effectiveness of their teaching assistants and how they can be best used to support learning and improve outcomes throughout the whole school.

The EEF's guidance report, *Making best use of teaching assistants* (2015), offers the latest evidence and makes a number of recommendations to help schools make best use of their teaching assistants. The overwhelming piece of advice from the report is: '*[Teaching assistants] should not be used as an informal teaching resource for low attaining pupils.*'

The report goes on to state:

> *The evidence on [teaching assistant] deployment suggests schools have drifted into a situation in which [teaching assistants] are often used as an informal instructional resource for pupils in most need. This has the effect of separating pupils from the classroom, their teacher and their peers. Although this has happened with the best of intentions, this evidence suggests that the status quo is no longer an option. School leaders should systematically review the roles of both teachers and [teaching assistants] and take a wider view of how [teaching assistants] can support learning and improve attainment throughout the school.*

Other important recommendations from the EEF's report include:

- Use support staff to add value to what teachers do, not replacing them. The expectation here is that the needs of all pupils should be addressed, first and foremost, through high quality classroom teaching.
- Deploy support staff to help pupils develop independent learning skills and manage their own learning. Teaching assistants should, for example, be trained to concentrate on helping pupils develop ownership of tasks rather than focus on task completion. They can intervene, for example by asking the pupil questions to help guide their thinking.
- Ensure support staff are fully conversant with the aims of the lesson. This can include speaking with them beforehand to ensure they understand the aims of the lesson, the concepts involved and what successful learning will look like.
- Teaching assistants can be deployed to deliver high quality, one-to-one and small group support and interventions, but only if they are appropriately trained in doing so.
- Schools should only be deploying support staff to deliver one-to-one interventions that have been proven by research evidence to be successful. Also, the support staff should have received extensive quality training from experienced trainers or teachers, and the intervention should include structured supporting resources and lesson plans with clear objectives. Support staff must closely follow the plan and structure of the intervention.
- Ensure that explicit connections are made between learning from everyday classroom teaching and structured interventions. There needs to be allocated time for teachers and TAs to liaise and pupils need to be helped to understand the links between the intervention and the work in class.

Other excellent research on teaching assistants is available, such as *The deployment and impact of support staff* (DfE, 2004).

When I first started teaching, the norm was to have your lowest-attaining pupils working (often outside the classroom) with a teaching or learning support assistant. But we now know that this was misguided, and that children who need the most support should be working with the main teacher.

Here are some top tips for effectively working with your support staff:

- Communicate with teaching assistants and ask for their advice.
- Recognise and use their strengths and allow them to make decisions.
- Provide professional development opportunities for them.

- Involve teaching assistants by asking them to interact with the class and make sure students know they have authority.
- Teaching assistants need patience, empathy and a caring attitude.
- They need to be able to adapt to changing circumstances and respond to the needs of both pupils and teachers.
- Recognise their communication skills and tone of voice, as these are important for behaviour management.
- Teaching assistants who are good at active listening can better support students and connect with them.
- Teaching assistants should work collaboratively with colleagues.
- Teaching assistants may find themselves overwhelmed by challenges, so make sure there are mentors or champions to support them.
- At the beginning of each day or week, consider giving your teaching assistant a copy of your daily lesson plans. This can help them become familiar with the material before the lessons so they can better assist pupils.
- One of the teaching assistant's duties involves working with pupils individually, so if there are any pupils you'd like them to work with during or after a lesson, let them know in advance so they can review the lesson and prepare the necessary materials for the pupils.
- Sometimes it will be more effective for you to work with a small group who needs the most help and for your teaching assistant to circle around the room offering support.
- Show them gratitude and try not to see them as part of the furniture.
- If you ask them to mark work, ensure they know how to do this in the same way that you would.

Working with support staff can be hugely rewarding, and often strong relationships are made between teachers and their support staff as well as with the pupils. Occasionally relationships may falter – if this is the case, seek advice from your mentor or senior leadership team.

Workload and wellbeing

How can you work hard, doing the best for all of your pupils and meeting workload demands, and *still* find the time and energy to look after yourself? You must remember to put on your own metaphorical oxygen mask first, otherwise you won't be able to do anything for your pupils.

Manage workload and wellbeing

Here are some good ideas relating to each of the statements at the beginning of this chapter (see pages 227–28).

Using and personalising systems and routines to support efficient time and task management

If you refer back to the chapter on assessment (Chapter 9) you will find ideas for timesaving and highly effective ways of carrying out assessments that mean you don't have to spend every evening marking. Marking in the moment can be more effective for your pupils, alongside saving valuable time for you. Having pupils marking their own or their peers' work in a low-stakes test, spelling test or list of maths questions works well.

In 2024, the UK government announced a £4m initiative aimed at developing AI tools to assist teachers with homework marking and reducing workload. This came as part of a government acknowledgement that teachers work tirelessly and that utilising some of the time-saving devices that AI can provide could be useful in supporting teachers.

Understanding the right to support

You don't have to deal with everything by yourself. Nobody expects you to be a fully competent teacher on day one. So, reach out and ask for help if you need it. This may be from colleagues (who love to help) such as fellow teachers, support staff, the senior leadership team, SENDOs (or SENDCOs) or even the headteacher. If you feel you aren't being supported appropriately, then try and ask again.

Collaborating with colleagues to share the load of planning and preparation

The principles of collaborative planning are that you do double, triple or quadruple the amount of work in half, a third or a quarter of the time. Use previously written schemes of work or lesson plans but adapt them to suit you and the needs of your pupils. Be smart with your planning time. You can refer to Chapter 7 (see page 133) for more on planning.

Making time for rest and recovery and being aware of help available to support good mental wellbeing

At different points in their career, teachers can feel overwhelmed or stressed. Most schools, certainly in the public sector, have access to occupational support services, either through the local authority or through the MAT if you work in one. You may have access to a chaplaincy service or school counsellor; either way, reach out for help if you need it. You may prefer to see a GP or seek support from outside school.

Here are some good tips for maintaining good mental health:

- Set boundaries around your time and workload to avoid burnout.
- Make self-care a habit that helps to prevent stress.
- Get enough sleep. Going to bed early can positively impact your emotions, mood, performance and effectiveness.
- Practice deep breathing: close your eyes and take 10 deep breaths. You could also go for a 10-minute walk.
- Practice gratitude. Gratitude can help establish a healthy classroom culture and increase feelings of optimism and joy.
- Look at the NHS '5 steps to mental wellbeing', which include connecting with other people, being physically active, learning new skills, giving to others and paying attention to the present moment (mindfulness).

Personal and professional conduct

Part 2 of the Teachers' Standards says:

> *A teacher is expected to demonstrate consistently high standards of personal and professional conduct. The following statements define the behaviour and attitudes which set the required standard for conduct throughout a teacher's career.*
>
> *Teachers uphold public trust in the profession and maintain high standards of ethics and behaviour, within and outside school, by:*
> - *Treating pupils with dignity, building relationships rooted in mutual respect and at all times observing proper boundaries appropriate to a teacher's professional position.*
> - *Having regard for the need to safeguard pupils' wellbeing, in accordance with statutory provisions.*
> - *Showing tolerance of and respect for the rights of others.*
> - *Not undermining fundamental British values, including democracy, the rule of law, individual liberty and mutual respect and tolerance of those with different faiths and beliefs.*
> - *Ensuring that personal beliefs are not expressed in ways that exploit pupils' vulnerability or may lead them to break the law.*

Teachers must have proper and professional regard for the ethos, policies and practices of the school in which they teach and maintain high standards in their own attendance and punctuality.

Teachers must have an understanding of, and always act within, the statutory frameworks that set out their professional duties and responsibilities.

These are really important statements, and failure to adhere to them may result in you losing your job and possibly being barred from teaching.

Your relationship with pupils

Always keep a social distance between yourself and your pupils. My first boss told me to be 'friendly, not matey' with pupils – it was good advice. Do not allow secondary-age pupils to speak to you informally, and avoid speaking to them informally yourself. Do not communicate with pupils through social media; if you are on social media, you must fix the privacy settings so pupils can't see your posts. You are the adult, and they must respect you.

Never be tempted to invite pupils to your house and never allow them to drink alcohol. If you take teenage pupils on a school trip, school rules must still apply as regards to smoking and alcohol. No teenager should be allowed to behave in any way that would embarrass you if their parents or your head teacher knew about it. If a pupil behaves in a way that you feel is inappropriate or wrong, always seek the advice of a more experienced colleague.

In 2025, a teacher with over 35 years of experience was dismissed from a primary school after a comment made during a maths SAT preparation class. She jokingly said she would 'whack' a pupil who did not hold their papers in place. Despite her argument that her comment was made in jest, it was deemed to be gross misconduct (*The Standard*, 2025).

Recently, a Year 6 teacher was dismissed for gross misconduct after referring to her class as 'a bunch of chattering monkeys'. Parents deemed the comment 'very racist', especially given the class's racial diversity. One parent also complained that the teacher 'told the class that they are getting on her nerves so much she wants to shoot herself or them' (Mail Online, 2024). Make sure you are careful how you speak to pupils, even if you think you are joking.

Similarly, I had a nice member of staff who once threw a tennis ball at a sixth former who was asleep in his lesson. The boy and his parents were not especially bothered about this, but the incident came to be reported to local social services and was the subject of a formal investigation.

A good teacher made the mistake of sending messages to their pupils on Teams that were far too informal. Their school suspended him for gross misconduct and informed the Teaching Regulation Agency, who found him guilty of 'failure to maintain professional boundaries'. Even if you feel you are simply being friendly to pupils online, the consequences can be serious.

So, these aspects of the Teachers' Standards are not friendly advice – they are rules by which you must live.

Before you start teaching in a school, you must know two things:

1. The child protection and safeguarding regulations, which are spelled out in the DfE's 'Keeping children safe in education' guidance. Your school must give you training and tell you who to report to if you have any concerns. Nothing is more important.

    It is a sad fact that some adults are sexually attracted to school-age children or young people, and not surprisingly some of them become teachers, so you must be aware of any signs you need to look out for.

2. Any other policies your school has about the behaviour of staff.

Some hints and tips for professional conduct

Here are some further suggestions for maintaining your professionalism:

- Maintain a distance and set boundaries. This is particularly important if you are taking teenagers on a trip, for example.
- Avoid touching pupils. Even an arm around the shoulders can be misinterpreted.
- Change social media settings and make yourself anonymous. Even if pupils don't try to track you down on social media, parents will, so ensure you change your name and don't have a recognisable photo of you on your socials. Don't accept friend requests from parents or pupils if you are using social media.
- Try not to frequent the same pubs or clubs as the parents of your pupils.
- Remember that when you are socialising, other people can hear what you say, so avoid speaking about pupils or parents. Always speak respectfully.
- Be careful about what you wear and how you present yourself.
- Ensure that all written communication with pupils and parents is checked for spelling and grammar.

Parental complaints

In 2024, Browne Jacobson published a report in which 90% of school staff said that the impact of dealing with complaints was having a detrimental impact on staff wellbeing. The poll found that 68% of teachers said personal attacks or aggression are the most common types of behaviour, while 70% of teachers believed parents and carers are now quicker to escalate concerns to a formal stage.

Browne Jacobson's study, which was completed by over 200 school leaders, found most grievances raised revolved around support for pupils with special needs. Other matters included behaviour and discipline, equality complaints such as discrimination and transgender issues and parental responsibility and safeguarding. Cited impacts of these parental complaints were poor recruitment and retention of governors (19%) and teaching staff (48%) and poor staff wellbeing (90%) who responded to the survey.

Hopefully, you will be working in a school that takes these matters seriously. You should be able to seek support from your mentor or a member of the senior leadership team if you are faced with parental complaints yourself. If you are able to, make an appointment with the parents to come back to discuss the matter and ensure you have your mentor or a senior leader with you at the allotted time.

However, sometimes a parent may catch you 'on the hop' and come in before or after school to complain about something. Before school is not the best time for a discussion, so ask them to come and have the discussion with you after school. If they do approach you out of the blue with a complaint, here is some advice:

- Welcome them politely. Stand up and shake hands. Ask how they are. Ensure they feel comfortable. Sit down with them, ideally at a 90-degree angle – this ensures that eye contact can be made but is less intimidating for you than sitting directly opposite them.
- Ask them what they would like to discuss.
- Make notes. This helps to avoid direct eye contact, while also showing that you are listening and taking the matter seriously.
- Ask them questions to gather more information, such as if other children are involved. Ask for the names of those involved if you need to carry out an investigation into an incident.
- Be polite and not defensive. Express empathy for their concerns, such as: 'If this is the case, I can understand it must be worrying for you; however, I will need to find out the facts and get back to you.'
- Be reassuring: 'As soon as I have found out what happened, I will get back to you.' Let them know how you will contact them (i.e. via a phone call, email or another meeting).
- Ensure you follow up. Sum up the exchange and be ready to set up a subsequent meetings.

- Keep in touch. Do this in a way that suits the parents, at the time that suits everyone, and regularly. If there are ongoing concerns, aim for every three weeks, even if it is a quick email or note in the homework diary.
- Discuss the meeting with a member of the senior leadership team or your mentor and ask for advice. They may take the matter off your hands themselves, or they may advise you how to proceed.

If a parent has been unreasonable or expressed anger, don't take it personally and remember they are concerned for their chid. If they have expressed anger directly at you or accused you of mishandling a situation, it's really important that you take steps to look after your own wellbeing:

- Try to vent to someone before you leave school.
- Don't drive until you are feeling calm.
- Try to do something in the evening to distract you.

It is important that you ensure you are not always readily accessible to receive complaints. Sometimes we need to take extra measures to ensure our privacy, particularly when we are not in the workplace during our own time. Try to avoid giving parents your email address, and *never* share your phone number with them.

Here are some additional tips to ensure you have the correct boundaries in place between yourself and the parents:

- Be vague about where you live.
- Don't mention names of family members.
- Change your name on social media to something different and add a profile picture that is not a photograph of you (I have had many teacher friends who have received private messages late at night from pupils or parents).
- Don't 'friend' parents on social media.
- Don't let the parents know where you will be or what you will be doing at the weekend, particularly if you live near the school.

Primary school parents' meetings

Most parents are nice, reasonable people who want the best for their children, and they will approach you in appropriate ways if they have a query. Your aim will be to nurture a good healthy relationship between yourself and them, with you as the professional and them as the parents. Having an effective school-home relationship is best for the pupils, as you are likely to be co-educating your pupils with the parents as first educators.

Nurture your relationships with the parents to find out more about their children. Parent-teacher consultations are a good means of doing this. However, your first consultation evening is likely to be daunting, so ask your mentor or a member of the senior leadership team to practise with you first. The school may have a proforma for you to complete on each pupil in preparation for the meetings, but if this is not the case, here are some useful tips to help you get through your first consultation meeting:

- Welcome them with a smile and introduce yourself (if necessary).
- Thank them for coming (remember, some of them will find this nerve-wracking).
- Start with a positive comment about their child ('Rosie has settled in really well and seems to be enjoying school').
- Ask them their opinion ('Is that your impression too?').
- Let them know about any friendships and relationships with others in the class.
- Update them on how their child is getting on in school in terms of progress.
- Advise them on any help their child may need at home to take the next step in class.
- Let them know the percentage of their child's attendance and whether anything needs to be improved.
- Ask them if they have any questions or anything to add.
- End by thanking them for coming, and reasserting anything you have agreed on as an action for either you or them.

Beginner teachers will soon realise that parent-teacher consultation evenings are not only useful but can be a very pleasurable experience. As long as you approach the meeting as an opportunity to work together for the sake of the child, the meeting will run smoothly – and you may even be told what a great job you are doing.

Be like Ella

Ella teaches Year 1 and greets all of her pupils in the mornings at the door with a smile and a few words. She is available if parents want to speak to her. At the end of the day, she walks into the area outside her classroom with a smile and ensures pupils are matched to caregivers. If a parent asks to speak with her, she says, 'Yes of course, shall we go into the classroom when everyone has gone?' She sits down with her notebook and invites the parent to sit at the same table. She asks, 'How can I help?' and the parent tells her. During

> the conversation, her body language and actions show that she is listening attentively, and she reassures the parent that she will deal with the matter immediately and get back to them to let them know about the outcome. She follows through with all of her promises and reassurances. Within just a few months, she has gained the trust and respect of all her Year 1 parents.

End-of-term reports

Your school will provide you with guidance and requirements for writing end-of-term reports, but here are some suggestions on what to do – and what not to do.

Do:

- Try to find something positive to say, if you can.
- Give an honest statement about the pupil's performance compared to others in the year group. Sometimes a simple rank order will tell the parent that.
- Distinguish between ability and effort.
- Have a formula you use for most reports, such as what the pupil has done well, what could be better and what they must do to improve.
- Get someone to check your spelling and make a note of any mistakes you make.

Don't:

- Predict exam results. This creates a difficulty if you are too optimistic, and the results are then disappointing.
- Describe the syllabus that has been 'covered'.
- Make personal comments about the pupil. Focus on the work, not the individual.
- Write a very critical report if the parents haven't already been told of the problems. They would rightly expect to know about them before the report arrives.
- Copy and paste so that all your reports are the same.

References

Bethune, A., 2023, *Wellbeing in the Primary Classroom: The Updated Guide to Teaching Happiness and Positive Mental Health*, Bloomsbury.

Bethune, A. and Kell, E., 2020, *A Little Guide for Teachers: Teacher Wellbeing and Self-care*, Corwin.

Department for Education, 2004, The deployment and impact of support staff in schools: Research brief, DfE.

Department for Education, 2024, Keeping children safe in education, DfE.

Education Endowment Foundation, 2015, Making Best Use of Teaching Assistants: Guidance Report.

Gilbert, I., 2018, The working class: Poverty, education and alternative voices, Independent Thinking Press.

Chapter 12
Age phases

When you are learning to be a good teacher, how you go about it will depend on which subjects you are teaching and how old the children are. In this chapter, we think about children of different ages.

Early years (age 2–5)

If you are teaching in the early years, you need to see three key documents:

- *Early years foundation stage statutory framework for group and school-based providers* (DfE, 2024)
- *Non-statutory guidance for the Early Years Foundation Stage* (Early Years Coalition, 2021)
- *Development Matters: Non-statutory curriculum guidance for the early years' foundation stage* (DfE, 2024)

Teaching in the early years can be a rewarding experience as all children develop in different ways and at different times. The guiding principles of teaching this age range are that each unique child is given opportunities to interact in positive relationships and enabling environments that encourage their engagement and recognise their strengths. It is based on an approach that acknowledges that all children have agency and curiosity to learn and therefore they will interact with other people and the world around them in different ways. Understanding these different ways of learning about the world is central to learning who these children are and how best to support their learning and development.

The guiding principles are described in the *Early years foundation stage (EYFS) statutory framework* (DfE, 2024) thus:

- Every child is unique and constantly learning. They can be resilient, capable, confident and self-assured.
- Children learn to be strong and independent through positive relationships.
- Children learn and develop well in enabling environments with teaching and support from adults, who respond to their individual interests and needs and help them to build their learning over time. Children benefit from a strong partnership between practitioners and parents or carers.
- Children develop and learn at different rates. The framework covers the education and care of all children, including SEND children.

Characteristics of effective teaching and learning

When planning and guiding what children learn, it's important for us to reflect on the different rates at which children are developing and adjust our practice appropriately. According to the DfE (2024), the three characteristics of effective teaching and learning are:

- **Playing and exploring** – Children investigate and experience things, and 'have a go'.
- **Active learning** – Children concentrate and keep on trying if they encounter difficulties, and they enjoy achievement.
- **Creating and thinking critically** – Children have and develop their own ideas, make links between ideas and develop strategies for doing things.

The importance of play

It is widely recognised that play supports children's development, as it affords opportunities to tap into their natural curiosity, explore interests and develop social skills. Play needs to be expertly supported by adults through quality interactions, to encourage with the development of understanding and help children to acquire specific skills.

When adults join children in their play and respond appropriately, valuable opportunities are created to develop learning through the introduction of vocabulary in context, adding a narrative to play and pointing things out. It also provides opportunities to get to know the children well and understand their interests, strengths and areas that need development.

Joining children in their play can provide valuable insights into what and how children learn. Practitioners can join children in their play to:

- Add a narrative to the play.
- Support with interactions.
- Model language.
- Model behaviour expectations.
- Model skills.
- Provide model 'think-alouds' in problem-solving situations.
- Support with communication.
- Introduce and use new vocabulary.
- Explain ideas and demonstrate things.
- Encourage children to explore and explain their ideas.
- Undertake assessment and plan next steps for learning.

Active learning

Active learning in the early years is a child-centred approach to teaching. It prioritises the child's active involvement in the learning process and encourages them to engage with their learning environment in a hands-on and exploratory way. Children are encouraged to investigate and discover new things for themselves using their natural curiosity to drive their learning. Through active learning, children have agency and take ownership of their own learning journey, and this is thought to promote the development of confidence and independence as they explore the world around them.

Learning can be either adult-led or child-initiated

When learning is adult-led, the teacher has clear expectations and knows in advance the skills, knowledge, abilities and vocabulary they intend to develop in their pupils. A natural part of the teaching process is to respond to the children's needs and plan subsequent learning. Some early years providers use a strategy called 'planning in the moment', where the idea is to capture the interest of a child or children in the present moment and plan activities that are intended for them to learn through whatever is interesting them at that particular time.

When learning is child-initiated, children themselves take the lead and choose the direction of the learning. Adults respond to their thoughts and ideas, but rather than having a clear plan, this is spontaneous. In these instances, it's essential to take the time to listen carefully, share the children's experiences, think about a variety of possibilities that may happen and work together to solve problems.

Quality interactions

We know from several decades of research that a high-quality early childhood has a positive effect on a child's educational, cognitive, behavioural and social development and leads to improved life chances. Effective early years provision combines care with education, focusing on both social and cognitive development.

The following strategies encourage children to engage in high-quality conversational interactions:

- Maintaining eye contact, where you look expectantly at children as you engage in conversation with them.
- Being warm and receptive and welcoming children's attempts to communicate.
- Promoting friendship by fostering their friendship skills, emotional understanding and emotional expression.

- Promoting cooperation by offering opportunities to 'practise' friendship skills, such as sharing through cooperative games.
- Acknowledging and valuing positive behaviours.
- Listening carefully and scaffolding language, expanding and extending on what the child says.
- Modelling by talking about what the child sees and does.

Continuous provision

Continuous provision refers to the resources and areas laid out in the early years or KS1 setting to encourage learning through play and exploration. Resources should be freely accessible to the children during any designated 'free play' or child-initiated learning and should stay the same throughout the school year. The resources in each area of learning should be engaging and relevant in order to challenge and promote critical thinking and problem solving, while remaining open-ended.

Emotional development

Development of the children's physical and cognitive skills in the early years is important, but so too is their social-emotional development, which is likely to lay the foundations for their emotional and mental health and social relationships going forward. This aspect of child development is more concerned with how children act towards and feel about others.

Emotional development is about gradually learning to deal with, discuss, control and express emotions such as fear, jealousy, anger and sadness. It also deals with how they learn to experience and react to feelings of love, happiness and excitement in an appropriate manner. Due to the close connection with social development, you often see emotional development referred to as 'social-emotional'.

The gender gap

Research carried out by the EPI (Education Policy institute) in 2024 found that girls consistently outperform boys in each of the five areas of the DfE's GLD ('good level of development') measure areas – literacy, maths, physical development, communication and personal, social and emotional. By age five, girls were 3.3 months ahead of boys in 2024 – a gap smaller than the 4.7-month disadvantage gap. The gender gap increased slightly from 2023 and is now 0.4 months higher than before the pandemic, returning to its 2016 level after previously declining since 2013.

The EPI's 2023 report found that among reception-aged pupils, girls were 3.2 months ahead of boys, a slight increase from the 2.9-month gap observed in 2019; however, this disparity remains nearly one month narrower than it was in 2013. Girls have consistently outperformed boys across all key learning domains, with the most significant differences historically observed in literacy (particularly writing) and the smallest disparities noted in mathematics.

Males are diagnosed with dyslexia more frequently than females, which could account for some of these results. Some think that this is because girls are more able to mask dyslexia, though there is a large amount of research suggesting that younger boys have slower processing speeds. Either way, the question we must ask ourselves is what is the emotional impact of underperformance in boys with regard to reading and writing?

Phonics and KS1

In 2022–23, the percentage of girls passing their phonics screening test was 78%, while it was 72% for boys. The gap is even wider for disadvantaged boys. In the KS1 reading SATs, attainment was 72% for girls and 65% for boys.

Summer-born boys

Children born in the summer are more likely to have lower self-esteem than their classmates born in the fall. This is due to a number of factors, including:

- **Being the youngest in the year** – Children born in the summer are often the youngest in their school year, which can impact their confidence and self-esteem.
- **Birth-date effect** – Children born in June, July and August are statistically more likely to perform less well than their older classmates

Why is this and what is the impact on self-esteem?

More and more these days, pupils will start school in the September before their fifth birthday. The gap in cognitive ability between four years and one month and five years is vast. Some schools still have a rising five intake, starting pupils in the term before their fifth birthday.

I was a summer-born pupil. When I started school during Easter before my fifth birthday, I remember feeling as though I was stupid as the other pupils seemed to know what was going on and I didn't. They knew the expectations and routines, and they could read and do simple sums. I didn't know any of this, and as a result my self-esteem was impacted.

Both of my sons are summer-born boys and both struggled in school until they caught up around the age of nine or 10. Typically, research shows that summer-born boys usually catch up with their peers by the end of their primary education, which is a long time to spend thinking that you are less able than your peers. Young children will not understand the reason for the difference, or that they can catch up. This can impact their self-esteem and how they view their ability for the remainder of their education.

In 2024, the APPG (All-Party Parliamentary Groups) released a concerning report about the under-achievement of boys at all stages of their education, which included the following information:

> *Boys perform worse than girls on most major educational indicators through their school years. In England, and in the 2022-23 academic year, boys performed worse on the following measures:*
>
> * **Exclusion** – *In the autumn term, boys were nearly twice as likely as girls to be suspended and slightly more than twice as likely to be permanently excluded.*
> * **End of reception year** – *Just under two-thirds of boys had a GLD aged around five compared to around three-quarters of girls.*
> * **End of primary schooling** – *63% of girls met the expected standard in all of English reading, writing and maths, compared to 56% of boys. However, boys did slightly better than girls in maths alone: 73% met the expected standard compared to 72% of girls.*
> * **End of compulsory secondary education** – *Girls do better across all headline DfE measures than boys. For example, in 2023, 68% of girls in state-funded schools achieved both English and maths GCSEs at grade 4 or above compared to 63% of boys*

The longer-term implications of these findings are that boys' underperformance impacts general wellbeing and mental health (including suicide, drugs related issues and rough sleeping) and employability. This is partly attributable to males being more likely to have ADHD or ASD and subsequently being viewed more negatively than their female counterparts. The APPG found that within the school system, more severe treatment of boys persists when teachers grade them more negatively or sanction them more heavily than girls.

Key stage 1 (age 5–7)

Years 1 and 2 of primary school are referred to as Key stage 1. KS1 marks a shift from early years to more subject-specific learning. KS1 covers all the compulsory national curriculum subjects.

The KS1 curriculum is designed to introduce children to the core and foundational subjects they will learn throughout their time at school. It is assessed on a regular basis to give teachers and parents an indication of how their child is progressing.

The compulsory taught subjects in the KS1 curriculum are:

- English
- Maths
- Science
- Design and technology
- History
- Geography
- Art
- Music
- Physical education (PE)
- Computing
- Religious education (schools must provide some form of religious education, but parents can ask for their children to be taken out of the whole lesson or part of it).

Schools sometimes also teach:

- Personal, social, health and economic education (PSHE)
- Citizenship
- Modern foreign languages

Emotional development in KS1

Over the course of KS1, children become more competent with expressing feelings and emotions, although they may need help and time to identify and talk about tricky emotions like frustration or jealousy. They often have much better control over feelings and may have fewer unexpected outbursts of anger or sadness. However, it's important that we support the children in their social and emotional development, which is why most primary schools include a programme of PSHE in their curriculum. It is important to teach them emotional vocabulary so they are able to express themselves and understand when they are feeling that something may be wrong.

Children of this age are continuing to develop their sense of self. They are learning how to cope with stress and manage their emotions. Additionally, they continue to develop their social skills and empathy, which can in turn help them to connect with others and build friendships.

They are developing empathy and beginning to ask big questions about the world. They are likely to be encountering loss, and may encounter the death of a loved one, prompting them to seek to find meaning in life, death, the afterlife and (in some cases) their religion. If they lose someone close, they are likely to start to worry about other members of their family who may disappear, as now they are realising that when people die, we don't see them again. This can cause anxiety and worry.

Social and emotional development can be covered in PSHE lessons, which are designed to help children learn to manage their feelings and behaviours, learn the language of emotions and build positive relationships. PSHE lessons help children in the following ways:

- **Recognise emotions** – Helping children identify their feelings and the words to label them.
- **Express feelings** – Encouraging them to express their feelings and develop strategies to cope with challenging situations.
- **Build relationships** – Helping them develop close relationships with others and learn to negotiate difficult situations.
- **Set goals** – Helping them to identify positive things about themselves and set personal goals.
- **Face challenges** – Teaching them to face challenges positively by making responsible choices and taking action.

Other strategies for helping with anxiety include:

- **Routines** – Routines help children feel safe and understand the structure of their day.
- **Role modelling** – Adults being role models and praising children who demonstrate desired behaviours, modelling turn-taking and polite conversation, for example.
- **Talking and listening** – Talking to children, using their name and listening to them.
- **Encourage independence** – Encouraging independence skills as soon as children are capable.

Concentration

Younger children can't concentrate for long. Sustained attention is not secure until approximately the age of six, so younger children will find concentration challenging, if not impossible. They need shorter tasks, lots of breaks and plenty of direct eye contact.

Young children also have more limited working memory, so they should be set simple tasks with limited distractions. They have to be taught simple things such as using scissors, applying glue and working with other children.

Gender

The gender gap continues in KS1. In 2022–23, the percentage of girls passing their phonics screening test was 78%, while it was 72% for boys. The gap is even wider for boys from lower income homes – in the KS1 reading SATs, attainment was 65% for disadvantaged boys and 72% for disadvantaged girls.

Children born in the summer are more likely to have lower self-esteem than their classmates born in the autumn. According to the LSE (2021), this is more pronounced in boys than girls, resulting in summer-born boys scoring below summer-born girls in GLD, phonics screening and KS1 SATs, with more boys being diagnosed as having additional learning needs than summer-born girls. This is in part due to the fact that these children are often the youngest in their school year, which can impact their confidence. Increasingly these days, pupils start school in the September before their fifth birthday. The gap in cognitive ability between four years and one month and five years is vast. Some schools still have a rising five intake, a term that refers to pupils starting school in the term before their fifth birthday.

I was a summer-born pupil. When I started school at Easter before my fifth birthday (as was common in the 1960s and 1970s), I remember literally feeling as though I was stupid, as the other pupils seemed to know what was going on and I didn't. They knew the expectations and routines, and they could read and do simple sums. I didn't know any of this, and as a result my self-esteem was impacted. Both of my sons are summer-born boys and both struggled in school until they caught up around the age of nine or ten. Typically, research shows that summer-born boys usually catch up with their peers by the end of their primary education, which is a long time to spend thinking that you are less able than your peers. Young children will not understand the reason for the difference, or that they can catch up. This can impact their self-esteem and view of their ability for the remainder of their education.

Key stage 2 (age 7–11)

The KS2 programmes of study for English, maths and science are presented in the national curriculum as 'lower' (years 3 and 4) and 'upper' (years 5 and 6). This distinction is made as guidance for teachers and is not reflected in legislation. The KS2 curriculum is an extension of the KS1 curriculum and is designed to build upon learning from the earlier stage. The addition of learning languages is the only key difference in the KS2 curriculum.

Tests and assessments at KS2

In June each year, Year 4 pupils undertake an assessment of their multiplication tables knowledge, known as the multiplication tables check (MTC). This is a statutory requirement for all Year 4 pupils registered at state-funded maintained schools, special schools or academies in England. The purpose of the MTC is to determine whether pupils can recall their times tables fluently, which is considered to be essential for future success in maths. It helps identify pupils who have not yet mastered their times tables so that additional support can be provided where needed. (At the time of writing, we are unsure how long this check will remain in place.)

In May each year, most pupils in Year 6 will take the KS2 national curriculum tests, commonly known as standard assessment tests (SATs). These tests, alongside teacher assessment of writing and science, are used to measure school performance and make sure individual pupils have the support that they need as they move into secondary school. The data will provide information to parents about their child's attainment, support the transition to secondary schools and can help identify where additional support is best targeted to individual pupils.

Body changes and puberty

Between the ages of seven and 11, children's bodies change as they approach puberty. During this time, their brains are also adapting rapidly. While they are becoming physically stronger and more coordinated, they are also becoming more abstract in their thought processes and more aware of their own feelings, those of others and the world around them.

Relationship and sex education (RSE) and PSHE lessons are designed to support pupils through some of these changes. Puberty may begin from the age of eight, with breast development for girls and enlargement of the testicles for boys. Alongside this, both girls and boys are likely to experience growth spurts, which can cause joint and muscle pain. Typically, a child will grow 6–8cm a year and gain 2–4kg each year.

The children's motor skills are likely to be improving and becoming stronger as they build muscle. Their coordination, balance and control are likely to be maturing as muscle mass increases. Children at this age are active and need plenty of exercise and playtime.

Emotional and social development

Throughout KS2, children may become more independent and more interested in their friends. They may also experience more peer pressure, so it's important for them to feel good about themselves to resist this. Children may also develop crushes, which are not sexual and can be same-sex. The majority of girls experience a preadolescent growth spurt around age nine or ten, while most boys experience the same growth spurt around age 11 or 12. As this growth spurt is often related to hormonal changes in the body, it can impact on the emotional development of the pupils.

In general, pupils in years 3 and 4 are more aware of themselves and others' perceptions of them. They may complain about friendships and the reactions of other pupils. Often, they want to behave well but aren't as attentive to directions and executive functioning tasks as older KS2 pupils. You may also find that they try to express feelings with words but may resort to aggression when upset.

Some features of emotional development during upper KS2 include:

● Sharing secrets and jokes with friends.
● Starting to develop more of their own identity by withdrawing from family activities and conversations.
● Being affectionate, silly and curious, but at times also selfish, rude and argumentative.
● Learning the skills involved in emotional regulation (though this is not the case for all pupils).
● Developing friendships, which can help to develop self-esteem and a sense of competency in the social world.
● Becoming more susceptible to peer pressure within friendships and relationships, adopting group norms as their own in an attempt to enhance their self-esteem.

In 2025, the website Everyone's Invited published a list of 1,664 primary schools whose former pupils had submitted stories about sexual abuse of girls by boys. The creators of the website said that primary-age boys had been corrupted by exposure to online pornography and proposed that teachers and parents improve relationship training at primary level.

Intellectual development

Children in KS2 are likely to develop a longer attention span and be able to take on more responsibility. They may also be able to understand fractions, money and the concept of space, and begin to think more logically about concrete events and understand the concept of conservation. The national curriculum takes account of all of these cognitive and intellectual changes, and you can see this reflected in how the programmes of study change as pupils get older.

Language development is part of this, and children may be able to use more advanced words and understand other points of view more easily and readily. They are much more likely to be able to keep a conversation going by giving reasons and explaining choices.

The changing lives of pupils in recent years

Everything we have covered so far in KS2 is understood and has been known to us for some time. What are not so well understood are the changes in pupils of this age over recent years, particularly since the advent of the internet and social media. This is particularly concerning, because we don't yet know the impact that this will have on our children. It simply has not been around for long enough for us to measure or understand the implications.

What we are seeing at the moment is changes in attitudes, respect for adults and other authority figures and vast amounts of time spent staring at a screen. Indeed, a recent TES headline (2024) reads:

> *Teachers face 'alarming' rise in verbal and physical abuse from pupils.*
> *Increase in challenging behaviour from children and parents is impacting teachers' mental health and wellbeing, charity warns.*

Let's look at some of these more recent phenomena to see how our children may be impacted.

Screen time

There has been a deluge of recent research on the impact of screentime on our preteens (ages 8–12). Here are some of the things this research has told us:

- Preteens spend about 5½ hours daily on devices, up an hour from a decade earlier; this means that some spend half of their waking day in front of a screen. Usage jumped in 2019 just before the Covid-19 pandemic started, and has continued to go up since (Yang, 2024).
- At least half of those hours are spent on televisions, not just on phones or tablets.
- For preteens and teenagers, this has had variable effects on mental health, academic achievement and social skills.
- More screen time can be associated with:
  - Higher anxiety.
  - Depression symptoms.
  - Lower quality of life.
  - Lower psychological wellbeing.
  - Lower school functioning.

- Lower academic achievement.
- Lower self-esteem.
- Poor language achievement.
- Poor achievement.

Additionally, we need to ask ourselves exactly what children are spending their screen time doing. Parents should be checking. Time spent may be purely innocent, such as chatting to friends online or playing Minecraft or Mario Kart, but equally it could be spent accessing adult content. Here are some guidelines for government-approved apps and games at various age groups, which adults often find surprising.

Age group	Apps and games
Any age	Nintendoland, EA Sports FC, Just Dance, Animal Crossing
7+	Roblox, Minecraft, Lego series
12+	Fortnite, Super Smash Bros, The Sims
13+	Snapchat, Facebook, Instagram, TikTok, X (formerly known as Twitter), Wink, Halo, Avengers, Spider-Man
16+	WhatsApp
18+	Call of Duty, Warzone, Grand Theft Auto, YouTube

A few years ago, a parent came to see me, concerned because her son had been having sleepless nights and nightmares. She then discovered that he had been on YouTube and was repeatedly watching films of beheadings taking place, which at the time were being posted online by ISIS.

Young children, if given unlimited access to these apps and games, start to believe that behaviours seen in these games are normal. They become 'normalised' in their minds. They start to see violence and prostitution and abuse towards women on their screens every day. We can't yet know the impact of this and won't until the children become adults.

Oversharing on social media

Children can sometimes feel pressure to share personal information online, such as:

- Names, addresses and phone numbers.
- The school they attend.
- Frequent locations.
- Other people's personal information, such as their parents'.
- Links to join private group chats.
- Photos of themselves, including their bodies.

Many apps and games give users the option to share their location. Some of the ways they may be likely to share their location include:

- Tagging photos with the geolocation.
- Checking into venues.
- Sharing journeys.
- Location settings on their device.
- Sharing images or videos that contain street names.

If shared publicly, a child's location could be seen by someone they don't know. Others, including adults, can find out where they live or go to school, allowing an accurate picture of their daily routine to be built up. This leads to significant risks to children, including cyberbullying, stalking, unwanted contact or becoming a target.

Other ways that screentime can impact on their mental health

Sending or receiving inappropriate content

Young people can feel pressured into sharing content that could be harmful to themselves or others. This could be in the form of sexting or sharing nude photos, or it may be sharing memes and images of others without their consent, which can be a form of cyberbullying.

Body image issues

With so many influencers and users sharing photos, children can feel under pressure to conform to the 'ideal' body and lifestyle. It is important to talk about positive body image with them and for them to know that many online photos have been enhanced, either with or without AI. They also need to know that the content they see is simply a carefully curated segment of someone's life, not the whole of their life.

Obsessive focus on likes and comments

Children may become focused on how many likes or comments their posts attract. They think that the more 'likes' they receive, the more popular they are (this, of course, works in reverse). This can leave children feeling that they aren't good enough or not as popular as someone else.

Labels and badges of honour

Picture the scene. I walk into a Year 5 classroom in a leafy small town and see the pupils quietly reading. Noticing me, the teacher asks, 'Ms Smith, please could you have a word with my pupils about giving each other (and themselves) labels?'

I ask the pupils what this is all about, and they proceed to tell me:

- 'He keeps telling me I have ADHD. I do have ADHD, but it's none of his business.'
- 'Well, I have autism, so you're lucky.'
- 'No, you don't have autism.'
- 'Yes I do, that's why I can't follow rules.'

Increasingly, both pupils and parents are using labels to classify themselves. Many parents are rightfully seeking diagnoses for their children to receive required additional support in schools, but some people think that there are parents who are referring to their children as 'autistic' as a means of justifying poor behaviour rather than accepting responsibility for their parenting.

Pupils have taken up the mantle for this labelling themselves as well, as the example above illustrates. In one school I visited, there were four pupils in Year 6 opting out of assemblies, music lessons, playground activities and whole-school events on the grounds that they were autistic and didn't like loud noises. None of them had an official diagnosis that had been reported to the school.

My advice for you, as the teacher, is to check SEND records if a pupil tells you they have a diagnosis and to speak to your SENCO. It may be the case that a diagnosis is forthcoming and the school is aware of this, but it hasn't arrived yet, or it may even be the case that a pupil does have a difficulty that the school is not yet aware of and the SENCO needs to investigate further.

Key stage 3 (age 11–14)

Pupils in KS3 face several challenges:

- They are in a new school, and it's much larger than their previous school. Only a few months ago they were the oldest in their school; now they are the youngest, and the older pupils can be quite scary. So, they need looking after, and their form teacher plays an important role in this respect. New pupils get lost and arrive late for lessons; they should be helped in the early days, not punished.
- They are in a three-year period when most are developing physically, which creates stress. Girls seem to be growing much faster than boys. Some boys are much less physically mature than others, which worries them.
- They come under the influence of their peers as much as their parents. Parents are right to worry about their children having 'the wrong friends'. There can also be inappropriate sexual behaviour.

- Adolescents start doing crazy things. Their emotional intelligence is weak, and they have a limited grasp of risks. So, teenagers can upset other people without fully realising the consequences of their actions. They take risks that one day they will grow out of.

- At this age teenagers are focused on forming their own identity. They are thin-skinned and self-conscious. They feel things intensely, so they can be easily upset. They want to be part of a group. They are greatly influenced by their peers, so it's often best to speak to a difficult teenager on their own.

- They seek autonomy and independence, so it's best not to be too authoritarian. If you can, create a culture of trust rather than control.

- The range of abilities arriving in the secondary school will depend in part on how effective their primary school was. Some will still have weak reading and writing, and this will prevent them from being able to access the secondary curriculum. They must be given additional literacy lessons, even at the cost of other subjects. If you are teaching a pupil with very weak writing, try to help them and speak to the SENCO.

- Perhaps for the first time pupils will find themselves in sets or ability groups of some kind. That is not a bad thing in a subject where pupils can exhibit a wide range of ability, such as maths. In other subjects, you may teach the full ability range.

Your teaching at KS3 has to do three things.

It must be interesting

GCSEs seem a long way off, and already some pupils are unsure about the purpose of school. Explain to them why KS3 matters and make your lessons pacy and interesting. Make sure you know what your pupils learned in KS2 in your subject and build on that.

It must lay the foundations for GCSE

This is especially important in the core subjects the pupils will take at GCSE (English language, English literature, maths and the sciences). Too many children seem to develop a belief that they are 'no good at maths', but we know that good teachers can gradually build their confidence to a point where they can pass the GCSE. Supporting struggling mathematicians at this stage is important.

The non-core subjects such as art, history, geography, religious studies and French will be taken by many pupils. Ambitious teachers will be keen to make their subject attractive so pupils opt for it at GCSE.

PE and games are very important regardless of GCSEs because the pupils need to learn how to be physically fit and they develop interests in sports, which can help them for the rest of the lives.

It must provide well-rounded education

Some schools start the GCSE syllabus in Year 9, others in Year 10. So, your subject might be dropped at the end of Year 8 or Year 9. That will be the end of their engagement with your subject for the rest of their lives, so it's important to use KS3 to teach the things that an educated person ought to know.

KS3 is the weakest part of the secondary school curriculum for two reasons: the motivation of external exams is not there, and for many subjects the number of periods per week is limited. No subject can be taught well on fewer than two periods a week, ideally one near the start of the week and one towards the end. But schools like to offer many subjects in KS3, and the temptation is to run some of them for half a term at a time or for only one period a week. So, some pupils exhibit a dip in performance compared to where they were in primary school.

The best schools make every effort to lift the performance of pupils in KS3. They set regular and serious tests and exams. They make a fuss about effort grades, and they reward achievement and effort. As a teacher, you have an important part to play by maintaining good behaviour and making your lessons interesting but also demanding.

Don't assume the pupils learned nothing in primary school – drive them forward as fast as is reasonable. There is no reason why a KS3 pupil can't learn a lot of French or Spanish vocabulary, for example, or be required to explore and understand classical music.

At the end of KS3, the pupils will choose their optional GCSE subjects. A wise form teacher or head of year is needed to ensure they are making sensible choices.

Key stage 4 (age 14–16)

Many of the trends that developed in KS3 become more obvious at KS4:

- The pupils become physically mature while still having the minds of children.
- They misbehave, form close peer groups and are sometimes tempted to bully other teenagers.
- They spend a lot of time on social media. Girls in particular can have mental health issues, which sometimes develop into eating disorders.
- Relationships with parents can worsen, so parents have to remain calm as well as firm.

Teenagers become more interested in sex, in socialising with friends, in experiencing new things even if that means taking risks. They take cues from their peers not their parents. They feel things intensely. They can be less good at taking instructions and may respond best if they are given a voice in school.

In 2020 the website Everyone's Invited was created to publish the anonymous testimonies of girls who had been sexually abused, mainly by boys, in and out of school. Many schools had little idea this was going on. In 2021 Ofsted published a *Review of Sexual Abuse in Schools and Colleges*. A number of issues were discussed including the danger of unsupervised parties and misogynistic behaviours by boys and young men partly influenced by pornography. The team behind the website visit schools to provide support and education in relationships and behaviour.

In 2025 research by the Youth Endowment Fund found that one in eight teachers surveyed had reported a child sexually assaulting another pupil at their school in the past term. Too few children report receiving lessons on topics such as consent, harassment and healthy relationships and teachers often lack the confidence and expertise to teach children about relationships.

Good schools will keep an eye on these nearly-adults, providing the right balance of discipline and pastoral care. As ever, the most important thing is attendance – if a pupil misses lessons, it's very difficult for them to be successful.

As teachers, we need to avoid diagnosing too many young people as having a mental health condition or disorder, as this is the remit of medical professionals. In 2024 James Dahl, master of Wellington College, warned that the Instagram generation are confusing normal stress and anxiety for mental health conditions because increased awareness has led to 'over interpretation' and 'over pathologisation'. Dahl claimed that online diagnosis tools on social media sites are convincing many children they have an issue when they are just experiencing 'the normal undulations of the teenage life cycle'. Social media was leading to 'normal transient forms of teenage upset and distress being interpreted as significant mental health issues'.

Schools will be pushing to get good GCSE results, and to some extent you will be judged by the results of your pupils. Test them frequently by getting them to do past papers and questions you have written which are similar to GCSE papers. Walk through model answers and check the notes they are learning from. Find time to give extra help to any pupils who fall behind. Aim to finish the GCSE syllabus by March of Year 11, leaving about six weeks of the summer term to do final revision.

If a pupil is struggling in Year 10, it's reasonable for them to drop one GCSE so they have more time to devote to the rest.

Give the parents of Year 10 and Year 11 pupils advice about how they can help their children. Keep them off smartphones and electronic games. The Easter holiday of Year 11 needs to be given over to revision at home in the knowledge that exams start in May – they will have long summer holidays to compensate. Parents should be told not to take them away in the Easter holiday – their teenager needs a quiet room to work in at home and should have a revision planner to work from.

A-level subject choice

In Year 11, all pupils will need informed advice on what to do in the following year. Some will stay in their existing school to take A-levels or other qualifications, while many will move to a different school or a sixth form college. Some will go to a further education (FE) college to take a vocational course.

For all pupils, what they do next will depend a bit on their GCSE grades. Most schools and colleges will require minimum GCSE grades for those thinking of taking A-levels and a minimum grade for specific A-level subjects (for example, a grade 7 or above in GCSE maths if you want to take A-level maths).

One of the most important things a teacher can do is give pupils good advice about subject choice. At GCSE the range of options is more limited, but at A-level they are extensive. For example, here are the A-level choices made in 2022 for A-levels that were sat in 2024:

Subject	Male (thousands)	Female (thousands)	Total (thousands)
Art	11	33	44
Biology	27	47	74
Business Studies	27	18	45
Chemistry	27	35	62
Classics	2	4	6
Computing	17	4	21
Design and technology	7	3	10
Drama	2	6	8
Economics	28	12	40
English literature	8	31	39
French	2	5	7
Geography	20	17	37

Subject	Male (thousands)	Female (thousands)	Total (thousands)
History	22	26	48
Maths	67	40	107
Further maths	13	5	18
Media	10	13	23
Music	3	3	6
PE	8	5	13
Physics	33	10	43
Politics	11	11	22
Psychology	21	58	79
Religious studies	5	12	17
Sociology	11	34	45
Spanish	3	6	9

Joint Council for Qualification

This data shows two interesting things:

● The most popular A-levels were maths and psychology.
● Most subjects had a gender bias. For example, far more girls take psychology, sociology and English literature, while far more boys take economics, physics and computing.

Why do fewer girls than boys opt for maths A-level? One reason is that girls get better GCSE results all round, so they have more subjects to choose from than boys who, if they are good at maths, sometimes do comparatively less well in the arts and humanities. Why do fewer girls opt for physics than boys? One reason is that they perceive physics to be a 'male' subject; they prefer to choose a subject like psychology instead.

As a teacher, you will be keen for good pupils to choose the subject you teach. Your school will usually have specific GCSE requirements based on their knowledge of the relationship between GCSE and A-level grades in different subjects. When giving pupils advice about subject choice, you will be weighing up three or four factors:

● What are their favourite subjects?
● Which subjects best support their career aspirations (for example, keeping the door open for medicine)?
● Given their academic level at GCSE, which subjects seem most likely to yield the good A-level grades required by most universities?

- What are their parents saying? Sometimes we have to be clear if a parent has aspirations for their child ('we want her to be a doctor') which may be unrealistic. Equally, you may need to tell parents that it could be good for their child to go to university even if they have never considered this option.

Parents make another serious mistake. They assume that non-vocational A-levels like English or history are 'useless' because they do not lead directly to a job. In fact, most subjects do not directly lead to a job and most jobs do not require a particular A-level subject.

What if A-levels are not the best option?

A-levels are the best option for a pupil who may wish to apply to university. But for pupils who are better off studying a vocational course or taking an apprenticeship, which can lead to a good job, they should be comparing vocational options offered by their current school with the options available in other sixth forms or FE colleges.

Too young to know?

Some children appear to have clear ideas what they want to do by the age of 14 or 16. But in reality, they base their ideas on a very limited understanding of what careers are possible and how to get there. So, advice from teachers matters greatly. Plenty of research shows that the advice given by just one teacher can transform the aspirations and career prospects of young people, including simple comments like, 'you ought to go to university' or 'you are clever – if you work hard, you will do well'. Many teachers and parents have little idea about vocational courses like T-levels, so schools need to bring in expert advice.

Key stage 5 (age 16–18)

The worst is now over. Relationships with parents may improve. The pupils are more grown up and have been sifted as a result of their GCSE grades, so they are taking courses which suit them, whether A-levels, BTECs, T-levels or another vocational course. Those who failed maths or English at GCSE will need to re-sit or take another similar or easier qualification.

It is important for any school to appraise pupils after a few weeks in sixth form and make plans for any who are clearly struggling. You are often aiming for three decent A-level grades, and if a pupil cannot cope with one of their chosen subjects it's not too late to change to another subject (ideally a subject that is good at picking up late starters, such as photography).

If the parents are recent immigrants or from a disadvantaged background, they may know nothing about higher and further education in England, so they need to be advised. I encountered this when I helped set up the London Academy of Excellence in East London. Common issues were:

- Parents who were reluctant for their daughters to go away to university.
- Parents who thought that university degree subjects like history or English (non-vocational subjects, are a waste of time), not realising that most jobs don't require a degree in a particular subject (though of course, some do).
- Parents who had no idea about the hierarchy of universities, thinking that it's fine for their child to go to the university nearest to where they live. But some universities are in fact better or more prestigious than others, and it's an advantage to go to a university that demands high grades if you can make it.
- Parents and sixth formers who were put off university by the student loan, not fully appreciating that the loan doesn't have to be paid off unless your income exceeds a particular threshold.

University choices should be made towards the end of Year 12. Pupils must be given talks about the options and encouraged to be sensible about their choices (ideally two courses that require grades that are challenging but realistic and two or three that are easier and will become insurance offers).

Is it a good idea to go to university? For most pupils the answer is 'yes', as university opens many doors. There are two exceptions:

- Some good firms, like Rolls Royce or Dyson, offer apprenticeships that are more likely than a university to result in a great job. Some offer degree apprenticeships so you get work experience and a degree.
- The students on some courses earn less in their lives than those who had similar academic backgrounds but didn't go to university. These students tend to go to lower-quality universities and study subjects that tend to be less well paid, such as the creative arts. This information can be found by looking at the DfE Longitudinal Education Outcomes data. The DfE takes the academic record of each person (what they studied, where and when) and they match this up with their tax records to show how much they earn in later life.

Earnings of first degree graduates by subject studied and sex, five years after graduation, UK domiciled male and female graduates from English HE providers, 2020/21 tax year

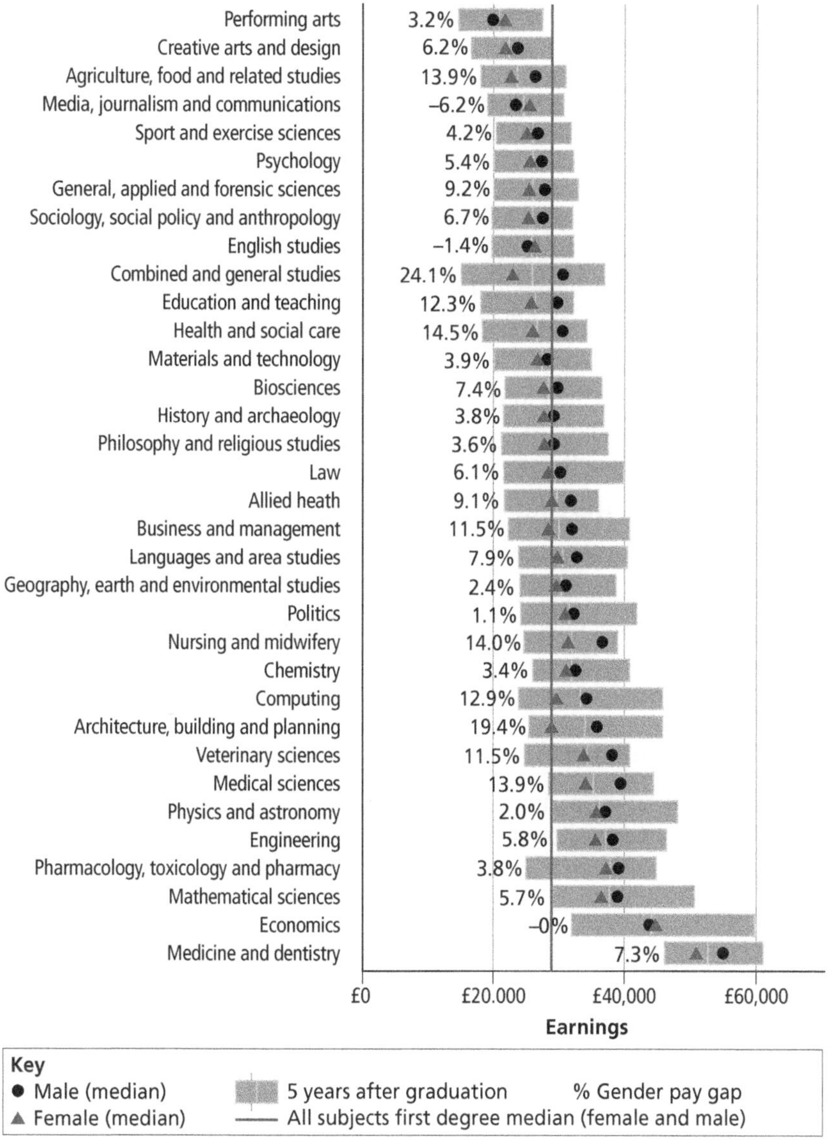

Subject	Gender pay gap
Performing arts	3.2%
Creative arts and design	6.2%
Agriculture, food and related studies	13.9%
Media, journalism and communications	–6.2%
Sport and exercise sciences	4.2%
Psychology	5.4%
General, applied and forensic sciences	9.2%
Sociology, social policy and anthropology	6.7%
English studies	–1.4%
Combined and general studies	24.1%
Education and teaching	12.3%
Health and social care	14.5%
Materials and technology	3.9%
Biosciences	7.4%
History and archaeology	3.8%
Philosophy and religious studies	3.6%
Law	6.1%
Allied heath	9.1%
Business and management	11.5%
Languages and area studies	7.9%
Geography, earth and environmental studies	2.4%
Politics	1.1%
Nursing and midwifery	14.0%
Chemistry	3.4%
Computing	12.9%
Architecture, building and planning	19.4%
Veterinary sciences	11.5%
Medical sciences	13.9%
Physics and astronomy	2.0%
Engineering	5.8%
Pharmacology, toxicology and pharmacy	3.8%
Mathematical sciences	5.7%
Economics	–0%
Medicine and dentistry	7.3%

Earnings: £0   £20.000   £40,000   £60,000

Key
- ● Male (median)
- ▲ Female (median)
- 5 years after graduation
- —— All subjects first degree median (female and male)
- % Gender pay gap

LEO Graduate and Postgraduate Outcomes, Tax year 2020-21 – Explore education statistics –
GOV.UK (explore-education-statistics.service.gov.uk)

269

It is a good idea to invite former pupils who were the first in their family to go to university to come to the school and talk about their experience. As a young teacher, you will be closer to the UCAS process than your older colleagues and can therefore have a big influence on individual pupils.

Applicants for Oxford, Cambridge, medicine and veterinary science face particularly demanding entrance requirements, so they need considered advice; for example, medics need to have done work experience in a hospital or GP surgery. Applications should be completed in September of Year 13. Oxbridge pupils (those who apply to either Oxford or Cambridge) need extra tuition long before they get to the application itself, and they will need help choosing which Oxford or Cambridge college to apply to. They must practice admissions tests before taking them, and this means they will need help from teachers.

Many Oxbridge applicants will fail, and for them it will be the first taste of failure in their lives. They will therefore need support and reassurance. Many parents of all backgrounds may think that their child's stellar GCSE results guarantee them a place at Oxford or Cambridge – this isn't true.

Where are we by the time young people are 19?

By the age of 19, 40% of young people have A-levels, 25% have a vocational level 3 qualification, 10% have retaken GCSEs and improved and another 20% did badly in GCSEs and have not improved. Just over a quarter (29%) of pupils eligible for free school meals at age 15 are in higher education at age 19, compared with almost half (49%) of their better-off peers (DfE, 2024).

Boys and young men

In 2024, an all-party parliamentary group on the attainment of men and boys released a report about the underachievement of boys at all stages of their education:

> Exclusion: In the autumn term, boys were nearly twice as likely as girls to be suspended, and slightly more than twice as likely to be permanently excluded.

> End of reception year: Just under two-thirds of boys had a 'good level of development' aged around five, compared to around three-quarters of girls.

> End of primary schooling: 63% of girls met the expected standard in all of English reading, writing and maths, compared to 56% of boys. However, boys did slightly better than girls in maths: 73% met the expected standard, compared to 72% of girls.

End of compulsory secondary education: Girls do better across all headline measures than boys. For example, 68% of girls in state-funded schools achieved both English and maths GCSEs at grade 4 or above, compared to 63% of boys.

Boys are also more likely to have identified special educational needs than girls. In January 2023, 22% of boys had identified SEN, compared to 12% of girls. 6% of boys had Education, health and care (EHC) plans, suggesting more complex special educational needs, compared to 2% of girls.

Men are considerably less likely to progress to higher education by age 19, than women, and this has been the case for many years. In 2021/22, 54% of women were in HE by 19, compared to only 40% of men. Men are also more likely to drop out of their HE courses.

House of Commons Library, Research Briefing, 2024, Educational attainment of boys

The longer-term implications of these findings are that boys' underperformance impacts general wellbeing and mental health (including suicide, drugs-related issues or rough sleeping) and employability. This is partly attributable to males being more likely to have ADHD or ASD (and then being viewed more negatively than their female counterparts). The group found that within the school system, more severe treatment of boys persists as teachers grade boys more negatively or sanction them more heavily than girls.

References

Campbell, T., 2021, Special Educational Needs and Disabilities within the English primary school system: What can disproportionalities by season of birth contribute to understanding processes behind attributions and (lack of) provisions?, LSE's Centre for Analysis of Social Exclusion (CASE).

DfE, 2024, Development Matters: Non-statutory curriculum guidance for the early years foundation stage.

DfE, 2024, Early years foundation stage statutory framework for group and school-based providers.

Early Years Coalition, 2021, *Birth to 5 Matters: Non-statutory guidance for the Early Years Foundation Stage.* St Albans: Early Education.

House of Commons Library, Research Briefing, 2024, Educational attainment of boys.

Yang, S., Saïd, M., Peyre, H., Ramus, F., Taine, M., Law, E. C., Dufourg, M. N., Heude, B., Cgarles, M. A., and Bernard, J. Y., 2024, Associations of screen use with cognitive development in early childhood: The ELFE birth cohort. The Journal of Child Psychology and Psychiatry, 65(5), 680–693.

Chapter 13
Trends in education

Let us think about the most important educational trends in the UK over the past few years.

Expansion of educational opportunities

In 1950, only 30% of 15-year-olds, 14% of 16-year-olds and 7% of 17-year-olds were in full-time education in England and Wales. In 2025, these figures are close to 100%.

In 1955, 10.7% of the relevant age group passed five or more O-levels at schools in England and Wales; now, with GCSEs, this figure is just above 65%. In 1955, 5.5% of the relevant age group passed one or more A-level; now this is more than 45%.

So, a much higher proportion of the population are being educated, and to a higher level. This is the most important long-term trend. And the most important component of this expansion of education has been the expansion of opportunities for girls. Look, for example, at rounded-up university entry figures since 1950:

Year	Male	Female	Total
1950	13,000	4,000	17,000
1990	43,000	34,000	77,000
2010	230,000	309,000	539,000
2021	235,000	320,000	555,000

Office for Students, 2023, Official Statistics
Bolton, P. and Lewis, J., 2023, Equality of access and outcomes in Higher Education in England, House of Commons Library

In 1996, more women than men were accepted through UCAS for the first time. Since then the gap has grown to around 85,000 a year.

Improving the opportunities of the least successful

In the 2010 Schools White Paper, the foreword, written by the Secretary of State for Education, states:

Our schools should be engines of social mobility, helping children to overcome the accidents of birth and background to achieve much more than they may ever have imagined. But, at the moment, our school system does not close gaps — it widens them.

65% of children get five GCSE grades 4–9 including maths and English, meaning 35% don't. 60% of white working class 14-year-old boys have a reading age of seven.

So, education inequality is seen by many as the biggest problem this country still faces. At the top, our levels of achievement are clearly world class; the problem is the bottom 30%. 70% of children in Britain do quite well at school, but 30% do quite badly in tests compared to other countries, especially East Asia.

But exams are far from being the only measure of progress, and teachers need to find other ways in which children can benefit from school, not least in subjects such as music, drama or sport.

Influence of other countries on our system

In the 2010 Schools White Paper, the foreword by the Prime Minister and Deputy Prime Minister states: 'What really matters is how we're doing compared with our international competitors.' In the past 40 years, Southeast Asia has rapidly developed, and its school systems have started to outperform ours.

The Programme for International Student Assessment (PISA) is the most important international measure of the proficiency of 15-year-olds in maths, reading and science. It is run by the OECD (Organisation for Economic Co-operation and Development). Comparing the most recent results with those of previous years shows how well individual countries are doing compared to other countries and whether these countries are making progress over time.

The PISA scores suggest that 15-year-old pupils in Singapore are 10 months ahead of those in the UK in English and 20 months ahead in maths. South Korea, Japan, Hong Kong and Shanghai have similar results. Why do we see these results? These countries believe everyone can achieve success, so the focus is on effort rather than natural ability. Diligence is rewarded. By contrast, in the UK and US there is too much emphasis on pupil ability and not enough on the virtues of hard work.

We should remember that only 10% of the population of the world lives in Europe, 60% in Asia, 15% in Africa.

The 2022 PISA results showed that:

● In maths, the UK was ranked 12th (but England was 11th) out of 81 countries, a big improvement on the 2018 ranks.

● In reading, the UK was ranked 13th (as was England), a slight improvement since 2018.

● In science, the UK was ranked 14th (England was 13th), the same as the 2018 ranks.

The results for England were better than those for Wales and Scotland. This is important, because the reforms introduced by David Cameron and Michael Gove after 2010 only applied in England. So, to some extent the 2022 results were a judgement on those wide-ranging reforms.

Who did best in 2022? In maths, six East Asian education systems – Hong Kong, Japan, South Korea, Macao (China), Singapore and Taiwan – scored highest. In reading, the top countries were Singapore, Ireland, Estonia, Japan, South Korea and Taiwan. In science, the highest performing countries or cities are the same as the highest six in maths, plus Canada and Estonia.

The PISA scores have some flaws. Many of the places that do best are either individual cities (like Macao) or very small countries (like Singapore). It is wrong to compare such places with a larger and much more socially diverse country like the UK. Indeed, if the UK just put forward test results from London, it would be higher in the PISA league table. Also, the focus on just three subjects devalues the excellence of other subjects in the UK, such as the arts.

Overall, we can say that the UK is doing fairly well. The standard of education in our schools and universities bears comparison with other rich countries. But there are still some weaknesses (Field, 2024; Lenon, 2018):

● **Poor parenting during the early years** – The gap between different children's reading ability is too wide at age five. Some parents teach their children to read, while others don't.

● **The tail of underachievement at age 16** – It is almost as if some pupils learned nothing much at secondary school.

● **The weakness of post-16 further education** – We can do better at developing strong courses that train our young people in skills that lead to good jobs.

Emergence of AI

There are many ways in which AI can save teachers' time:

- Creating lesson plans.
- Finding information about topics.
- Data inputting and analysis.
- Help with redrafting.
- Generating reports.
- Generating checklists.
- Establishing misconceptions to be explored.
- Generating action plans.
- Creating tests of prior knowledge.
- Promoting inclusivity and diversity through adaptive resources.
- Creating an assessment rubric.

Research by the Massachusetts Institute of Technology in 2025 showed that people relying on ChatGPT to write essays had lower brain activity than those using their mind alone. They remembered much less and thought critically less because their brains switched off when using AI. The same was not true of those simply using internet search engines. The conclusion of the research was that AI damages brain function.

Government support for teachers

In 2024, the UK government announced a new project designed to enhance the ability of AI generative tools to learn from a new bank of lesson plans and curriculums. The idea was to support teachers with workload reduction, and it came about as a result of the government finding, through research, that parents would prefer teachers to be using AI to reduce out of hours work as a way of boosting the amount of time they could be spending teaching and supporting children in the classroom with face-to-face teaching.

Backed by £4 million of investment, the government will make available documents including curriculum guidance, lesson plans and anonymised pupil assessments that would then be used by AI companies to train their tools to generate accurate, high-quality content. The resources, such as tailored, creative lesson plans and workbooks, could then be reliably used in schools.

What should we teach our pupils?

If the potential of generative AI is harnessed appropriately, it's likely that pupils may have better access to a knowledge-rich curriculum that allows them to become well-informed users of technology and understand its impact on society. Some of the recommendations suggest that the education sector needs to:

- Prepare pupils for changing workplaces of the future.
- Teach them how to use emerging technologies such as generative AI safely and appropriately.
- Teach them about the limitations, reliability and potential bias of generative AI.
- Help them to understand how information on the internet is organised and ranked.
- Teach enhanced online safety to protect against harmful or misleading content.

Online learning

Major benefits of online learning include cost, convenience and scale, as well as the opportunity to reach a significant number of pupils. Online teaching also has massive potential for raising the quality of education.

Udemy, MasterClass, Oak National Academy and many other education platforms are being used in schools. MasterClass has some content taught by practitioners in the field, often celebrities, such as learning about film making with Martin Scorsese or about conservation from Dr Jane Goodall. Virtual reality (VR) simulation platforms are also being used in schools and universities.

In 2023, Unesco published *An Ed-Tech Tragedy?*, which describes how ed tech has led to poorer education. The online methods used during the Covid-19 pandemic have led to greater inequality and learning systems which put profits before people. Education was narrowed and impoverished.

Global test scores in literacy, science and maths have been falling since 2012, just as the use of tech in schools has been rising.

Private tutoring

Tutoring offers more options for home schooling or educating at home, which is a growing trend. 'Microschools' are being set up, where small groups of pupils meet in person outside a traditional learning environment. Private tutors are also used in schools (who source and pay for them) for pupils with neurodiverse needs who find the traditional classroom challenging. More and more private tutoring will be delivered by AI.

Nothing stands still. We have rising aspirations for our children and our schools. We can learn from what the most successful countries and schools are doing – but teachers rightly fear the turmoil of constant change.

Further reading

Field, S., 2024, Inequality in English post-16 education, Oxford Open Economics, 3(1), i828–i841 or see the *Institute for Fiscal Studies Deaton Review*

Lenon, B., 2018, *Other People's Children: What Happens to Those in the Bottom 50% Academically?* John Catt.

UNESCO, 2023, *An Ed-Tech Tragedy?* UNESCO.

Chapter 14
Where does your school fit in?

There is a bewildering number of types of school in England, mostly due to the historical evolution of the system. Only by looking at this history can we understand where these different types of school came from.

The earliest schools appeared around the end of the sixth century, such as King's Canterbury (597AD) and King's Rochester (604AD). They were attached to cathedrals and monasteries and taught Latin, the language of the Church; many of the pupils would become priests or monks. Later schools were independent of the Church, such as Winchester (1382) and Eton (1440). King Edward VI established many schools, including King Edward's School, Birmingham in 1552. After 1500, many new grammar schools were created, largely for the commercial middle classes. They were fee-charging.

In general, there was strong resistance to state involvement in education before 1870 – education was seen as a matter for parents, not the government. Before the Industrial Revolution, most people were engaged in farming, so children didn't need much education as they were useful working on the farm. Many children didn't go to school, and those who did went to so-called voluntary (often Church of England) primary schools.

The 1870 Elementary Education Act

Also known as the Forster Act, this act allowed school boards to be set up to run schools for children aged 5–12 in England and Wales. It didn't make education free or compulsory, but it did require that a school should be placed within the reach of every child. Local authorities were required to submit data about the number of school-age children in their area and the number that were in school. If there was a shortfall, a school board for the district was set up. This elementary education largely comprised Church of England, nonconformist and Catholic schools. This was the first small step in the long journey towards free and compulsory education up to the age of 18.

The Forster Act was passed because the Industrial Revolution was leading to the creation of large cities and there were concerns about the behaviour of the urban working class. As the number of skilled jobs in manufacturing grew, it was clear that the population needed to be more educated – British schooling was falling behind Germany. The 1867 Reform Act had given the vote to more of the population, and it was felt that voters needed a better education so that they could vote 'wisely'.

So, the government began to provide elementary education in 1870, with secondary education following in 1902. The government also continued to increase funding to the voluntary schools run by the churches. In return, these schools were increasingly influenced by the state and were subject to inspections.

The Elementary Education Act of 1880 specified the minimum age or educational standard that needed to be reached before a child could leave school. It imposed compulsory attendance from 5–10 years. Children under 13 who were employed were required to have a certificate to show they had reached a defined educational standard. State primary education became free of charge in 1891.

The movement of the school leaving age is important because this has always been the age when most children or young people do indeed leave school. These are the school leaving ages from 1880 in England and Wales:

- 1880 – 10
- 1893 – 11
- 1899 – 12
- 1909 – 13
- 1918 – 14
- 1947 – 15
- 1972 – 16
- 2015 – 16 but in education or training to 18

1944 Education Act

Also known as the Butler Act, the aim of this act was to address the needs of the UK in the post-war era. Under this act, fees were abolished in all state schools. Education was divided into primary (ages 5–11) and secondary (ages 11–15). Secondary education was divided into grammar, technical and modern schools. The act also provided for nursery schools and further education (FE) colleges.

Schooling in England and Wales reflected social class, as four types of secondary schools were established:

- Private schools were for wealthier families.
- Grammar schools were mainly for the middle classes. Their curriculum was largely based on that of private schools, with some focus on the classics. To obtain entry to a grammar school, you had to take an entrance exam – the 11-plus. Grammar schools were intended for the most able 25% in the country.

- Secondary modern schools were for children who didn't sit or failed the 11-plus, which was the majority. These schools trained pupils in basic skills in subjects like arithmetic, woodworking and cookery.
- Technical schools were supposed to be for those with a technical aspiration, but few were built because of a shortage of money after the Second World War.

In 1926, secondary voluntary schools had been required to choose between being 'grant-aided' by the local authority or receiving a 'direct grant' from government. Under the 1944 act, most of the direct grant schools became direct grant grammar schools. The direct grant grammar schools offered free places to some families, while others paid fees. They were the most successful schools academically.

Exams

It seems extraordinary to us now that before 1965, only the top 20% of the ability range (those in grammar schools and independent schools) took any exams, which at the time were O-levels. The rest left school at 15 without qualifications, although many moved into apprenticeships with day-release to study at a technical college.

In 1965, the certificate of secondary education (CSE) was introduced for both vocational and academic subjects. If the O-level was for the top 20% of ability, CSEs were for the next 40%. The remaining 40%, it was thought, shouldn't take any nationally recognised leaving exams. So, the population of children was clearly divided into three: academic, technical or vocational and the rest.

After 1984, O-levels and CSEs were scrapped and replaced by the general certificate of secondary education (GCSE), with the intention that most children would take the GCSEs when they were 16. In many ways this was a good thing, but it resulted in 'dumbing-down' compared to the previous O-levels. It also had some consequences for those pupils who had benefited from vocational CSEs: there was less hands-on learning and courses most relevant to work were lost. The assessment of oral skills gave way almost completely to assessment by writing.

Comprehensive schools

After 1965, the country started to move away from academic selection at age 11 (grammar schools and secondary moderns) towards all-ability intakes (comprehensive schools). This happened for numerous reasons:

- A growing demand for skilled workers due to economic advance and technological change. The secondary modern schools weren't supplying the skills the country needed.
- Failing the 11-plus exam (the fate of most children) was inevitably demotivating.
- There were doubts about validity of selection at 11 – too many pupils in grammar schools did badly at O-level, and many children in secondary moderns were perfectly capable of a more academic education.
- Selection at age 11 had the effect of limiting social mobility – very few children from secondary moderns went to university. The division between middle-class grammar schools and working-class secondary moderns cemented social class.
- More and more parents wanted their children to have a good education, and on the whole this wasn't being provided by the secondary moderns, which received less funding than grammar schools.

In 1965, local education authorities were instructed to move towards comprehensive systems of secondary education. This led to the abolition of most but not all grammar schools, some of which went independent at that point. Around 160 state grammar schools still survive in various parts of the country.

Direct grant schools

In the 1960s and 1970s, the most successful schools in England were the direct grant schools, which were often ancient grammar schools like Bradford Grammar, Leeds Grammar and Manchester Grammar. These were independent schools who admitted pupils on the basis of a good score in the 11-plus exam. Children from lower-income families had their fees paid by their local authority. The direct grant was abolished by the government in 1976, and most of the direct grant schools became fully fee-paying.

The Thatcher years

In 1980, then Prime Minister Margaret Thatcher set up the Assisted Places Scheme to allow free or subsidised places at independent schools. This was to compensate for the removal of the government grant from the direct grant schools in 1976.

The 1980s saw a move to greater central government control of schools. Margaret Thatcher's government disliked local authorities, who ran most schools in England and Wales. Many of these authorities believed in 'progressive' forms of education such as mixed-ability teaching and project work rather than traditional school subjects. Most had proved incapable of improving very weak schools.

So, the 1988 Education Reform Act included several measures to remove schools from local authority control:

- Devolution of budgets to schools gave them more control over their budgets.
- The establishment of city technology colleges, which specialised in science, technology and maths and were sponsored by private businesses, who met 20% of the capital costs. Financial control was transferred from local authorities to the head and governors of the school. In due course 15 were created, and they are considered to be the forerunners of academies.
- If enough parents agreed, a school could opt out of local authority control and become a grant maintained school (GMS), which received funds direct from the government. The government gave these schools more money as an incentive to become a GMS.
- The Inner London Education Authority was abolished.

The act also introduced a national curriculum (for the first time anywhere in the UK), which made it compulsory for schools to teach certain subjects and syllabi. National curriculum assessments were introduced at ages 7, 11, 14 and 16 (the tests at 16 being GCSEs) and also gave the Secretary of State for Education control over exams in English and Welsh schools. School league tables were introduced from 1992 to promote competition and inform parents.

The Blair and Brown years

There were many reforms to schools under Tony Blair and Gordon Brown from 1997–2010:

- Literacy and numeracy hours became compulsory in state primary schools, with targets for improved reading, writing and maths.
- All secondary schools were allowed to become 'specialist' in something like science or sport. Specialist schools were allowed to select 10% of their pupils.
- City academies were set up. These were new schools that took over from failing local schools. They were part-funded by local businesses, charities or private individuals and were outside local authority control.
- The Assisted Places Scheme was abolished.

The London Challenge programme (2003–2011)

The London Challenge was a school improvement policy aimed at secondary schools in London; it was later extended to primary schools. In the late 1990s,

London schools were the worst in the country. Today, they outperform schools in the rest of England, achieving the highest proportion of students obtaining good GCSEs, the highest percentage of schools rated 'outstanding' by Ofsted and the highest GCSE attainment for pupils from poorer backgrounds.

In the London Challenge, which was managed by the DfE, the exam results of socially similar schools in London were compared, and this made it possible to challenge underperformance on the compelling grounds that if other schools were doing much better with a similar intake of students, significant improvement was possible. The use of data, therefore, generated both optimism and urgency about the need for change. An important element was buy-in from schools, which was driven by a moral imperative to improve the results for disadvantaged pupils. Improvement work was to be done *with* them, not *to* them.

The focus was on training existing teachers to be more effective. This was done by external experts and the best teachers in the area. The main cost was providing cover for the teachers to have time off to be trained or to train others. The training took place in teaching schools. The host schools' teachers gave training to around 15 teachers from the schools being supported. A teacher in each supported school was appointed the in-house mentor to help the trainee develop back in their own school.

So, the key elements of the London Challenge were:

- A focus on data and data literacy.
- A culture of accountability.
- The creation of a more professional working culture.
- A collective sense of possibility.
- Highly effective practitioner-led professional development.

An Ofsted report (2010) summarised the effect of the London Challenge:

> *Working with teachers from other schools with similar challenges, outside the confines of their home school, enabled frank discussions of strengths and weaknesses in their own teaching, free from concerns about performance management or the disapproval of peers. In particular, a high proportion of time was dedicated to reflecting on and reviewing their own teaching and their understanding of pedagogy. This taught teachers to become reflective practitioners, and they began to share that skill with their colleagues at their home school under the guidance of the school mentor.*

Four other things helped schools in London to improve:

- The Academies programme helped to raise standards in London because it removed some of the worst-performing schools from local authority control and, in the most successful cases, transferred them to very effective groups of independent trustees.
- Teach First programme helped because it recruited some of the brightest graduates coming out of university and put them in the worst London schools. By 2010, these graduates made up around 6% of all London teachers and a much higher proportion in Inner London.
- London has a stronger and more diverse economy than other parts of the country, and this makes it easier for young people to see the link between school and a job. Many London-based companies are involved in improving their local schools.
- Finally, there has been large-scale immigration to London from abroad. To start with, these immigrants were at a disadvantage – they had limited resources, and some spoke very little English. But over time, some of their children became the highest-achieving group in the country, as they were hard-working and ambitious.

The Coalition and Conservative years

Under the Conservative and Liberal Democrats coalition government (2010–15), there was a new focus on social mobility and meritocracy (reward for merit regardless of background). They started the Pupil Premium, which provided extra money to schools for each low-income pupil.

More use was made of data that highlighted the different performance of children by gender, ethnicity or SEND. Government league tables became even more important, with a focus on value added (the progress made by a school from one stage to another compared to the national average). Progress 8 compared the scores achieved by every child in their English and maths SATs results at age 11 with their GCSE results in English, maths and six other subjects.

The national curriculum, GCSE and A-level syllabi were reformed on the basis that international tests told us that other countries' systems were more effective than those in England. The content of the syllabi was increased, and exams were changed to be more stretching. There was an increase in the amount of maths in the curriculum.

There was also an increase in the amount of knowledge that pupils were required to possess. The government was greatly influenced by the US writer E. D. Hirsch, who authored works such as *Cultural Literacy: What Every American Needs to Know*

(1987). Hirsch made the compelling argument that knowledge had to come before either critical thinking or general 'skills' in the school curriculum, because without knowledge in subjects like history or science you don't have the basis for either critical thinking or skills. You need to know things before you can think about or use them.

After 2014, the government reduced the number of exams taken by secondary-age pupils by scrapping GCSE and A-level 'modules'. Every A-level had been divided into six modules that could be taken at any point in the two-year course (such as January in the first year) and then retaken at any point to rack up more marks. This resulted in grade inflation, but it also meant that by the end of the course pupils had forgotten the modules that had been assessed in the first year.

The coalition government also increased the number of academies, which side-lined local authorities further. It made it possible for all state schools in England to become academies that are still publicly funded but with an increased degree of autonomy, including the setting of teachers' pay and deciding the school curriculum.

In 2025, 40% of primary schools and 80% of secondary schools are academies. There are two types of academies:

- Sponsored academies, which had been doing badly and were handed over to a government-approved sponsor.
- Converter academies, which are good schools that chose to convert to academy status.

After 2015, there was a big push to encourage schools in England to join multi-academy trusts (MATs). Regional schools commissioners were appointed for each region to help organise this.

MATs have several advantages. Grouping schools allows economies of scale and the employment of specialist advisers, including turn-around experts. Some of the earliest MATs, such as Harris and Ark, showed how successful they can be. However, one disadvantage of MATs is that the strong centralised systems can result in an erosion of teacher autonomy.

The evidence about the success of academies is mixed – some are brilliant, others are less so – but most academies and academy chains are quite new and it's unfair to judge any of them too quickly. There are outstanding local authority schools and outstanding academies.

Free schools

Free schools were established in 2011 based on the success of charter schools in the US. They are normal state schools, but they are set up and run by groups such as teachers, parents, businesses, charities, independent schools and universities. So, they are funded directly by the government. Quite a few are SEND schools, and some have been set up by local authorities.

There are now over 700 free schools. Inevitably, some have been more successful than others. Some failed to attract pupils and closed. But on average, their exam results have been better than other state schools and several have been outstanding.

Free schools have generated worthwhile innovation, such as the behaviour and academic standards set by Michaela School in Wembley, or the focus on oracy of School 21 in Newham.

Maths schools

In 2017, the government announced its intention of opening specialist sixth-form maths free schools across the country, an idea copied from the Soviet Union. The first two, King's London and Exeter, have been successful. The number of students is small, and the very narrow choice of A-levels on offer means it's unlikely that such schools will make a great impact.

University technical colleges

There are about 40 university technical colleges (UTCs) in England, which are sponsored by universities and local employers. They are for pupils aged 14–18. A UTC curriculum includes one or two technical specialisms linked to the skills gaps in its region. For example, Silverstone UTC, which opened in September 2013 on the Silverstone racetrack, specialises in high-performance engineering and event management.

UTCs have struggled to attract pupils because few pupils at the age of 14 wish to change schools and few schools want their pupils to leave. But they are a good idea. In the future, they may adapt to take more pupils at age 16.

Grammar schools and academic selection

There are 163 grammar schools in England today.

Grammar schools have survived in some places because they are popular with local parents. Chris Cook's research (2016) showed that in local authority areas with grammar schools, the minority of pupils in the area go to the grammar schools and they do better than they may have done in a comprehensive, but the majority left in the comprehensive schools do worse than they may have done had the grammar schools not existed.

The reason that comprehensive schools do less well in areas with grammar schools nearby is that all the high attainment pupils have been stripped out. This makes it harder to push pupils towards the top marks and harder to attract good teachers. Those who have been rejected by the grammar schools (the majority) may be demotivated. Cook's research in Kent and Medway, an area with grammar schools, shows that poorer children lag further behind than they should do, richer children move further ahead and the losses at the bottom are much larger than the gains at the top.

All analysis of the effectiveness of grammar schools is compromised by the fact that 74% of grammar schools are single-sex. Because being single-sex influences results, it's hard to disentangle this influence from that of selection by ability.

It is also important to note that academic selection doesn't just happen with entry to grammar schools at age 11:

- There is selection within schools into streams and sets, and this often determines which subjects pupils will take and, for GCSEs, which tier of exam they will sit.
- There are many comprehensive schools who are allowed to select up to 10% of their pupils on the basis of their ability in a specialism, such as science.
- Schools select pupils in part by the proximity of their homes to the school. When schools deliver good results, this drives up house prices. In this way, social selection becomes established – only wealthier parents can afford to live near the best schools.
- Schools with a religious character may apply religious criteria when selecting pupils, and when they do, the entry is often more middle class.
- Almost all state sixth forms are academically selective. Most comprehensive schools in England only allow a limited proportion of their Year 11 pupils to continue onto A-levels. So those who argue for comprehensive education are really only arguing on behalf of pupils aged 11–16.

So, there is plenty of selection taking place without grammar schools.

Faith schools

Faith schools are generally normal schools that are designated as having a religious character. Schools with a faith designation can use faith criteria in their admissions criteria. They can choose what they teach in religious studies. Parents often like faith schools, sometimes because they reflect their own religious beliefs but more often because they are good schools, and they like their moral code.

The two main providers of faith schools in England are the Church of England and the Catholic Education Service. Around one third of the 20,000 state-funded schools in England are faith schools, approximately 7,000 in total, of which 68% are Church of England schools and 29% are Roman Catholic. Other faith schools are Methodist, Jewish, Muslim, Sikh and Hindu. Around one million children attend Church of England schools, which account for around 25% of primary schools.

Funding agreements for entirely new academies and free schools with a religious character provide that where the school is oversubscribed, at least 50% of places are to be allocated without reference to faith. Catholic schools took exception to this rule, because it meant some Catholic children were displaced by non-Catholic children. For this reason, Catholic schools refused to join MATs or establish Catholic free schools.

Faith schools in England show distinctive geographical distributions. For example, Church of England schools are often located in rural areas around large conurbations, while Catholic schools are most prevalent in the north-west of England.

Faith schools tend to deliver better academic results at both primary and secondary phases, but these effects vary by faith type and seem to be mainly a result of differences in intake rather than anything that goes on inside the schools themselves.

SEND schools

SEND schools with pupils aged 11 and older can specialise in one of the four areas of SEND:

- Communication and interaction
- Cognition and learning
- Social, emotional and mental health
- Sensory and physical needs

Schools can further specialise within these categories to reflect the special needs they help with, for example autism, visual impairment or speech, language and communication needs.

Further education colleges

After GCSEs, where do pupils go? There are four options:

- School sixth form
- Sixth form college
- Apprenticeship with a firm
- FE college

FE colleges are a very important part of the education system in England. Every year, about 100,000 16-year-olds enroll at an FE college to do technical or vocational courses, and yet they are rarely talked about in the media and receive scant attention from politicians. Their funding has been poor and their courses are of mixed quality. In some colleges, teaching is not demanding enough and attendance at lessons is too low.

State boarding schools

State boarding schools are designed for parents who need boarding for their children, for example where both parents work long hours or change job location frequently, such as members of the armed forces. A few boarding schools take overseas pupils as an additional source of income. Boarding schools often get good academic results, and their fees are generally lower than those of independent schools.

Boarding schools have two other advantages: they create a strong sense of community within which many pupils thrive, and they can offer a far wider and deeper range of co-curricular activities than day schools. Pupils at boarding schools tend to become more socially adept as a result of their boarding experience and have a strong sense of belonging to the institution, especially their boarding house.

Independent schools

Independent schools educate 7% of all pupils and 14% of those taking A-levels. Their fees average about £20,000 a year for a day place.

Independent schools have been around for much longer than state schools. A third of pupils at independent schools are on a reduced fee. For example, Manchester Grammar School has 220 bursary holders, and the average bursary is 93% of the fee.

Reforms to the English education system have often mimicked best practice in private schools, such as the notion of independence (in academies and free schools), a focus on traditional academic subjects, character development, soft skills and extra-curricular activities. The international GCSE, similar to GCSEs but designed for overseas schools and much loved by many private schools, was the model for the GCSE reforms in the 2010s.

Research into value-added at GCSE from the Centre for Evaluation and Monitoring (CEM) at Durham (Ndaji et al., 2016) showed much higher levels of value-added in independent schools than in state schools and suggested that attending an independent school is associated with the equivalent of two additional years of schooling by the age of 16. If independent schools were measured on international PISA outcomes, they would outperform the best European nations and be on a par with Japan and South Korea.

34% of pupils at independent schools are from a minority ethnic background (ISC census, 2025). In many independent schools in London and Birmingham, the majority of pupils are non-white.

Independent schools do much good apart from exam results. Many have a specialist provision, which is thin on the ground in the state sector, such as:

● SEND
● Single-sex education
● Boarding
● Schools for very high attainment pupils
● Schools offering the International Baccalaureate
● Specialist music and dance schools

Independent schools generally perform well in sport, music and drama. These are some of the reasons why these schools attract pupils from around the world.

The main limitation of independent schools is their cost, which restricts the number of children who can apply. It is unfair that some children have more spent on their education than others.

Prep schools

Prep schools are junior independent schools for pupils aged 5–11 or 7–13. One of the great merits of prep schools is that they employ subject specialists, who are specialist teachers (often secondary trained) who teach their subject vertically across a school.

Prep schools tend to have dedicated subject rooms for a range of academic subjects, and children go to those rooms for the subject lessons, particularly in KS2.

Some (but not all) pupils at prep schools take the Common Entrance exam at age 11 or 13 across a wide range of subjects as the necessary entry qualification for the senior school they are applying for. For children taking the 13-plus exam, this drives them to a higher level than that achieved by KS3 pupils in the state sector.

Montessori schools

Montessori schools were founded in 1907 by Maria Montessori, Italy's first female doctor, to educate poor Italian children. Her philosophy was that children learn best if they are independent. According to her beliefs, working independently builds confidence and motivation.

So, in a Montessori school children are given freedom to work at their own pace with no fixed lesson times, set assignments or formal testing. They are not expected to learn the same things at the same speed as the person next to them. There is an emphasis on creativity and exploration. They study what they are interested in, and this develops a love of learning.

Montessori schools teach good manners and respect for others. Mixed-age classrooms are common, with younger and older children learning to work together. Educational materials are often made out of natural materials such as wood rather than plastic.

Montessori methods are quite expensive, so many are fee-charging.

Types of schools and colleges in England today

To summarise, the different types of school can be classified in different ways:

- Nurseries, primary schools and secondary schools.
- Single-sex and co-educational schools.
- Day and boarding schools.
- Independent and state schools.
- Maintained schools funded by the local authority and academies, free schools, studio schools and university technical colleges funded by the government.
- Faith schools and non-faith schools.
- Grammar schools and their counterpart, comprehensive schools without the highest attaining pupils and fully comprehensive schools.
- Sixth form colleges.
- FE colleges.
- SEND schools, both private and state.

● Pupil referral units. These are small schools arranged by local authorities for pupils who, because of exclusion, illness or other reasons, would not otherwise receive a suitable education. Often these are pupils whose behaviour has been disruptive. Sometimes these are called alternative provision schools.

So, there are many types of schools and colleges in England because of the historical evolution of the system, the involvement of the Church and the fact that the UK government hasn't been able to agree on one model they can follow consistently.

Where does your school fit in?

References

Ndaji, F., Little, J., and Coe, R., 2016, A comparison of academic achievement in independent and state schools, Centre for Evaluation and Monitoring, Durham University.

Chapter 15
The sociology of schools

Every teacher will need to be aware of the social background of the pupils in their school and classes. In this chapter, we are going to look at the sociology of school-age pupils in England and what, if anything, this means for teachers.

The most important point to consider is that national averages, such as the national average proportion of pupils on free school meals, can be misleading for two reasons:

- Pupils of any one type are not spread evenly across the country or even across classes in your school. Poorer parts of big cities have many more pupils on free school meals than wealthier parts. In the north-east of England, over 30% of pupils are on free school meals, whereas in the south-east the proportion is under 20%.

- National averages can be misinterpreted. For example, the statement 'two in five pupils from the poorest one-third of postcodes fail GCSE maths, nearly twice as many as those from the richest third' may imply that pupils from low-income postcodes are less good at maths.

  But three in five of these children on free school meals pass GCSE maths. And in the Greater London area, many fewer pupils from poorer postcodes fail maths. As a teacher the worst thing you can do is create a self-fulfilling prophecy, where you believe that pupils of a particular background, gender or ethnicity are likely to do more or less well because of their sociology. A teacher who demands less of a boy because he is a boy is creating a self-fulfilling prophecy – the boy does indeed do less well, but that may be because you expected less of him.

  Here is another example: 'Of the bottom 20% of pupils academically at age 16, 25% are on free school meals.' How could you rewrite that sentence to present a different picture?

When Michael Gove was Secretary of State for Education (2010–2014), he often spoke about 'the soft bigotry of low expectations'. Low expectations tend to damage the education of disadvantaged children most.

Children We Care For

Children We Care For ([CWCF], previously known as 'looked after children') are those in the care of the local authority – around 84,000 at any one time. Reasons for being looked after include the following:

- Because they were at risk of abuse or neglect. In 2024, this applied to 54,810 children, which at 65% of all looked after children is the most common reason identified.
- Living in a family where the parenting capacity is chronically inadequate (family dysfunction) – 10,570 (13%).
- There being no parents available to provide for the child (absent parenting) – 7,290 (9%).
- Living in a family that is going through a temporary crisis that diminishes the parental capacity to adequately meet some of the children's needs (family being in acute stress) – 6,160 (7%).
- The child's or parent's disability or illness – 4,010 (5%).

The majority of looked after children are put in foster placements, where an approved carer looks after the child. The largest group are aged 10–15. Most such children will be vulnerable and need the support of their schools. They may have changed schools several times and will need extra help catching up.

Free school meals and family income

25% of children in England are eligible for free school meals, a status given to children whose parents are in receipt of income support benefits. There are plenty of other families who don't qualify for free school meals but who are on low incomes – the so-called 'working poor'.

When you look at the DfE 'Compare the performance of schools and colleges in England' tool, you will see that data is broken down into the comparative performance of pupils who are on free school meals and pupils who are not. You can compare the free school meals numbers and performance of your school with other schools in the area and the country as a whole.

Schools are given additional funding if they have pupils on free school meals – this is called the pupil premium. At the time of writing, this was £1,515 for every primary age pupil and £1,075 for every secondary age pupil. Pupils are defined as disadvantaged if they are known to have been eligible for free school meals at any time in the past six or seven years, they are recorded as having been 'looked after' for at least one day or they are recorded as having been adopted from care.

The term 'Ever 6 FSM' means eligible for free school meals at any point in the past six years.

A child is defined as being in relative poverty if the income of the household they live in is below 60 per cent of the median wage.

Here are the DfE primary school SATs results:

Percentage of pupils meeting the expected standard in reading, writing and maths by disadvantage status, 2019, 2022, and 2023 (England, state-funded schools)

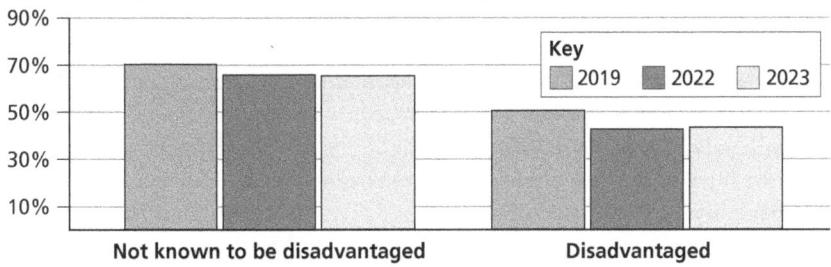

Department for Education, 2023, Key Stage 2 attainment

Research by Professor Steve Strand (2022) showed that GCSE results are influenced by pupils' social class or household income – far greater than the impact of ethnicity or gender. The lowest achieving groups were white British boys and black Caribbean boys from low-income homes, but income was a more important influence than either gender or ethnicity.

There are two important points to make about pupils from low-income homes. First, it's impossible to generalise about their lives. Many have two good parents who support their reading and school life, but some have family lives that are chaotic and where managing school life is the least of their concerns. Try to find out about the backgrounds of your pupils so you can avoid stereotypes.

Second, if you work in a school with a comprehensive intake, you will have pupils from challenging backgrounds who will be difficult to manage for many reasons. Some will come to school hungry, and in general their diet is poor – because of this, they will have health problems. Some pupils will have lost a parent to prison or an unstable partnership, while others will have parents with drug or alcohol addictions. Many will be in homes that are cold, have no place to do homework and lack a computer or internet access. They may have high rates of absenteeism, as there will be very little discipline at home or respect for the rules at school.

These children will need extra help from their school and especially from individual teachers. They will need food, and they will need patience. They can't be permitted to disturb lessons for the other children. Pupil premium money will be spent to support them. If they have suffered from a traumatic childhood, they may not easily be persuaded to take much interest in school life, learning and GCSEs. They will feel that children like them rarely benefit from good exam results. They need a curriculum and teachers than can excite them, including art, music and drama.

The philosopher Pierre Bourdieu (1977) makes the point that advantage and disadvantage should be thought of in three strands:

- **Economic capital** – Money and other assets.
- **Social capital** – Our friends and acquaintances who can broaden our knowledge of experiences and careers.
- **Cultural capital** – Knowledge of music, literature, the theatre and other arts that allow us to think about the human experience and understand choices in our lives.

Children from poorer homes can be disadvantaged in all three of these strands.

Schools have been encouraged to focus on tests and exam results as the main measures of success. But a proportion of pupils in a school with a comprehensive intake are never going to contribute to this success. Some are cognitively limited, while others are more able but lack motivation. In a system where the proportion of pass grades is rationed, a high proportion must fail (see 196–97). The challenge for schools is to find aspects of school life other than grades, which will enhance the lives of such pupils and give them self-confidence, self-regulation and motivation.

Effective practice for teaching disadvantaged pupils

As with teaching SEND pupils ('what works for SEND pupils works for all pupils'), the same is true for teaching disadvantaged pupils. Creating a supportive and inclusive environment by understanding students' needs and having a climate of high expectations will obviously help, but there is no single targeted academic strategy that schools can implement that will fully close the advantage gap. Schools receive extra funding for pupil premium pupils, which may be spent on extra teaching assistants for classes or extra tuition for these pupils. It is also used to fund trips and extra-curricular activities that their families struggle to afford.

The EEF (2024) suggests that the best ways of spending the funding are:

- High quality teaching.
- Targeted academic support.

- Wider strategies (looking at non-academic challenges such as attendance, behaviour and social and emotional learning).
- Diagnosing your pupils' needs carefully.
- Using strong, research-based evidence to support strategies.

Some other support that schools give include:

- Providing access for parents to foodbanks, second-hand clothes, uniform and bedding.
- Mental health support for parents.
- Free school places for young pupils.

Cultural capital

'The best that has been thought and said.' (Matthew Arnold)

Matthew Arnold's famous phrase from *Culture and Anarchy* (1869) is a call to pursue knowledge of the best ideas and writings in the world. Arnold believed that culture was a pursuit of perfection that could help to remedy social ills. He was critical of the idea that culture should be used to create social and class distinctions, and he believed that culture should be available to everyone, not just those from certain backgrounds.

In the 2024 'Early years inspection handbook', Ofsted defined 'cultural capital' as the essential knowledge that children need to prepare them for their future success. It is about giving children the best possible start to their early education.

In recent years, Ofsted has placed an increasing emphasis on the concept of cultural capital and its inclusion in school inspections. They examine the school's curriculum and how it has been designed to promote cultural capital and provide pupils with a broad and balanced curriculum that reflects diverse cultural perspectives. They are looking for a wide range of cultural experiences, including literature, arts, history, and traditions from different backgrounds. This should be planned carefully to help pupils develop a deeper understanding of the world around them.

By providing all pupils with equal access to cultural resources, exposure to diverse experiences and opportunities to develop their cultural awareness, schools can promote social inclusion and academic success for all pupils and support the wellbeing of staff.

Teaching vocabulary explicitly

Research carried out in 2016 by Oxford University Press found that the word-knowledge gap represents a significant and widespread challenge to both primary and secondary schools. Primary school teachers who took part in the research reported that 49% of Year 1 pupils have a limited vocabulary to the extent that it affects their learning. Prior to this, research by Hart and Risley in 2003 found that there is a strong correlation between the number of words a child comes in contact with on a daily basis and the breadth of their vocabulary, and that the 'word gap' widens as pupils get older.

Exposure to rich language is important, and research has demonstrated that explicit instruction and practice with new words is necessary for pupils to develop a deep understanding of vocabulary. Wide reading should also be encouraged and scaffolded, with explicit opportunities to explore, discuss and apply new vocabulary pupils are exposed to when they read. Some schools pre-teach the vocabulary that will be needed for a lesson before it begins and have this vocabulary displayed on walls.

For some great ideas on teaching vocabulary, have a look at 'Why Closing the Word Gap Matters: Oxford Language Report' (2016).

Ethnicity

According to the DfE census (2023–24), 37% of school pupils in England are from a minority ethnic background, with most of the rest (61%) being classified as white British. The largest minority ethnic groups are black African (4.8%), Pakistani (4.6%) and Indian (4%).

For primary schools here is the DfE data for 2023 SATs results:

Percentage of pupils meeting the expected standard in reading, writing and maths (combined) by ethnicity. 2023 (England, state-funded schools)

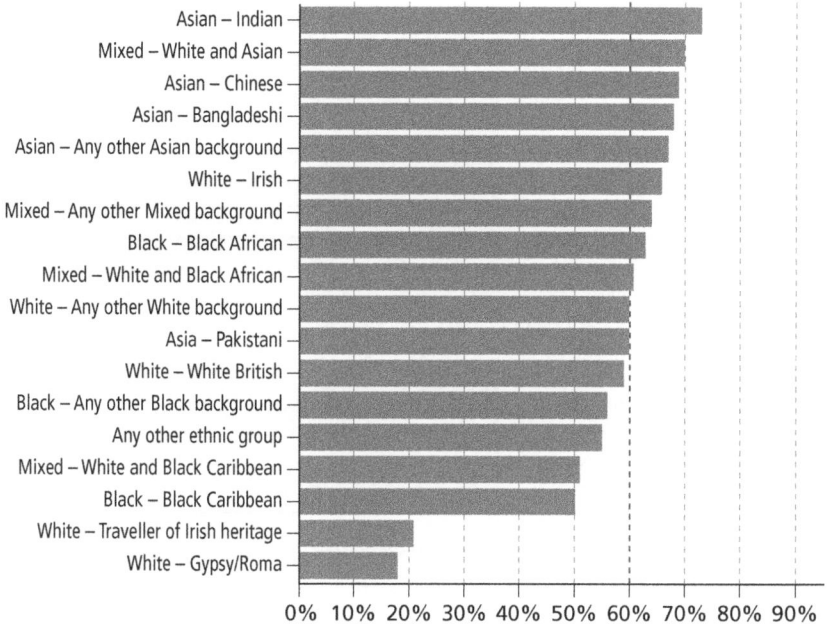

Department for Education 2024 Key Stage 4 Performance

This is the average GCSE Attainment 8 score for 2022 by ethnicity:

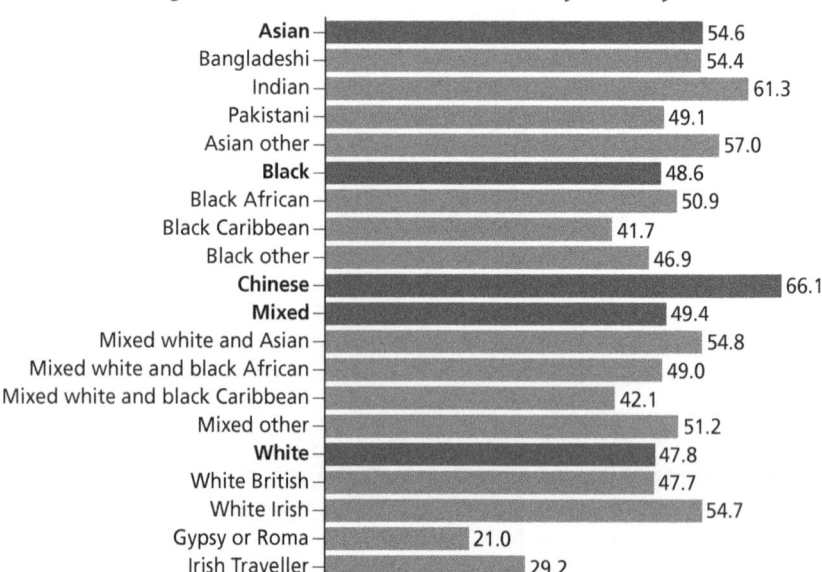

Ethnicity	Score
Asian	54.6
Bangladeshi	54.4
Indian	61.3
Pakistani	49.1
Asian other	57.0
Black	48.6
Black African	50.9
Black Caribbean	41.7
Black other	46.9
Chinese	66.1
Mixed	49.4
Mixed white and Asian	54.8
Mixed white and black African	49.0
Mixed white and black Caribbean	42.1
Mixed other	51.2
White	47.8
White British	47.7
White Irish	54.7
Gypsy or Roma	21.0
Irish Traveller	29.2

Department for Education 2023 GCSE results (attainment 8). The highest available score is 90

White boys from poorer homes do least well other than Gypsy, Roma or Irish Travellers. Children from most minority ethnic groups do better even though many do not speak English at home. The parents of these children came to England to forge a better life and, for many, ensuring that their children take school seriously was and is the priority. Schools (including independent schools) have been the ladder to success for many children of immigrant families in the UK.

But even these statements are generalisations that conceal much detail. For example, Strand et al. (2015) found that among black African pupils, speakers of Igbo from Nigeria got far better GCSE results than Portuguese-speaking black African children. It is important to avoid simplistic interpretations.

EAL

20% of school pupils have English as an additional language (EAL). At age 5, the percentage of EAL pupils achieving a good level of development tends to be lower than that of other pupils, but this evens out as they get older. Pupils who speak Portuguese, Somali, Lingala or Lithuanian tend to have lower outcomes at age 16, while children with Mandarin as their first language tend to perform well, averaging between a B and a C at GCSE in Attainment 8.

The most effective strategy with EAL pupils involves the following:

- Teach them vocabulary and grammar explicitly – don't rely on osmosis.
- Teach them terminology and then model the use of the word in sentences.
- Make them practise over and over again.

The Bell Foundation is a great online platform for getting ideas for supporting your EAL pupils in the classroom. They have identified five key principles to guide EAL pedagogy:

- **Multilingualism is an asset** – Encouraging learners to use and develop their full linguistic repertoire is highly beneficial.
- **High expectations with appropriate support** – Having high expectations of learners using EAL while offering them the language support they need is beneficial to their learning.
- **Integrated focus on content and language** – Focusing on language while teaching subject content is crucial to the progress and attainment of learners using EAL.
- **Effective and holistic pupil assessment** – EAL assessment builds a broad picture of the learner, which enables teachers to plan appropriate and targeted support.
- **Social inclusion** – Including learners using EAL and their family in all aspects of school life improves their wellbeing and motivation for learning and is beneficial for the school.

Gender

At ages five and 11, girls are well ahead of boys. The graph below shows the distribution of SATs results by gender:

Percentage of pupils meeting the expected standard in reading, writing and maths by gender, 2019, 2022 and 2023 (England, all schools)

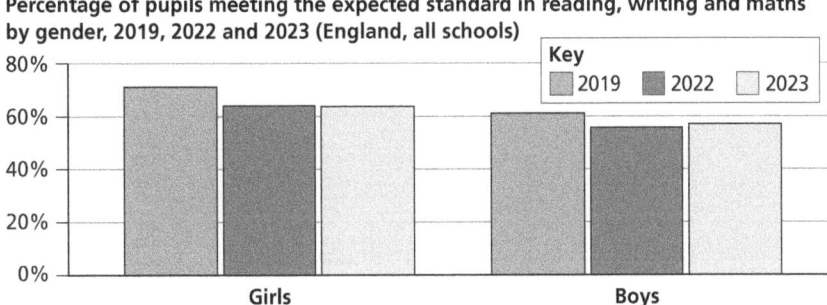

Department for Education, 2023, Key Stage 2 attainment

At GCSE, boys do worse than girls in most subjects. This is because generally boys are less mature than girls of the same age, which means they struggle to concentrate and behave to the same level of the girls. For pupils achieving all grades 9s in their GCSE subjects in 2024, 35% were male and 65% female.

Progress 8 is the measure of progress each child makes between the age of 11 when they took the SATs and the age of 16 when they took GCSEs compared to all other children with similar SAT results. The average progress of all children is set as zero in Progress 8. Even though girls are already well ahead of boys by the age of 11, the 2023 GCSE scores showed that girls averaged a Progress 8 score of 0.12, whereas boys averaged a score of –0.17. This means girls, on average, progressed more than expected when compared to similar pupils in their prior attainment group, whereas boys achieved nearly 20% of a grade less than expected by the end of KS4.

Intersectionality

Intersectionality means the way that the three variables discussed above (income, ethnicity and gender) relate to each other. For example, different ethnic groups have different income profiles, meaning that statements like those above that imply that boys do much worse than girls are not entirely true. White working-class girls do quite poorly, not least in maths, so income, ethnicity and gender intersect in this case.

Another example is that the proportion of pupils at the end of KS4 eligible for free school meals varies by ethnicity in England, as shown in the following table for school year 2023–24.

Ethnicity	Proportion of pupils eligible for free school meals
Irish Traveller	64.9%
Gypsy/Roma	58.3%
Black Caribbean	44.7%
Pakistani	26.6%
Indian	7.3%
Chinese	7.5%
White British	23.8%

Department for Education, 2024, Schools, pupils and their characteristics: academic year 2023–2024

Closing gaps in attainment

We know that there are differences between the average attainment of children when considering social class, gender and ethnicity.

In his 2010 study, Professor Steve Strand looked at how well different schools achieved progress for pupils aged 7–11 in relation to prior attainment, ethnicity, free school meals and gender using an English national dataset of 530,000 pupils attending over 14,200 primary schools. He found that no school appeared to eliminate or reverse the typical within-school attainment gaps in relation to free school meals pupils, black Caribbean pupils or white British pupils. Some schools were much better than others in terms of the results achieved on average by all pupils, but the gaps between groups remained the same regardless of the school's performance.

In a 2016 study, Strand analysed the national test results at age 7–11 of over 6,000 pupils attending 57 mainstream primary schools over three successive years in a socially and ethnically diverse London borough. The pupil groups with the poorest progress were white British pupils on free school meals and black Caribbean pupils (both eligible and not eligible for free school meals). Differences between schools in average pupil progress were large, but there was no evidence of differential school effectiveness in relation to closing gaps relating to social class, ethnicity or gender. All pupil groupings benefited from attending the more effective schools to a broadly similar extent, so these schools 'raised the bar' but did not 'close the gap'.

Why is it that attainment gaps between rich and poor, black and white, boy and girl remain the same whether the school gets good results or bad results? The answer may be that the attainment gap has little to do with the school and more to do with the family background. Or it may be the case that schools do things that limit their ability to close the gaps such as setting, which usually places the more disadvantaged children in lower sets, which may reduce motivation.

Closing gaps in attainment is very hard and ultimately may be less valuable for the individual children than getting good or very good results for *all* pupils regardless of their background.

Professor John Goldthorpe is the doyen of UK sociologists and works from Nuffield College, Oxford. His work on England since the Second World War shows that education has had little impact in terms of social mobility. What mattered most for social mobility was the creation of better jobs, such as the growth of good service-sector jobs after 1960 that provided opportunities for the children of working-class families whose parents had worked in dying, mining and manufacturing sectors (Goldthorpe, 2012; Bukodi and Goldthorpe, 2019).

Schools were less important than job creation in terms of social mobility. Parents with superior (economic, social and cultural) resources are well able to deploy those resources to ensure that their children retain a competitive edge. Of course, at the level of individual children, good education can create social mobility relative to the economic status of their parents, but this is not true on the national scale. The best way to achieve social mobility more broadly is to create more good quality professional and managerial jobs.

What about gaps in attainment between the north and south of England?

Analysis of GCSE data over years shows that, although on average pupils in London do better than, say, those in the north of England, this gap is due to differences in ethnicity and social class, not geography. The striking fact is that the differences in GCSE grades between different regions of England are small compared to the gap in attainment between different schools in almost every local area (Burgess and Thomson, 2023). London has some low-performing schools, while the north has plenty of high-performing schools, so regional gaps in attainment are not fully explained by some regions having better schools than others.

So why do some children do less well at school?

The evidence suggests that the main reasons some children do badly is not 'bad schools' but the characteristics of the children themselves and their families. A report for the Institute for Public Policy Research (Clifton and Cook, 2012) found that 'about 20% of variability in a pupil's achievement is attributable to school-level factors, with around 80% attributable to pupil-level factors'.

Those results are similar to the findings of Professor Robert Plomin of the Institute of Psychiatry, Psychology and Neuroscience, King's College, London. Plomin took 10,000 pairs of twins born between 1994–96 and he has tracked them through their lives. Some were identical twins, some were not; some were brought up together, while some were separated and brought up by different parents. These traits enabled Plomin to determine the relative influence of genes and environment.

In terms of GCSE results, Plomin found that school accounted for 20% of the variance in achievement, genes explained 60% of differences and the rest was the environment. This doesn't mean that schools can't make up for any lack of genetic ability – Plomin is very clear that they can. Genes predict the mean outcome for groups, but there is a wide range of individual differences within each group. So, you can possess genes that on average may predict poor ability, but you can still do very well in your GCSEs. As we all know, pupils who may be less academically able can compensate by working hard.

As schools have become better, the relative impact of genes has become greater. Two hundred years ago there was a low national level of reading ability, so genes were less important in terms of explaining variability in reading than environment, as so few children went to school. Today, there is a high national level of reading ability because everyone is taught to read at school, so genes have become more important in explaining variations in reading ability than the competence of your parents or the school you went to.

Other authors place greater emphasis on differences in the home environment. For example, Gilbert (2018) describes the fact that children from lower-income homes have a narrow range of experiences than better-off children, including holidays abroad, day trips out and parents reading books to them. These experiences develop schema in the brain, which are sets of interconnected knowledge to which new knowledge can be more easily attached and are more easily understood by the child. For example, if a child has been to an art gallery they will be more likely to understand the meaning of words like 'exhibition' or 'picture frame'. Language development depends less on being taught words than hearing words spoken in a relevant context.

Children from middle-class homes will arrive at school with a greater range of schema in their brains based on a range of experiences that cost money. They will, as a result, pick up new ideas more readily. They will also have a wider vocabulary linked to this wider range of experiences, alongside the fact that their parents were more likely to read to them.

So, children start school with very unequal levels of cognitive development that are closely associated with their parents' social class and income, and those inequalities persist through the school and after leaving school (Johnson, 2024).

Children from poorer homes have worse nutrition and health. They are more likely to suffer from housing insecurity and broken homes. They are much less likely to have a quiet space to do homework and are more likely to have caring responsibilities for parents and siblings.

Diane Reay (2024) writes about the fact that many parents in poorer households had a negative experience at school themselves. This reduces their ability to help their children, and quite quickly their attitude towards education infects their children. School is seen as an obstacle to success rather than a ladder to opportunity.

Children from poorer homes can be more likely to form friendships with other pupils who don't like or enjoy school. They may cement their position in the friendship group by misbehaving and being anti-learning.

Once a school develops a reputation for being a good school, better-off parents buy houses in the catchment area, which drives up house prices. These schools become more and more middle class. The Sutton Trust found that the top performing 500 comprehensive schools in England based on GCSE attainment are highly socially selective, taking just 9.4% of pupils eligible for free school meals, under half the rate of the average comprehensive (Cullinane et al., 2017).

Children from poorer homes are much more likely to change schools frequently, often because of insecure housing tenure or a deterioration in their parents' ability to afford the rent. Children who move school other than at age 11 and 16 will often find that the only places available are in the lowest-achieving schools in the area.

Schools in disadvantaged areas find it harder to recruit good teachers. A Teacher Tapp survey found that 77% of primary heads in the most affluent areas had found that recruitment was difficult, jumping to 84% in the most deprived areas. 28% of schools in poor areas had experience of new teachers never turning up for the job at all compared to 20% in affluent areas (Teacher Tapp, 2024).

So, is the problem weak pupils or bad schools? It is probably better to direct government policy at improving struggling pupils within all schools rather than focusing on so-called 'weak' schools. The pupil premium is an example of the former – it recognises that there are disadvantaged pupils everywhere and it's paid to all schools.

There is a lot of variation in results between neighbouring schools, but there is also a lot of variation in GCSE outcomes within schools. This is important to bear in mind, because improving low performing schools won't help *all* low attainment pupils since there are many low attainers in high-performing schools (Burgess and Thomson, 2023).

Extra reading

Arnold, M., 1869, Culture and Anarchy, In R. H. Super (Ed.), *The Complete Prose Works of Matthew Arnold*, Volume 5, Ann Arbor: University of Michigan, 1960.

Bourdieu, P., 1977, *Outline of a Theory of Practice*, Cambridge University Press.

Bukodi, E. and Goldthorpe, J,. 2019, *Social Mobility and Education in Britain: Research, Politics and Policy*, Cambridge University Press.

Burgess, S. and Thomson, D., 2023, Differences in school performance are local not regional (mostly), Education DataLab.

Clifton, J. and Cook, C., 2012, *A Long Division: Closing the Gap in England's Secondary Schools*, London: Institute for Public Policy Research.

Cullinane, C., Hillary, J., Andrade, J., and McNamara, S., 2017, *Selective Comprehensives 2017: Admissions to High-Attaining Non-Selective Schools for Disadvantaged Pupils*, London: The Sutton Trust.

Department for Education, 2024, Schools, pupils and their characteristics: Academic year 2023-2024.

Gilbert, I., 2018, *The Working Class*, Crown House.

Goldthorpe, J. H., 2012, Understanding and misunderstanding - social mobility in Britain: The entry of the economists, the confusion of politicians and the limits of educational policy, Oxford: Oxford Institute of Social Policy and Nuffield College, University of Oxford.

Hart, B. and Risley, T., 2003, The Early Catastrophe – The 30 Million Word Gap by Age 3. American Educator, 27, 4–9.

Johnson, P., 2024, *Educational inequalities*, Oxford Open Economics, 3(1), i758–759 or see the Institute for Fiscal Studies Deaton Review.

Oxford University Press, 2016, Why Closing the Word Gap Matters: Oxford Language Report, Oxford.

Plomin, R., 2018, *Blueprint: How DNA Makes Us Who We Are*, Penguin.

Reay, D., 2024, *Measuring and understanding contemporary English educational inequalities*, Oxford Open Economics, 3(1), i861–i878 or see the Institute for Fiscal Studies Deaton Review.

Strand, S., 2010, Do some schools narrow the gap? Differential school effectiveness by ethnicity, gender, poverty and prior attainment, School Effectiveness and School Improvement, 21(3), 289–314.

Strand, S., Malmberg, L., and Hall, J., 2015, English as an Additional Language and educational achievement in England: An analysis of the National Pupil Database, Department of Education, Oxford University.

Strand, S., 2016, Do some schools narrow the gap? Differential school effectiveness revisited, Review of Education, 4(2), 107–144.

Strand, S., 2022, *Education and achievement at 16*, Sociology Review.

Chapter 16
The politics of teaching

Schools in England are always going to be the subject of political debates because governments control most of them. Politicians can't afford anything other than success, and of course the future of the country depends on England having good schools. There are a number of key debates surrounding politics and education.

Growing government control of schools

This includes what is taught (the national curriculum determines the subjects taught and the syllabus content of those subjects), the funding of schools (a powerful lever of control for the government) and the inspection of schools by Ofsted.

Members of parliament determine government policy, but ministers typically spend a short amount of time in the DfE and most of them have limited experience of schools. They have special advisers (SPADs), who are young people whose power may exceed their experience. There are professional educators that the government of the time chooses to call upon, but they are often only there because they support the opinions of the current DfE ministers.

This question has a counterpart – do we agree with the reduction in the role of local authorities, who know their area better than the government but have sometimes been disappointing in the past?

Choice for parents

In theory, giving parents the freedom of choice regarding their children's education should allow good schools to grow and poor schools to decline. This was one of the ideas behind the creation of free schools after 2010. But in practice, less densely populated parts of the country can't afford to build a diversity of schools accessible to all pupils. Even in cities, most parents don't have much choice – they select the nearest school.

Do MATs work?

MATs have not been around long and are still an experiment. They achieve economies of scale, which is good for budgets. But some MATs are more successful than others.

How much money should be spent on education?

Education spending is the second largest element of public service spending in the UK behind health, totalling £116 billion in 2023–24, or around 4.4% of national income. Education is in competition with spending on the NHS, defence and welfare support. It is the job of every government to determine where the priorities lie. The amount of money available depends in part on whether any given government believes in low or high taxation.

What should we teach?

There is a debate, which may never be resolved, between those who believe in a traditional academic curriculum and those who think that in the era of advanced technology there should be more focus on skills. These skills are needed for a twenty-first century economy where AI will play an increasingly prominent role. The problem is that skills, like creativity, team-work and critical thinking, are best taught in the context of traditional school subjects. It is hard to teach 'skills' in isolation.

In 2023, the then prime minister, Rishi Sunak, proposed that all sixth formers should study maths – as happens in a number of countries, and is an element of the sixth form International Baccalaureate (IB). Sunak believed that a strong grasp of maths was necessary for individual success in many careers in the modern-day economy and economic growth in the UK. It was a reasonable view.

As things stand, 30% of young people fail GCSE maths, so for them the priority is presumably to continue to work at basic maths – the sort of maths we all need in everyday life. Over 100,000 a year study A-level maths, so there is no need to force more maths onto them. The rest (in the middle) have passed GCSE maths and so are already quite competent. So, sixth form maths would have at least three streams.

Of course, if sixth formers all do maths, there will be less time available to do traditional A-levels. So, A-level syllabi will need to be cut, and that will impact what students know when they go up to university.

A curriculum is only worth having if it motivates pupils, as unmotivated pupils rarely succeed. The current English model of 3–4 sixth form subjects (or one T-level) chosen from a wide range of possibilities is the best possible way of ensuring motivation. The pupils are choosing subjects they like.

A third of pupils fail English and maths GCSEs (below grade 4). These are what the teachers' union, the Association of School and College Leaders (ASCL) call the 'forgotten third' (Education Policy Institute, 2019). After 11 years in school, these pupils have got little from these two crucial subjects in terms of qualifications. Should we accept that this is simply a fair reflection of their work ethic and academic competence? Or is this a cruel or ineffective way to treat young people?

Before 1986, many children didn't take any public exams before they left school. From 1986 onwards, GCSEs were introduced and were designed to be suitable for the whole school population. Over time, many schools also introduced vocational alternatives to GCSEs. It may seem like it was a sensible road to go down, but experience suggested that there were three big issues:

1. Higher attainment pupils found GCSEs too easy and rather dull. That is why, after 2012, the government introduced harder, more stretching questions into GCSEs and created a new top grade (grade 9) to recognise the high attainment pupils who could manage these tougher questions.

2. The vocational alternatives to GCSEs were investigated by Baroness Alison Wolf in 2011, and she concluded that not only were they rather poor qualifications but possessing these qualifications turned out to do more harm to a pupil's prospects than not having them. They were, in effect, a negative qualification.

3. The schools' minister, Nick Gibb, found evidence that children with high potential from disadvantaged homes were wrongly put in for sub-standard vocational qualifications and GCSE subjects that did not pave the way to good A-levels and access to university. This raises two questions:

   - Can schools be trusted to pick the right pathway for pupils if they are to be divided into academic and vocational streams?
   - If you are going to divide pupils into these streams, at what age should the decision be made? (At present, the decision is made when they are 14 or 16.)

Russell Group universities published a list of A-level subjects that were most likely to lead to the degree subjects they offered ('facilitating subjects'). This inspired Gibb to introduce the EBacc, a list of GCSE subjects that most pupils should take in order to keep the door to university open.

There are those who say that children are different from each other, and some are much more suited to academic GCSEs than others. There are those who say that dividing children into academic and vocational streams at age 14 is too early and is tantamount to dividing them into sheep and goats in the way we did with the 11+ exam after 1944 (see page 280).

How should we teach?

There are many teachers who will not agree with some aspects of the teaching methods described in this book. If you wanted to classify different approaches to teaching, you could call them 'traditional' and 'progressive'.

Traditional teaching methods focus on the teacher transmitting knowledge to the pupil through:

- traditional subjects
- direct instruction
- a focus on memorisation and grades
- use of textbooks
- learning that occurs according to a set pace and schedule.

Progressive teaching methods are pupil-centred and focus on the learning process rather than the curriculum. They include:

- Learning by doing, such as hands-on projects.
- Learning that takes place through dialogue and interaction.
- A focus on critical thinking and problem solving.
- Group work.
- Less use of textbooks.
- Giving children the freedom to choose activities.
- The teacher acting as a guide and facilitating learning rather than directing it.

Both methods have merits and limitations, and many teachers use elements of both. Do read Peal (2014), Birbalsingh (2016) and Gibb and Peal (2025).

What is the future of assessment?

Those who support written exams are adamant that they are the simplest and fairest way of 'sorting' pupils, identifying good and less good schools and encouraging young people to commit what is taught to the memory. On the other hand, those who oppose exams like GCSEs claim that exam preparation takes too much of the time that could be spent more productively, exams are stressful and assessing pupils by means of written exams fails to capture the full range of their abilities.

There are two specific issues with exams that will continue to be debated:

- The fact that we use written, end-of-course exams in most cases. Some pupils find these stressful, and they may be better at other forms of assessment such as coursework. But coursework can be dull and is easily corrupted by cheating.

- Grades awarded to the more subjective subjects are unreliable. In 2018, Ofqual published some analysis of marking consistency. It summarises the results of a double marking project in which each exam script is marked by a chief examiner as well as a standard examiner.

For maths and science subjects, the standard examiner and chief examiner awarded the same grade in well over 80% of cases. However, corresponding figures were around 60% in English and history. Since the grade associated with the mark given by a senior examiner – referred to by Ofqual as the 'definitive' grade – is by definition 'right', then on average around 40% of the awarded English and history grades could be wrong.

Why are these grades so unreliable? Not because essay marking is sloppy, but because essay marking is not precise. Different examiners can legitimately give the same script (slightly) different marks.

Should state grammar schools still be allowed to exist?

They are good for the few pupils who get in, bad for the majority who do not (pages 293–94).

Should we still have private schools?

It seems reasonable that if parents have the money, they should be allowed to spend it on their children's education if they wish to. Independent schools do a good job (they have to), but the system is unfair because the amount spent per pupil in independent schools is greater than in the state sector.

Independent schools are good schools, and any future government may ask the question of whether can they be opened up to disadvantaged children or, for boarding schools, children in care. Can we introduce a scheme whereby such parents take the money that the government spends on each pupil in the state sector (about £8,000 per year) to an independent school?

School inspections

Ofsted plays a useful role in identifying good and struggling schools. Without Ofsted, many parents would only have exam results to look at. But many state schools place too much emphasis on 'preparing for Ofsted', and fear of Ofsted drives down teacher motivation. We're still trying to find the balance between holding schools to agreed standards while allowing them the freedom and flexibility to improve the education they deliver.

Should so many young people go to university?

According to the Higher Education Statistics Agency, there are 2.4 million students in higher education. For most of these students, going to university is very worthwhile and boosts lifetime income. But for others, it may have been better not to have gone – around 25% of graduates aged 21–30 are in low- to medium-skilled jobs.

Over the next few years, we need to increase the number of young people taking qualifications that lead directly to the skilled jobs where there is a shortage of qualified people at the moment, such as digital skills, health and life sciences, the green economy, house building and infrastructure development. Many such qualifications should be at level 4–5, which means above A-level but below degree level.

References

Birbalsingh, K., 2016, *The Battle Hymn of the Tiger Teachers: The Michaela Way*, John Catt.

Education Policy Institute, 2019, The forgotten third: a rapid review of the evidence, ASCL.

Gibb, N. and Peal, R., 2025, *Reforming Lessons: Why English Schools Have Improved Since 2010 and How This Was Achieved*, Routledge.

Ofqual, 2018, *Marking consistency metrics: An update.*

Peal, R., 2014, *Progressively Worse: The Burden of Bad Ideas in British Schools*, Civitas.

Willingham, D., 2021, *Why Don't Pupils Like School*, 2nd edition, Jossey-Bass.

Wolf, A., 2011, Review of vocational education: the Wolf report, Department for Education.

Chapter 17
What is the purpose of education?

It is a great pity that the syllabus for QTS ignores any consideration of the philosophy of education, preferring instead to focus on the mechanics of classroom management. All teachers should think about the purpose of schools.

Here are some quotes about education:

- 'Education is not the filling of a pail, but rather the lighting of a fire.' (W. B. Yeats)
- 'Education is not preparation for life; education is life itself.' (John Dewey)
- 'An investment in knowledge pays the best interest.' (Benjamin Franklin)
- 'Education is the key to unlock the golden door of freedom.' (George Washington Carver)
- 'The content of a book holds the power of education, and it is with this power that we can shape our future and change lives.' (Malala Yousafzai)
- 'Education is the passport to the future, for tomorrow belongs to those who prepare for it today.' (Malcolm X)
- 'Education's purpose is to replace an empty mind with an open one.' (Malcolm Forbes)
- 'Give a man a fish and you feed him for a day; teach a man to fish and you feed him for a lifetime.' (Maimonides)
- 'The aim of education is the knowledge, not of facts, but of values.' (William Burroughs)
- 'Intelligence plus character – that is the goal of true education.' (Martin Luther King Jr)
- 'The ability to read, write, and analyse; the confidence to stand up and demand justice and equality; the qualifications and connections to get your foot in the door and take your seat at the table – all of that starts with education.' (Michelle Obama)

The aims of education

The main purpose of education should be to transmit important human knowledge in a way that will ensure the pupil is able to recall a good proportion of it in the years after school. Important knowledge is that which provides essential life skills, which allows pupils to understand the world, which provides a basis for developing related interests after school, which leads directly or indirectly to employment.

Essential life skills can in large measure be taught by parents. Where parents can't manage this, it's up to schools to plug the gap by teaching the following:

- The ability to read and write well.
- The ability to speak well.
- Basic numeracy.
- IT skills.
- The ability to concentrate, memorise and work hard.
- The ability to be an effective part of a team.
- The ability to be resilient in the face of difficulties.
- The ability to be organised.
- The ability to form good relationships.
- The ability to live a healthy life.

For those with more effective parents, the essential skills a school will teach include English, mathematics and ICT. For those with less effective parents, schools have much more to do, including teaching pupils how to behave, how to organise themselves and how to eat well and be healthy. Children starting primary school are increasingly having to be taught bladder control, how to dress themselves and how to eat with cutlery.

Enabling pupils to understand the world is the particular function of history, geography, science and religious studies. These subjects allow us to make sense of the world and our place in it. They give us life perspective.

Providing the basis for developing interests after school is a function of many school subjects. Most have the capacity to do this, including sport, art, design and technology, drama, music, languages and literature – areas of human endeavour that are part of what makes life worth living. Latin and Ancient Greek are two 'useless' subjects that bring great enjoyment to some of our highest attaining pupils.

In many schools, inadequate emphasis is placed on sport, societies and activities, which develop qualities of leadership and teamwork. Too little time is devoted to them. Too much weight is placed on exam results because of DfE accountability measures, and too little emphasis is given to the non-examined areas of the curriculum by Ofsted.

We have been surprised by the number of pupils we have taught whose lives were influenced by activities they did at school outside the mainstream curriculum.

Some joined the armed forces – an interest they developed at school through the cadet force. The areas of the Harrow curriculum that inspired Winston Churchill were art, history and the Harrow rifle corps – the basis of lifelong interests salvaged from a curriculum that otherwise passed him by.

Several subjects can lead, after further training, to employment, including computer science, design and technology, A-level sciences and FE college vocational courses.

Another purpose of school is to improve children's health – more than a third of children in England are overweight, especially in the poorest areas. Providing healthy food and plenty of exercise are useful functions for schools.

The purposes of school education are that which can be achieved in 10,000 hours, but not all purposes of education can be achieved in that time. If you spend time specifically teaching character, citizenship, British values or PSHE, then something else has to be cut. Parents and politicians are always quick to suggest that schools solve the problems of society by 'teaching it', but never say what should be cut to make room. The multiple purposes of education exceed the time available.

Some people will rightly make arguments such as, 'the purpose of education is to create nice people or good citizens'. These are reasonable aspirations but are largely the responsibility of parents. If you take your eye off the main game – improving children's knowledge – then you tend to lose the match. All schools aim to create nice people and good citizens, but that should come as a by-product of the main function of the school. There will also be some who say, 'the purpose is to produce a fairer society'. Yes, but perhaps this shouldn't be the main purpose; it should be an important side effect of educating all children well.

So, education has many possible purposes, and it's not a bad idea to decide what you think they are, putting your ideas in some sort of rank order. For example:

1. Learning things that adults believe are worth knowing.
2. Getting good exam results that open the door to good universities and better jobs.
3. Developing skills that are going to be most relevant by 2050 and will help grow the country's economy.
4. Creating happy pupils.
5. Improving social mobility by helping pupils from disadvantaged backgrounds do better.
6. Saving the planet by educating children about climate change.

These are not mutually exclusive, but different politicians as well as different philosophers have held these different beliefs in recent years.

What do we do about vocational courses?

International comparisons tell us three things about what we do as a country:

- We place less emphasis on mathematics but more emphasis on other subjects compared to East Asia.
- We do well at the top of the attainment range compared to other high-performing jurisdictions.
- We do particularly badly at the bottom of the attainment range.

The fact that our public exam results correlate closely with social class means that, on average, pupils from disadvantaged backgrounds do poorly compared to their peers in England and to pupils from disadvantaged backgrounds in places like East Asia. There are two very different reactions to this.

View 1: We must try harder with academic courses

For the successive governments between 2010 and 2024, a priority was to improve the public exam results of the bottom 30% of pupils, including white working-class boys. Pupils who failed the English or maths GCSE when they were 16 were required to attend extra English and maths classes and resit these exams when they went on to vocational courses at FE colleges. Unfortunately, only 15–20% of those resitting pass. Of course, some excellent comprehensive schools achieve a much higher pass rate at age 16. This suggests that, if some schools can do it, we should not abandon the aspiration to get many more pupils up to the pass level.

The 2010–2024 governments took the view that vocational equivalents to GCSEs had been a mistake. No university or employer treated them as being an equivalent – they were effectively a negative qualification, something that implied that a young person was less intelligent. So, these vocational courses were scrapped.

What is more, research showed that pushing children, mainly from disadvantaged backgrounds, into a vocational pathway at age 14 had the same impact as the 11-plus exam (see pages 319–20) – a good number were misclassified.

View 2: We should stop pretending that academic courses are the correct diet for all pupils

The resitting of maths and English GCSEs policy has been a failure; most people don't need to learn the algebra or trigonometry elements of GCSE maths. There is a hard core of pupils who lack motivation, and they would be much better off taking vocational courses that may lead to a skilled job. There is currently too much emphasis in Westminster on the academic route.

David Goodhart explains in his book, *Head, Hand and Heart* (2020), there are three types of job:

● Jobs of the head, which require memorisation and are measured by academic qualifications.
● Jobs of the hand, which require a manual skill.
● Jobs of the heart, which require a particular personality, such as in social care.

Too much emphasis has been placed on jobs of the head and, as a result, England has a shortage of skilled technicians and care workers compared to many other countries.

Parity of esteem

Politicians have long fretted about the failure to achieve 'parity of esteem' between academic and vocational subjects, with some obvious exceptions like medicine and law. This is beginning to seem like a mistake. Now that 50% of people go to university there is less prestige attached to that achievement, and the government's own longitudinal outcomes data shows that many degrees leave young people worse off than if they had not gone to university.

When T-levels started in 2019, they were designed to be the equivalent to A-levels for technical courses. But for many less academic young people they were too demanding. This was a mistake caused by politicians being anxious about parity of esteem.

Further reading

Goodhart, D., 2020, *Head, Hand and Heart*, Allen Lane.

O'Hear, A., 2023, *In Defence of Liberal Education: Philosophy and Controversies*, University of Buckingham Press.

Some educational philosophers

Jean-Jacques Rousseau (1712–78) thought that formal education was inherently corrupting and rather it should enable the "natural" and "free" development of children, a view that eventually led to the modern movement known as "progressivism".

John Dewey (1859–1952) argued that education should be tailored to the individual child, though he rejected Plato's hierarchical sorting of students into categories.

Rudolf Steiner (1861–1925) focused on imaginative, aesthetic and holistic methods to support children to reach their full potential as creative, intelligent and well-rounded human beings.

Michael Oakeshott (1901–1990) said education should liberate students from their immediate surroundings and help them understand themselves. He believed that education should introduce students to a cultural inheritance of beliefs, imaginings, and activities that are distinct from their own experience.

E.D. Hirsch's (1928–) philosophy of education is based on the idea that students should be taught a core body of knowledge that is shared across the school system and that is able to promote equality, create a common cultural identity, enable students to participate in society and help students become effective citizens.

Chapter 18
Your career and money

Your career

Once you have passed through the early career framework and established yourself as a successful teacher in your school, you should be thinking about promotion. Here is some useful advice:

- It is often quicker to gain promotion by moving schools, but a CV that tells us that a person moves their job every 2–3 years is not very impressive. Schools will look for a sense of loyalty from their employees.
- Before you apply for a job in another school, tell your head teacher and any other referees. It goes down badly if they receive a reference request that they weren't expecting.
- If you work in a MAT, see whether you can receive promotion to another school within your trust.
- If you are applying to work in another school, find out about it and tailor your covering letter and CV to that job and school. You must explain why you are right for that particular post.
- When you go for an interview, know that everyone you meet may be asked to give their impression of you.
- You will probably have to teach a lesson as part of your interview. You will be told what to teach but you may not know much about the pupils or what they have studied previously. The most common mistake is that teachers try to get through too much in the observed lesson, so plan a lesson with different end points just in case it goes faster or slower than you expected. Make sure you teach the pupils something concrete and leave time to demonstrate they have actually learned it. Don't rely too much on technology, which may take too long to set up and may not work well in an unfamiliar school.
- Your age is rarely a factor – you can apply for promotion when you are quite young.
- If you are unsuccessful, don't worry. The most successful people have usually applied for many jobs; the least successful are those who give up after one rejection.

The most common routes to promotion are:

- Head of a subject or school department

- Head of year
- Assistant head
- Deputy head (academic or pastoral) or director of studies
- Head or principal
- Head of a MAT

Your money

Some teachers tend to be slightly vague about their own finances, so try to understand your monthly pay slip. When you are offered a job, ask someone to explain the pay scales to you – HR, your mentor or a union rep can help. You need to know that you have been put on the correct point on the pay scale, and you need to know how you can rise up the pay scale.

Unqualified teachers are paid on the unqualified teachers' scale, which in 2024–25 was £21,731 to £33,901 outside London.

The main pay scale for qualified teachers in England outside London in 2024–25 was as follows:

- M1 £31,650
- M2 £33,483
- M3 £35,674
- M4 £38,034
- M5 £40,438
- M6 £43,606
- U1 £45,646
- U2 £47,338
- U3 £49,084

New teachers usually start at M1. Teachers on the main scale generally progress through the pay points annually, moving from M1 to M2 and so on, until they reach M6. This progression is typically based on satisfactory performance and meeting set objectives. In each step up, the pay points reflect increased experience and competency, and results in a corresponding salary increase.

Teachers move onto the upper pay scale (U) only if the school is satisfied that the teacher is highly competent in all elements of the relevant standards and that the teacher's achievements and contribution to an educational setting are substantial and sustained. So, you can be given a pay rise based on length of service and your performance.

There are two other ways your pay can increase over time:

- The annual rise that all teachers get and that should reflect inflation to some degree. This is influenced by the annual recommendations of the independent School Teachers' Review Body.

  The government decides on the annual pay increase and this applies to state schools. Independent schools have their own pay scales but these are influenced by the state school pay scales.

- You can be given a pay rise because you have been given promotion or have taken on a specific responsibility. You need to be clear from the outset what will happen to your pay once you cease to carry that responsibility.

Deductions from your pay

Three or more sums are taken from your pay, normally by the school:

- **Income tax** – Levels of income tax are fixed by the government. In a recent tax year, for example, an employee paid 20% on income between £12,571 and £50,270 (you are not taxed on the first £12,570). Those who had an income higher than that were taxed at 40% on anything between £50,271 and £150,000, and 45% on anything over that.

- **National Insurance** – National Insurance is a second tax. It is used to fund social services such as the NHS and the state pension. Recently, employees have paid 8% of their gross pay as National Insurance. Your school also pays around 15% of your gross pay, but this doesn't come out of your pay.

- **Pension contribution** – Most (but not all) teachers are in the Teachers' Pension Scheme (TPS). The level of pension contribution you pay into the TPS depends on your salary. The bands usually change each year; for the school year 2024–25, they were as follows:

Annual salary rate for eligible employment from 1 April 2024	Member contribution rate
Up to £34,289	7.4%
£34,290 to £46,158	8.6%
£46,159 to £54,729	9.6%
£54,730 to £72,534	10.2%
£72,535 to £98,908	11.3%
£98,909 and above	11.7%

Teachers' Pensions

In addition, your school pays a sum based on your gross pay into the TPS. Again, this does not come out of your salary. In 2024–25, this figure was a whopping 28.68%. So, you can see that teachers are much more expensive to a school than just the basic salary. Some independent schools have withdrawn from the TPS because of the huge cost of the employers' contribution. In this case, the school will provide full details of your options.

● **Student loan** – If you have a student loan, a percentage of this may be deducted from your pay depending on how much you earn.

Keep a record of your payslips and pension contributions – you may need them one day.

Chapter 19
What does success look like for a teacher?

In the short term, there are several ways you will measure your success:

- You passed the QTS or PGCE qualification.
- You have got a job.
- You successfully completed the early career framework statutory induction.
- You are enjoying your job and pupils seem to enjoy your lessons. The work is stressful but worthwhile.
- You are good at your job. Pupils and colleagues like you. Your classes make good progress or get good exam results relative to their ability. At secondary, your pupils choose to continue with your subject to GCSE and A-level.
- If you are a secondary school teacher, you are a member of a subject association (such as the Royal Geographical Society).

In the medium term:

- You are now a confident teacher. You don't have to worry too much about controlling your classes and your subject knowledge is good.
- You have become more deeply involved in your school, such as taking responsibility for a subject, being a head of year or running a sport. You apply for promotion and are successful.
- You form a view about the type of school you want to work in for the rest of your career.

In the longer term, you will need to decide whether you wish to teach less and gain promotion to become a head of department, assistant head, deputy head or head.

If you take maternity or paternity leave, you will hopefully return to teaching at a time that suits you. Having school holidays is a great advantage to young parents and their children. Flexible and part-time working will become more and more common in schools in England.

Bibliography

Anderson, J. and Taner, G., 2023, *Building the expert teacher prototype: A metasummary of teacher expertise studies in primary and secondary education*, Educational Research Review.

Aubin, G., 2022, EEF blog: The Five-a-day approach: How the EEF can support a range of resources to support high-quality teaching for all pupils.

Ausubel, D., 1960, The use of advance organizers in the learning and retention of meaningful verbal material, Journal of Educational Psychology, 5, 267–272 1.

Ausubel, D. P., 1968, *Educational Psychology: A Cognitive View*. New York: Holt, Rinehart & Winston.

Bandura, A., 1977, Self-efficacy: Toward a unifying theory of behavioural change, Psychological Review, 84(2), 191–215.

Barton, C., 2018, *How I Wish I'd Taught Maths*, John Catt.

Baumer, N. and Frueh, J., 2021, What is neurodiversity?, *Harvard Health Blog*.

Bethune, A., 2023, *Wellbeing in the Primary Classroom: The Updated Guide to Teaching Happiness and Positive Mental Health, 2nd edition*, Bloomsbury.

Bethune, A. and Kell, E., 2020, *A Little Guide for Teachers: Teacher Wellbeing and Self-care*, Corwin.

Birbalsingh, K., 2016, *The Battle Hymn of the Tiger Teachers: The Michaela Way*, John Catt.

Bjork, R. A., 1994, Memory and meta-memory considerations in the training of human beings. In J. Metcalfe and A. Shimamura (Eds.), *Metacognition: Knowing About Knowing* (pp. 185–205), The MIT Press.

Bourdieu, P., 1977, *Outline of a Theory of Practice*, Cambridge University Press.

Black, P. and Wiliam, D., 1998, *Assessment and classroom learning*, Assessment in Educational Principles, Policy and Practice, 5(1), 7–74.

Black, P. and Wiliam, D., 2009, Developing the theory of formative assessment, Educational Assessment, Evaluation and Accountability, 21(1), 5-13.

Browne Jacobson LLP, 2024, School Leaders Survey Findings.

Burgess, S. and Thomson, D., 2023, *Differences in school performance are local not regional (mostly)*, Education DataLab.

Bukodi, E. and Goldthorpe, J., 2019, *Social Mobility and Education in Britain: Research, Politics and Policy*, Cambridge University Press.

Campbell, T., 2021, Special Educational Needs and Disabilities within the English primary school system: What can disproportionalities by season of birth contribute to understanding processes behind attributions and (lack of) provisions?, LSE's Centre for Analysis of Social Exclusion (CASE).

Carroll, J., Bradley, L., Crawford, H., Hannant, P., Johnson, H., and Thompson, A., 2017, SEN support: a rapid evidence assessment, UK Government (Home Office).

Christodoulou, D., 2014, *Seven Myths About Education*, Routledge.

Churchill, W., 1930, *My Early Life*, Charles Scribner's Sons.

Clark, J. and Paivio, A., 1991, Dual coding theory and education, Educational Psychology Review, 3, 149–210.

Clark, R. and Felton, D., 2014, *Cambridge Handbook of Multimedia Learning*, 2nd edition, Cambridge University Press.

Clifton, J. and Cook, C., 2012, *A Long Division: Closing the Gap in England's Secondary Schools*, London: Institute for Public Policy Research.

Coe, R., 2013, *Improving Education: A Triumph of Hope Over Experience*. Centre for Evaluation and Monitoring.

Coe, R., Aloisi, C., Higgins, S., and Major, L. E., 2014, *What makes great teaching. Review of the underpinning research*, Durham University: UK.

Cook, C., 2016, Why not bring back grammar schools?, BBC news report, 14 July 2013.

Cook, C. R., Fiat, A., and Tyler, R., 2018, Positive greetings at the door: Evaluation of a low-cost, high-yield proactive classroom management strategy, Journal of Positive Behavior Interventions, 30(3).

Cordingley, P., Higgins, S., Greany, T., Buckler, N., Coles-Jordan, D., Crisp, B., Saunders, L., and Coe, R., 2015, Developing Great Teaching, Teacher Development Trust.

Craik, F. and Lockhart, R., 1972, *Levels of processing: A framework for memory research*, Journal of Verbal Learning and Verbal Behaviour, 11(6), 671–684.

Cree, J. and McCree, M., 2012, A brief history of forest school in the UK – Part 2, Horizon Magazine, 62 (Summer), 32–35.

Cree, J. and McCree, M., 2012, A brief history of the roots of forest school in the UK, Horizon Magazine, 60 (Winter), 32–34.

Crehan, L., 2016, *Cleverlands: The Secrets Behind the Success of the World's Education Superpowers*, Unbound.

Cullen, M., et al., 2020, Special Educational Needs in Mainstream Schools: Evidence Review. Online at: EEF_SEND_Evidence_Review.pdf (d2tic4wvo1iusb.cloudfront.net) [Accessed 8th May 2024].

Cullinane, C., Hillary, J., Andrade, J., and McNamara, S., 2017, *Selective Comprehensives 2017: Admissions to High-Attaining Non-Selective Schools for Disadvantaged Pupils*, London: The Sutton Trust.

Deans for Impact, 2015, The Science of Learning.

Department for Education, 2004, The deployment and impact of support staff in schools: Research brief, DfE.

Department for Education, 2019, ITT core content framework. www.gov.uk/government/publications/initial-teacher-training-itt-core-content-framework.

Department for Education, 2024a, Initial teacher training and early career framework. www.gov.uk/government/publications/initial-teacher-training-and-early-career-framework.

Department for Education, 2024b, Initial teacher training: Criteria and supporting advice.

Department for Education, 2024, Keeping children safe in education.

Department for Education, 2024, Initial teacher training and early career framework. www.gov.uk/government/publications/initial-teacher-training-and-early-career-framework.

Department for Education, 2024, Development matters: Non-statutory curriculum guidance for the early years foundation stage.

Department for Education, 2024, Early years foundation stage statutory framework for group and school-based providers.

Dix, P., 2017, *When the Adults Change, Everything Changes:Seismic Shifts in School Behaviour*, Independent Thinking Press.

Dunlosky, J., Rawson, K., March, E., Nathan, M., Willingham, D., 2013, Improving students' learning with effective learning techniques: Promising directions from cognitive and educational psychology, Psychological Science in the Public Interest, 14(1), 4–58.

Dweck, C. S., 2006, *Mindset: The New Psychology of Success*. Random House.

Dweck, C. S. and Leggett, E. l., 1988, A social-cognitive approach to motivation and personality, Psychological Review, 95(2), 256–273.

Early Years Coalition, 2021, *Birth to 5 Matters: Non-statutory Guidance for the Early Years Foundation Stage*. St Albans: Early Education.

Eaton, J., 2022, EEF blog: Moving from 'differentiation' to 'adaptive teaching'.

Ebbinghaus, H., 1885, *Memory: A contribution to experimental psychology*. Reprinted in Annals of Neurosciences, 20(4), 155–156.

Education Policy Institute, 2019, *The Forgotten Third: A Rapid Review of the Evidence*, ASCL.

Education Endowment Foundation, 2018, Improving Secondary Science Guidance Report.

Education Endowment Foundation, 2015 Making Best Use of Teaching Assistants: Guidance Report.

Education Endowment Foundation, 2021, Cognitive science approaches in the classroom: A review of the evidence. Online.

Education Endowment Foundation, 2021, Education Endowment Foundation Teaching and Learning Toolkit, Mastery Learning. Online.

Education Endowment Foundation, 2021, Education Endowment Foundation Teaching and Learning Toolkit, Phonics. Online.

Education Endowment Foundation, 2021, Teacher Feedback to Improve Pupil Learning Guidance Report. Online.

Education Endowment Foundation, 2022, Working with worked examples – Simple techniques to enhance their effectiveness. Online.

Ellis, P., Kirby, A., and Osbourne, A., 2023, *Neurodiversity and Education*, Corwin, UK.

Field, S., 2024, Inequality in English post-16 education, Oxford Open Economics, 3(1), i828–i841 or see the Institute for Fiscal Studies Deaton Review.

Gardner, H., 1983, *Frames of Mind: The Theory of Multiple Intelligences*, Basic Books.

Gardner, H., 2013, Frequently asked questions—Multiple intelligences and related educational topics.

Gilbert, I., 2018, The *Working Class: Poverty, Education and Alternative Voices*, Independent Thinking Press.

Goldthorpe, J. H., 2012, Understanding and misunderstanding social mobility in Britain: The entry of the economists, the confusion of politicians and the limits of educational policy, Oxford: Oxford Institute of Social Policy and Nuffield College, University of Oxford.

Goodhart, D., 2020, *Head, Hand and Heart*, Allen Lane.

Grossman, P. (ed.), 2018, *Teaching Core Practices in Teacher Education*, Harvard Education Press.

Haidt, J., 2024, *The Anxious Generation: How the Great Rewiring of Childhood Is Causing an Epidemic of Mental Illness*, Allen Lane.

Hart, B. and Risley, T., 2003, The Early Catastrophe – The 30 Million Word Gap by Age 3. American Educator, 27, 4–9.

Hattie, J., 2008, Visible Learning: A Synthesis of Over 800 Meta-Analyses Relating to Achievement, Routledge.

Hattie, J., 2023, *Visible Learning: The Sequel*, Routledge.

Hirsch, E. D., 1987, *Cultural Literacy: What Every American Needs to Know*, Houghton Mifflin.

Honeybourne, V., 2018, *The Neurodiverse Classroom*, Jessica Kingsley Publishers, UK and USA.

Howard, E., Khan, A. and Lockyer, C., 2021, *Learning during the pandemic: review of research from England*, Ofqual.

Institute of Education Sciences, 2008, *Reducing Behavior Problems in the Elementary School Classroom*.

Jensen, E., 2009, *Teaching with Poverty in Mind: What Being Poor Does to Kids' Brains and What Schools Can Do About It*, ASCD.

Johnson, P., 2024, *Educational inequalities*, Oxford Open Economics, 3(1), i758–i759 or see the Institute for Fiscal Studies Deaton Review.

Koenig, J., 2021, *The Musical Child: Using the Power of Music to Raise Children Who Are Happy, Healthy, and Whole*, Harper Collins, London.

Kalyuga, S. and Sweller, J., 2014, *The redundancy principle in multi-media learning* . In R. E. Mayer (Ed.), *The Cambridge handbook of multimedia learning* (2nd ed). Cambridge University Press.

Kim, S. and Webb, S., 2022, *The Effects of Spaced Practice on Second Language Learning: A Meta-Analysis*. Language Learning.

Kirschner, P. and Hendrick, C., 2020, *How Learning Happens: Seminal works in educational psychology and what they mean in practice*, Routledge.

Kirschner, P., Sweller, J., and Clark, R., 2006, Why minimal guidance during instruction does not work: An analysis of the failure of constructivist, discovery, problem-based, experiential and inquiry-based teaching, Educational Psychology, 41(2), 75–86.

Kluger, A. and DeNisi, A., 1996, The effects of feedback interventions on performance: A historical review, a meta-analysis and a preliminary feedback intervention theory, Psychological Bulletin, 119(2), 254–284.

Knight, S., 2024, Forest School Forward, Horizon Magazine, May 2024, pp 14-16.

Lemov, D., 2021, *Teach Like a Champion 3.0*, Jossey-Bass.

Lenon, B., 2017, *Much Promise: Successful Schools in England*, John Catt.

Lenon, B., 2018, *Other People's Children: What Happens to Those in the Bottom 50% Academically?*, John Catt.

McGill, R., 2021, *Mark, Plan, Teach 2.0*, 2nd edition, Bloomsbury.

McGill, R., 2022, *The Teacher Toolkit Guide to Memory*, Bloomsbury.

McGill, R., 2023, *The Teacher Toolkit Guide to Questioning*, Bloomsbury.

McGill, R., 2024, *The Teacher Toolkit Guide to Feedback*, Bloomsbury.

McLeskey, J., Maheady, L., Billingsley, B., & Brownell, M., 2018, *High Leverage Practices for Inclusive Classrooms*, Rouledge.

Mould, K., 2021, EEF blog: Assess, adjust, adapt – what does adaptive teaching mean to you?

Mueller, P. and Oppenheimer, D., 2014, The pen is mightier than the keyboard: Advantages of longhand over laptop note taking, Psychological Science, 25(6), 1159–1168.

Mullin, S., 2020, *What They Didn't Teach Me on My PGCE*, Word and Deed Publishing.

Ndaji, F., Little, J., and Coe, R., 2016, A comparison of academic achievement in independent and state schools, Centre for Evaluation and Monitoring, University of Durham.

Oates, T, 2014, *Why Textbooks Count*, Cambridge Assessment.

Ofqual, 2018, Marking consistency metrics: An update.

Ofsted curriculum research reviews and subject reports.

O'Hear, A., 2023, *In Defence of Liberal Education: Philosophy and Controversies*, University of Buckingham Press.

Oxford University Press, 2016, Why Closing the Word Gap Matters: Oxford Language Report, Oxford.

Pashler, H., McDaniel, M., Rohrer, D., and Bjork, R., 2008, Learning styles: Concepts and evidence. Psychological Science in the Public Interest, 9(3), 105–119.

Peal, R., 2014, Progressively Worse: The Burden of Bad Ideas in British Schools, Civitas.

Pemberton, M., 2025, Labelling is too easy and this over-diagnosis is dangerous to children, The Times, January 4 2025.

Pink, D., 2011, *Drive: The Surprising Truth About What Motivates Us*, Canongate Books.

PISA, 2022, What is PISA?, PISA 2022 Assessment and Analytical Framework. OECD iLibrary: oecd-ilibrary.org

PISA., 2015, PISA in Focus: Do teacher-student relations affect students' well-being at school? OECD.

Pritchard, B., 2022, EEF Blog: Working with worked examples – Simple techniques to enhance their effectiveness. Online at: educationendowmentfoundation.org.uk

QAA, 2024, The Frameworks for Higher Education Qualifications of UK Degree-Awarding Bodies, 2nd edition.

Qin, X., Kaufman, T., Laninga-Wijnen, L., Ren, P., Zhang, Y., and Veenstra, R., 2021, *The Impact of Academic Achievement and Parental Practices on Depressive Symptom Trajectories Among Chinese Adolescents*, Research on Child and Adolescent Psychopathology, 49(10), 1359–1371.

Reay, D., 2024, Measuring and understanding contemporary English educational inequalities, Oxford Open Economics, 3(1), i861–i878 or see the Institute for Fiscal Studies Deaton Review.

Richmond, T. and Regan, E., 2023, Examining exams: Are there credible alternatives to written examinations? EDSK.

Rogers, B., 2007, *Behaviour Management: A Whole-School Approach*, Sage.

Rogers, B., 2015, Classroom Behaviour: *A Practical Guide to Effective Teaching, Behaviour Management and Colleague Support*, 4th edition, Sage.

Rosenshine, B., 2012, Principles of Instruction: Research-based strategies that all teachers should know, American Educator, 12–20.

Scarborough, H. S., 2001, Connecting early language and literacy to later reading (dis)abilities: Evidence, theory, and practice. In S. Neuman and D. Dickinson (Eds.), Handbook for Research in Early Literacy. New York: Guilford Press.

Sing, S., 2015, Pedagogical approaches to delivery of a knowledge-led, content rich GCSE and A level curriculum: Learning with independent schools - RESEARCH REPORT, London Schools Excellence Fund.

Speckesser, S., Runge, J., Foliano, F., Bursnall, M., Hudson-Sharp, N., Rolfe, H., and Anders, J., 2018, *Embedding Formative Assessment: Evaluation Report and Executive Summary*, Education Endowment Foundation.

Stephen, M. and Warwick, I., 2015, *Educating the More Able Student*, Sage.

Strand, S., 2010, Do some schools narrow the gap? Differential school effectiveness by ethnicity, gender, poverty and prior attainment, School Effectiveness and School Improvement, 21(3), 289–314.

Strand, S., 2016, *Do some schools narrow the gap? Differential school effectiveness revisited*, Review of Education, 4(2), 107–144.

Strand, S., 2022, *Education and achievement at 16, Sociology* Review.

Sweller, J., 1988, Cognitive load during problem solving: Effects on learning, Cognitive Science, 12(2), 257–285.

Tabarrok, A., 2022, *Direct instruction produces large gains in learning, Kenya edition*, Marginal Revolution.

Van der Weel, F. and Van der Meer, A., 2024, Handwriting but not typewriting leads to widespread brain connectivity: A high-density EEG study with implications for the classroom, Frontiers in Psychology, 14.

Verkoeijen, P. and Delaney, P., 2008, Rote rehearsal and spacing effects in the free recall of pure and mixed lists, Journal of Memory and Language, 58(1), 35–47.

Walker, S., 2016, The Tribe Effect: Measuring the non-cognitive impacts of state day, independent day and boarding education, Mind World.

Ward, A., Duke, K., Gneezy, A., and Boz, M., 2017, *Brain drain: The mere presence of one's own smartphone reduces available cognitive capacity*, Journal of the Association for Consumer Research, 2(2), 140–154.

Willingham, D., 2021, *Why Don't Pupils Like School*, 2nd edition, Jossey-Bass.

Yang, S., Saïd, M., Peyre, H., Ramus, F., Taine, M., Law, E. C., Dufourg, M. N., Heude, B., Cgarles, M. A., and Bernard, J. Y., 2024, Associations of screen use with cognitive development in early childhood: The ELFE birth cohort. The Journal of Child Psychology and Psychiatry, 65(5), 680–693.

Zimmerman, B., 1989, A social cognitive view of self-regulated academic learning, Journal of Educational Psychology, 81(3), 329–339.

Index

Acknowledgments

We would like to acknowledge and give our thanks to our colleagues in the many schools in which we have worked and at the University of Buckingham faculty of education.

We would also like to thank George Vlachonikolis for his wise words on the value of AI.

Personalised professional development from Hachette Learning Academy

A simple way to boost career progression, staff motivation and educational excellence.

Our online courses are:

 Aligned with **teaching competency frameworks**

 Written by experts in education, including Hachette Learning authors (formerly John Catt)

 Created to enable educators to **develop competencies** linked to their professional development aspirations

 Powered by adaptive learning, to accommodate a diverse range of skills, knowledge and understanding

 Designed to support **effective learning and high-impact teaching**

www.hachettelearning.com/academy